PROVE
THEM
WRONG

PROVE
THEM
WRONG

DEFYING ALL ODDS, HOW A TRIPLET
SURVIVED A CHICAGO GANG AND
GRADUATED FROM
THE U.S. NAVAL ACADEMY

DRE EVANS

LIONCREST
PUBLISHING

PROVE THEM WRONG
Defying All Odds, How a Triplet Survived a Chicago Gang and Graduated From the U.S. Naval Academy

ISBN   978-1-5445-3695-8   *Hardcover*

       978-1-5445-3696-5   *Paperback*

       978-1-5445-3697-2   *Ebook*

Stock image Designed by Rwdd_studios / Freepik.com

CONTENTS

ACT II: THE UNITED STATES NAVAL ACADEMY • 161

ACT III: DYING EMPTY BY LIVING LIFE TO THE FULLEST • 369

ALSO BY DRE EVANS

"The League of Wealth" Real Estate Comic Book:
How to Buy a Large Multifamily Property

That's My Property: How Purpose Turned a Chicago
Gang Member Into an Apartment Investor
& How You Can Become One Too

Did this book inspire or add value to you in some way? If so, I'd love to read your review and hear about it. Honest reviews impact the lives of other readers by helping them find the right book for their needs.

Thank you for your time and support.

GANGS: AN ANTIDOTE FOR ANSWERING THE QUESTION "WHO AM I?"

*This book is dedicated to the city
that formed my foundation as a man: Chicago.
For all the underdogs that fight to make something
of themselves, I hope that God leads you
to find inspiration in my story.*

*Lastly, this book is dedicated to my mother, Adrienne;
my father, Dwayne; my two brothers, Anthony and Alexander;
and my grandparents, Clarence and Mildred Johnson.
Everything I do flows from all of you.*

READER DISCLAIMER

The words within this text are exclusively of my own opinion. They do not reflect the official values or views of the Department of Defense, the United States Government, the Department of the Navy, the U.S. Naval Academy, or any components thereof.

Some names, places, and dates have been changed within this book to protect the identity of others. Some will hurt over the events described. Please respect that privacy.

Please respect that the events described in this book are not meant to glorify violence, but to depict realistic accounts of what life was like in Chicago. They are a means to an end that was survival. I relate them for an educational purpose only. The events described are meant to truly portray the extreme shift in journey and mindset I went through. Please do not attempt to replicate or promote any of the violence narrated within the text.

gang *noun*

1. : GROUP such as

   a. a group of persons working to unlawful or antisocial ends

   b. a group of persons working together

   c. a group of persons having informal and usually close social relations

   —MERRIAM-WEBSTER DICTIONARY

Gangs define:

- Our sense of who we are

- What we think and feel

- How we act

EVERY GREAT STORY STARTS WITH A VISION.

VISION IS THE ART OF THRIVING WITH BLINDNESS IN A STORM OF ADVERSITY.

GANG VIOLENCE IN CHICAGO IS A NATIONAL CRISIS.

Over 3,700 people have been shot in Chicago this year alone.

—THE CHICAGO TRIBUNE

AND I WAS CONTRIBUTING TO IT...

PROLOGUE

ONE OF THE PROUDEST MOMENTS OF MY LIFE WAS MY FIRST DRIVE-BY SHOOTING.

I was twelve years old.

It started with wearing baggy clothes. My pants sagged below my butt, and my hat was cocked back to the side. Yet, no matter how determined I was to look like a thug, I wasn't stupid. Never in my life did I dare walk in the house dressed for the streets— my mother didn't play that. But that didn't stop me from chasing the concrete.

The gloomy October sky frowned over Chicago on the day of my initiation into gang life. The clouds sat, depressed, over the city with their black-gray-purple hues. It was the middle of the day, and not a speck of light protruded from the weary skies. The city seemed to be trapped in a snow globe, dark on the inside but light all around. I knew that day could grow darker. I knew guys who died or were severely injured during their initiation ceremonies. Gang members broke my best friend's jaw with a gun when he attempted to join. I didn't know what happened to him at first, if he was alive or dead. He didn't call me or come to school for days. The next time I saw him, my mind was flooded with a mix of emotions. His bulky neck support and the thick metal brace around his face made him look so frail. I thought about all the moments we had spent joking around and the deep conversations about our families and manhood. I felt relieved that he was alive. But I also felt fear. I was about to put myself in the same situation—and at what cost?

If there was a Bill of Rights for Chicago's children, the most important would be the right to feel safe at home, school, and on the streets. With over 100,000 gang members defining the social structure of Chicago, the Windy City has the highest number of homicides. And with a murder rate twice the number of U.S. soldiers killed in Iraq and Afghanistan, newspapers around the nation gave Chicago the nickname "Chiraq."

I had physical ability, I had ambition, and I was searching for opportunity. These are traits necessary to succeed at the U.S. Naval Academy, which I would eventually learn as a student there. These are also the traits that lead thousands of kids on the streets of Chicago to join gangs.

And I was one of them.

"Why do you want to join a street gang?" the leader asked in a deep gladiator voice. His body was decorated with tattoos. He went by the name of Smoke, and he was one of nine guys standing in a circle around me. Like a gym without AC, the room felt hot.

"Shit. Umm...I wanna feel like I'm a part of somethin'. I want excitement. I wanna feel like I belong. Like a real family. Ya know?" I said with a hardness in my eyes. Despite what I saw my friend experience, I still wanted to join because I was hurting inside. My biological father's absence in my life left a hole in me. I felt abandoned and unloved. I found a new family on the street, and whenever I was with them, it filled that void of loneliness and allowed me to not view myself as a failure. There was even a sprinkle of hope inside me that my fate would be different.

"I got all the family you need right here," another male named Boogie said with a cracked laugh.

Boogie grabbed the butt stocks of the two black pistols tucked into his waistline and held them up in the air. Smiling, he waved the pistols back and forth before his face. The grips of the handguns were worn from use. It was not unusual to have a gun in Chicago. Like candy, they were everywhere and easy to acquire. It was a necessary form of protection on the South Side.

"Shut up, Boogie. Ain't no time for jokes right now," Smoke rasped back. He stepped forward into the middle of the circle and stopped right in front of my face. "There's no turning back from this, Dre. Once we start. That's it. You sure you wanna do this?"

"Yeah," I said with a large gulp. "I have to. I gotta prove I'm somebody."

"Bet."

The way ahead was uncertain.

Smoke stepped back into the circle. The room was so quiet that I heard a cockroach scurry across the gritty floor. The lights were out, and the dirty windows blocked most of the gray daylight.

A host of unfamiliar sensations came over me as the men took two steps toward me, shrinking the size of the circle. Their breath caused the hair follicles on the back of my neck to stand straight up, like a Marine being told to snap to attention. The men were panting while my heart was trying to Spartan kick through my chest. The palms of my hands grew moist.

"Now," Smoke ordered.

Like a swarm of bees, they attacked me.

The full force of two hands dug into my shoulder blades, and I hit the floor with a loud *bang*.

They were like hyenas attacking prey. All nine gang members commenced a rapid thunder of punches and kicks on my body. Their spit and sweat rained down on me. I held my arms up and squeezed them as tight as I could to shield my face. Getting "beat-in" was a mandatory rite of passage to join the gang. I felt like I was in one of those movies where the entire screen goes dark and the spotlight shines on the main character lying on the ground helpless and all alone.

After about five minutes, my body went numb.

I passed out and laid motionless on the cold floor.

As I came to, I wondered if I was about to die. Was proving my worth and attempting to be a part of something really worth dying for?

The kicking stopped, and the circle eased up. The room went silent.

"Oh shit, I think he's dead," I heard Boogie say. He gave me a slight kick to the leg.

I didn't move.

"You good, Dre? Get up, yo," Smoke yelled.

No response.

"Damn. I guess it was too much for him," somebody said.

"Alright, pick him up. We gotta toss the body," Smoke said.

Two of the members reached down and began to grab my arms and legs.

"AGHHHHH!!!"

Like a mad animal, I kicked my feet with fury and sprang from off the ground, screaming. I was fully awake then from being passed out.

I thought I was dead.

I swung my fists and tried to hit every member I could. Boogie grabbed me from behind and locked my hands in place.

"That's enough," he said.

"Well, that's different. I've never seen that befo. You got heart, kid. You don't give up. I like that," Smoke chuckled, his hands in his pockets.

As I exited the basement, I looked back at the nine shadows that, just a few moments before, had me in the jaws of their hands. I emerged from my ceremony as a new man. I was now a member of one of the most prominent street gangs in Chicago. They could be found on the news, in my neighborhood, and in school. With friends, associates, and classmates plugged into the life, it wasn't hard for me to become affiliated. My decision to join the gang was driven from pain and the lack of a positive male role model I could identify with. I wanted to be understood in some way. I wanted to walk the streets of Chicago with my head held high, unafraid. I wanted self expression. I wanted freedom. And I needed a way to survive and protect my family.

The next day, we all climbed into two gray Chrysler vans.

"Here, put this on," Boogie said, sitting next to me. He threw a black ski mask into my chest. I did as I was told and pulled the wool three-holed mask over my head. My face turned warm, and my breath felt hot as I attempted to breathe through the little hole cut for the mouth. I was wearing all black. Two of my other homies, Phil and Nate, were in the back seat of the van. Everyone was strapped and ready, their weapons lying in their laps.

"You better not chicken out like no bitch, Dre," Phil blurted out. He was a real skinny dude with big ears.

"I won't. I got this."

My initiation wasn't complete until I finished this task. The hit was against the two dudes who had beaten up and hurt my brother Anthony.

The day it happened, my brothers and I had borrowed a basketball from our neighbor. The three of us were walking back from the park when we noticed two older high school guys "posted up" on the porch. I didn't know them.

"Yo, young blood, hold up." We all stopped and looked their way. One of the guys jumped down from the porch and ran toward Anthony.

"Let me get that ball," he said.

"No. I can't. I borrowed this from a friend," Anthony shot back.

"I *said* give me the ball."

The older guy got right up into Anthony's grill, his six-foot frame towering over him. He was wearing an all-white muscle shirt and had dark chocolate skin full of tattoos. Not intimidated by the height difference, Anthony held his ground. The older guy pushed Anthony. Anthony pushed him back, but the large opponent barely moved.

Anthony pushed him again with all his might.

Then again.

And again.

The other guy on the porch ran over.

"Yo, chill. He's just a kid. Let 'em go."

"Fuck that," the first kid responded.

Smack.

The guy punched Anthony swiftly in the jaw.

My brother hit the cracked street pavement hard. The basketball rolled to the edge of the curb. As my brother got back on his feet, a tear rolled down his bruised red cheeks.

Smack.

Before Anthony got his balance back, the older guy hit him again. Then he grabbed the ball and walked away. I ran over and helped Anthony up. We walked back home with our heads down in dismay. I don't know why I didn't jump in to help my brother. It all happened so fast; I just froze. Maybe I was intimidated by how much bigger they were. Or maybe I was in shock because my brother fought the way he did for a basketball. But now I know it was deeper than that. Since birth, we have looked out for one another. He took the hit for us.

Now, it was my turn to repay the favor.

We turned on the block and slowed the van down to about twenty miles per hour. The two Black guys were outside smoking on the front porch. They still lived with their mother apparently. They both had on long-sleeved jackets and sweatpants. I placed my hand on the black door latch inside the van and braced myself to thrust it open when my opportunity came to fire. The instant the nose of the car crossed the house I slid the door back hard.

One of the guys was taking his final cigarette puff when he saw a black steel MAC-10 submachine gun pointed at him.

Have you ever been in a situation where you felt like time froze and everything around you happened really slowly?

Well, that's how this moment was for me.

In slow motion, the red-orange butt end of the guy's cigarette lit up, his eyes widened, and he made an "oh shit" face when he saw the barrel of the gun.

The gun was cold in my hands, but it also felt warm, almost like it had a soul of its own. I felt powerful for the first time in my life.

"Let them have it, Dre. Get they ass," Nate shouted, breaking the silent pause in time. He had a weapon in his hand as well.

I took a deep breath. This was it. My hands were now hot and sweaty from nervousness.

FRAAAAAAKatatata.... FRAAAAKKKKatatatatat....

Bullets sprayed all over the place until the full clip was unloaded.

ACT I: GROWING UP

When I was a child, I talked like a child, I thought like a child, I reasoned like a child. When I became a man, I put the ways of childhood behind me.

—1 CORINTHIANS 13:11

CHAPTER 1

THE ORIGINS OF THE CHICAGO KID

I WAS BORN INTO A GANG.

This is a Chicago story. However, its genesis starts 280 miles away in a place commonly referred to as "The Motor City" or "D-Town." On September 6, everything that mattered to my mother, Adrienne R. Johnson, and my father, Anthony H. Evans, changed. The average pregnancy for multiples was thirty-three weeks, but within the course of several minutes, none of that even mattered.

My mother loves telling the story of the day we were born. She remembers every detail.

"Augghhhhhh," the crowd moaned on the TV in disappointment while my mother sat on the gray-black patterned couch and watched *Wheel of Fortune.* She wore open-toed sandals with maroon painted toe nails, and a plain orange sundress: her favorite color. She must have looked like a divine

goddess—the light from the nearby square window beaming down on her tall and slender frame, Milky Way brown eyes, and buttermilk caramel skin. Her beauty has always been captivating.

My mother was born and raised on the South Side of Chicago by my grandparents Clarence (or Papa as we called him for short) and Mildred Johnson. A native of Kannapolis, North Carolina, Papa was a disciplined family man with a reputation for being very outspoken; he didn't hold his tongue for anyone. Despite only having a high school education, he didn't allow that to limit his exposure to opportunities.

My grandmother, on the other hand, hailed from Atlanta, Georgia. She was sweet and soft-spoken—in some ways shy— and didn't have much of an education. After experiencing an unpleasant family and social scene down South, she moved to Chicago with a friend in search of a better life. Papa had just returned home from the Air Force, and he, too, moved to Chicago in search of work. And that's where he met Mildred. It was history from there.

Starting out, they lived in a dark basement with nothing but a raggedy, worn-out mattress. But that didn't last long. All of Papa's hard work as a cab driver and handyman came to fruition in 1956, when he put years of his savings to use and purchased a home on the South Side for $15,000. He worked a full-time job during the week and, on the weekends, drove a cab. He always took pride in his work.

He paid off the entire house in one year.

My mother was in the middle of her TV episode when—*pop*—her water broke and fluids came gushing down the front side of the coach. This is a story my brothers and I have heard many times over the years.

"Tony!!!" my mother screamed. She rose from the sofa and started to walk toward the door. My biological father came rushing down the stairs in concern.

"What?! What is it, Adrienne?!"

"My water just broke."

She was about to give birth four weeks early.

Tony helped my mother to the car, and they sped off down the street toward the hospital.

"Mrs. Evans, could you please sign this consent form?" the doctor uttered underneath his clean white face mask. He looked down on my mother while she was quickly wheeled into the operating room. He forced a hopeful smile. His light brown eyebrows arched upward, and his clear blue eyes gave a friendly sparkle.

The hospital wanted to view and record her during labor. The birth of multiples was rare and considered high risk during the 1990s—especially when it was not drug-induced. Statistically speaking, the rate of higher order births was 3,547 per 100,000.

My mother reached out, grabbed the pen, and scratched out her signature.

Everything was white. The stiff hospital bed my mother laid on
was cold and creaked with each movement she made. Goosebumps sprinkled all over her caramel arms from the cold. My
mother lifted her hand and grabbed the flat silver railing that
surrounded her bed. She moved her body to a more comfortable position.

Like a bunch of eager visitors taking pictures of an exotic
animal at the zoo, my mother said she saw at least twenty people
beaming down on her from the balcony above in amazement.
She was in a large viewing delivery room.

"Hey, Mrs. Evans, are you doing okay?" her main doctor asked.
She was a short Black lady with hazelnut swirl skin and dark
brown hair and eyes. She could see the level of concern on my
mother's face. Everything was happening so fast.

"Yes, I'm okay. I'm just amazed at how many people are here
to watch."

"I understand. This is going to be quite the experience for all of
us. As a hospital, we are just as excited about this as you are."

She gently placed her hand on top of my mother's to comfort
her.

Another White male doctor—the anesthesiologist—walked up
to the bed with a fine 3½-inch-long needle. She was getting an
epidural to block the pain.

My mother flipped her body over and rested the side of her
head against the bed. She could feel a slight pinch as the

anesthesiologist slid the sharp needle into her back, near her spine. After about forty-five seconds, her lower abdominal area went numb. She could feel movement but no pain.

Anthony (or Atna as I call him) was the first to come out, at three pounds and ten ounces. He was named after my biological father. He grew to be six foot eight and was the tallest and silliest among us three. He always had this big, infectious smile etched across his face, as if it brought energy to his mood. He was the type of guy to laugh at his own jokes or engage in comical acts that made everyone in the family laugh. Because of his lanky height, strangers and friends attempted to push him into sports. But Anthony never took an interest. Nor did he engage in much physical or aggressive activity. Ultimately, music seemed to resonate with him the most. When he first started playing piano and later saxophone, he had a natural way of grasping concepts and playing with passion. Music just made "sense" to him in a way that Alex and I didn't understand.

Like Simba being lifted up by Rafiki before the kingdom of animals in *The Lion King*, the doctor raised Anthony into the air and showed my mother and the entire viewing room his crying face.

Two minutes later, my mother gave birth to me at three pounds, six ounces.

I didn't know it yet, but I was called to be a warrior.

In the book of Revelation, there was a protector: a strong, fierce angel that led God's army against the forces of evil. My mother gave me my middle name, Michael, after the archangel Michael in the Bible. That name would come to manifest its strength many times throughout my life. As a gang member, I looked out for my friends and my brothers, even when they didn't realize it. As a Naval Officer leading our nation's finest sailors into harm's way, I was required to protect and serve them. And just like Michael, who helped the children of Israel as a warrior, I, too, would become a fighting force to advocate for and provide outreach to minority youth in underserved and underrepresented communities.

Another two minutes later, Alex (or Ala) was born at three pounds, eleven ounces. He was the most generous of us three. Even as kids, when most are selfish about their things, Alex shared. He could be eating a package of gummy bears and would offer you his last. He was the sweetest, most kind-hearted of us. A quiet spirit, Alex was passionate about video games and anything related to the realm of technology. He built computers, always had the latest tech devices, and hacked phones. Years later, Alex would go on to major in cybersecurity studies at the Naval Academy.

My mother wanted all our names to start with an "A" just like hers. She didn't pick Anthony, Andre, and Alexander for any exact reason—only because she just really liked those names.

As we popped out, each of us was assigned our own team of nurses and taken away for further testing. My mother gave birth to three healthy triplet boys in Detroit, Michigan, at Hutzel Women's Hospital. Ever since that mid-afternoon day, she would always say she was "triple blessed."

But not all gang initiations are bloody and brutal: becoming a triplet was a beautiful process.

Right away, a close bond and helping out one another was innate.

During our infancy, my mother bought a thick white security gate to prevent us from leaving our upstairs bedroom. She feared we would hurt ourselves because there was a long, steep stairway that led from our bedroom downstairs to the main area of the house.

"Ehhh. Ahhhh. Ahhh. Augh," I spoke to my brothers in baby talk. We had our own special language as infants. On multiple occasions my mother would hear us laughing and talking to one another in the back of the car or in our bedrooms. Of course, she didn't understand a word we were saying.

I motioned to Alex that I wanted to get on his back. He was wearing a bright green polo with faded blue jeans. My shirt was red and Anthony's was blue. Our mother liked to dress us alike as toddlers but in our own colors. Coincidentally, those exact colors became our favorites. I gently placed my two small, chubby feet on top of Alex's back and leaned myself up against the gate. Like a tree branch, I put my arms together and stuck them out to give Anthony a support to grab hold of as he climbed over me and up above the white gate.

"What in the world? How did you three get down here?" my mother said when she saw us crawling on the floor in the kitchen. To her surprise, we had made it over her barrier.

A few days later, she bought two gates and stacked them on top of each other. For sure this would stop her small triplet boys. But we accepted that challenge, too.

Alex was always the anchor because he was the heaviest. He ate the most in our mother's tummy. This time Alex stood up on his two feet and leaned against the bottom of the first gate like he was hugging it. He extended his hand, and using my left foot first, I raised myself up to crawl and stand on his shoulders. Alex and I pressed all our weight against the gate to allow Anthony to crawl on our backs until he reached the top of my shoulders. We formed a human staircase by stacking ourselves on each other's backs and were able to reach the other side of my mother's two-story gate.

Again, we made it down the stairs to the kitchen where she was cooking. We also used that tactic to reach the cookie jar on the top shelf in the pantry.

"Hahahaha," she laughed when she saw us on the floor. "You guys are funny."

"Eghhh. Ehehehe," we laughed back in our little baby voices.

The third time, she removed the entire entry and replaced it with a screen door. That way she could hear and see us while keeping the door locked with a latch. We made it through that, too. Somehow my brothers and I managed to work together to unravel the rubber cord that held the screen in place and pushed it out from the inside.

Our bond is a testament to how our mother raised us and the amount of time we spent together growing up. We didn't have much of a sibling rivalry. My mother taught us to love one another, but like all siblings, we argued and fought. Yet there was a line we didn't cross: we never dared fight each other like we would someone on the street. In the end, we all developed into mature men with different personalities, and despite being apart, we are still close. My brothers and I communicate with one another often.

* * * *

THE FIRST TIME my mother got to hold us was when we were in the nursery. She described the nursery as open candy boxes on display for sale in a store. We were placed right next to one another in open plastic bins.

"Are you ready to hold them?" the nurse asked.

"Yes," my mother responded with a bright smile. She had a gentle, smooth, comforting voice.

She pulled up a chair right next to our bins and opened up her hospital gown, and the nurse helped lay all three of us on her chest. As premature babies, we were small, but already had long arms and legs, the physical gifts we inherited from Tony. He was six foot eight. It is vital for newborns to have contact with their mothers within the first few days because it releases a set of hormones that benefit their health, help control body temperature, and provide an initial connection. While the three of us lay on my mother's chest and napped, a moment of wonder overcame her. She could not believe she had three babies at one time. Multiples didn't run in our family.

"Because your sons were born early, we have to keep them in the incubator for a few weeks to monitor their health before we send them home with you. They need to gain a little bit more weight," the Black female doctor told my mother when she walked into the nursery.

"Okay. How often can I visit?"

"You are more than welcome to visit them whenever you like."

Each day my mother came to visit. Back then, patient health charts were in the room. Just like when she was a student at Loyola University and graduated magna cum laude, she read every bit of information the doctors had on us. If she didn't understand a term or concept, she would ask. When my mother came to see us that second week, she noticed something strange.

My first test at adversity and life's random punches occurred within that incubator. The nurses placed an IV near my bin. The fluid was supposed to go in my veins, but somehow mine slipped out.

So where did the fluid go?

The liquid dripped on my foot for a couple of hours, scarring my skin. The nurses should have caught it sooner.

"What happened to his foot?" my mother asked when she saw the large mark.

"The IV moved," the nurse responded. My mother said she was angry at first, but then she took a second and observed me.

My foot was all bandaged up, yet I lay there at peace. I didn't holler or cry or make a face. My mother turned toward the nurse.

"Did he cry or express any pain when the fluid dripped on him or when you wrapped his leg up?"

"No. He's been calm the entire time."

"Mhmm," my mother mumbled while nodding her head up and down, intrigued.

Right then, I showed my mother that I was the type of kid who could face adversity head-on.

And she knew it, too.

CHAPTER 2

CRACK DADDY

I BET MY MOTHER DIDN'T KNOW THAT DAY WOULD MARK THE END OF HER MARRIAGE.

My brothers and I were two years old.

"Hello?" my mother answered the phone.

"Yes. I'm here."

"Who's speaking?"

"Hi. Umm. Can I speak to Tony?"

My mother said the voice on the other end of the phone answered her nervously.

It was a woman's voice.

My mother said she was thinking, "What the hell? Why is a woman calling our home in the middle of the day asking to speak to my husband?"

25

"He's not here. What do you need?" my mother responded, her tone more aggressive this time.

"It's really important. I just really need you to have him call me back as soon as possible," the woman said.

So many more thoughts flooded my mother's mind at that instant. She told me that she wanted to know who this mysterious woman was. She wasn't anyone my father had mentioned before. Was he having an affair? Could the woman be pregnant?

My mother was sitting in a chair at the door waiting for Tony when he returned home.

"You got a phone call today from some woman. She said it was urgent. Who was that?"

"It was no one, Adrienne. It's nothing. She just had a family emergency. Don't worry about it," Tony responded in defense.

"What do you mean it's no one?! If she had a family emergency, then obviously she's someone to be calling you about it!"

"I said it's nothing, Adrienne. Just leave it alone," Tony said and walked away.

Since the time I was old enough to understand, I learned that my biological father was a Detroit native with a knack for deception. When my mother first met him, he was an engineer for a Fortune 500 company. Some of his jobs involved designing architectural plans for various buildings. My family described him as a self-centered, low-key type of guy; his moves and motives were always very calculated. He never followed through with the things he said he would do.

A few days later, my mother's checks started to bounce because their account had been overdrafted. Call it a hunch, but after multiple issues with how their money was spent, something in my mother's gut told her that her husband might have a drug problem. So she called a drug line.

"I think my husband is an addict."

"What is he doing that makes you think he's using?" the lady on the other end of the line asked.

"Well, my checks have been bouncing. He says things that make no sense. And the other day this woman called the house in a panic to speak to him. I think they might be using together."

"Okay. But those are not obvious signs," the lady replied.

Tony was a functional user and was good at hiding it.

The truth came out one Michigan morning on my mother's way to work.

My mother was five minutes down the street from our three-bedroom colonial style home when she realized she forgot something and quickly turned back around. Our home had an attached two car garage and a door that opened into the kitchen.

Tony didn't hear her when she came rushing back in.

The house was still, like no one was home.

When she stepped inside, my mother smelled a funny smoke, but she couldn't recognize the scent. She said it wasn't a cigarette or marijuana—she knew what that smelled like from growing up in Chicago.

As she stood there in the entryway for a few minutes, she still couldn't make out the smell of the strange substance. "*Tony!!!*" my mother yelled. The high-pitched octave in her voice indicated a level of concern.

"Yes," my biological father answered while rushing up the stairs from the basement.

"What is that smell?"

"I'm smoking a cigarette, honey." His dilated eyes wandered around the room to avoid looking at her directly.

Sweat dripped from his forehead.

"That doesn't smell like a cigarette, and when did you start smoking?"

My mother took a few steps forward to head down to the basement to investigate the smell.

Tony cut her off.

He was smoking crack.

"Adrienne, I'm sorry. I have a drinking and drug problem."

My mother was already running up the stairs before Tony could finish the rest of his words.

Where were her triplet boys? Were we okay? Did we inhale any of the fumes?

She said her defensive instincts as a mother kicked in full force. She described how her body temperature spiked and her heart beat violently through her chest. Her eyes grew watery, but she fought back the tears.

Like an Olympic sprinter, my mother made it to the top of the stairs and poked her head into our bedroom.

My brothers and I were sound asleep, cuddled up with each other.

After my mother saw that the three of us were okay in our room, she began to worry about the communication between her and Tony.

She rushed back downstairs.

"You've been doing drugs while my babies have been in the house?!"

Tony gave her a dejected look.

"What kind of drugs? And for how long?" she asked. "Why didn't you tell me?"

"I don't know, Adrienne. I guess I felt ashamed. It's been a while now. Mostly smoking and snorting cocaine." His shoulders were slumped and his demeanor told my mother that he knew he was caught. Tony was later fired from his job as an engineer at FedEx because his addiction to narcotics affected his ability to perform. He took a couple of different jobs soon after but either quit or was fired from those positions as well. Eventually, Tony lounged around the house and refused to work.

Unfortunately, drug addiction was commonplace among all the men my mother loved.

Her brothers experienced the same struggles.

All four of my uncles—Tyrone, Cedric, Gregory, and Clarence Jr.—had substance abuse and alcohol problems. Clarence and Tyrone were the only two who made a consistent effort to keep my grandmother's well-being a priority. They did the best at taking care of their responsibilities as men. Whenever they saw my brothers and me, they would say how proud of us they were or that they loved us. Their words felt genuine.

Like a deadly wasp, drugs stung Cedric hard at a young age. I'm not sure exactly when, but years ago he left Chicago for Minneapolis to attend a drug rehab program. Uncle Cedric has been addicted to narcotics for over twenty years now. It got so bad that he even tried to steal from my grandparents.

It happened on a typical workday. When Papa would come home, the first thing he would do was place his pants on top of the brown living room chair. His wallet was always tucked away in the back pocket. Papa was walking from the back porch toward the front of the house with his tools when he saw Cedric going through his pants.

"What are you doing?"

"I need money," Cedric responded.

He continued to reach into the pocket to remove the wallet.

"No. I'm not giving you any money. You need to work for it," Papa told him. There was never a time that Papa wasn't fixing something or working. He was the type of man who would move from one job to the next, each opportunity better than the last. He embodied the word "hustle." My family believes I inherited his ambitious spirit and confidence. Papa lengthened his stride to reach his son at a faster pace. His face was furious.

Not taking no for an answer and in dire need of cash, Cedric grabbed the pants and bolted for the door. Papa leaped forward to cut him off.

Then my grandmother Mildred jumped in to join the tussle.

There they were, the two of them, united in marriage and as parents, wrestling away with their son in the middle of the living room. Cedric broke free and ran out the front door. He was not successful at stealing Papa's wallet.

But this was a common scene in the late 1980s and early 1990s— addicts robbing loved ones to get their fix. Chicago gangs had a monopoly on the flow and sale of drugs within the city.

Cocaine was a staple only wealthy Caucasians could afford, and snorting it was common in the 1970s. By combining free-base cocaine with baking soda, drug dealers could sell a cheap yet effective drug that could be smoked: crack.

Crack spread rapidly in low-income neighborhoods on the South Side due to its addictive nature. Many dedicated users committed crimes, sold drugs, or, as in Cedric's case, even stole from loved ones to continue to support their habits. My mother's brothers came up in an era when crack was rampant. Nobody within the city realized how big of an impact crack would have on the Black community.

* * * *

THE BLACK DELL keyboard *clickety-clacked* as my mother's fingertips pressed against the square keys. It had been three days since her big fight with Tony. As a global account manager at FedEx, she spent most of her time completing calls and admin tasks at her desk. It was a Thursday afternoon, and she was going through an account profile to prepare for a meeting when one of her coworkers walked up. This is another one of my mother's stories we all know by heart: her opportunity to move back home.

"Hey, Adrienne. How's it going?" her coworker asked.

"I'm good, just finishing up reviewing an account."

My mother looked up to see a gloomy frown on her colleague's face.

"What's wrong?" my mother asked.

"I've been having some issues at home with my husband and our kids. The kids are out of control, and I feel like I'm raising them all by myself," she said.

"I get it," my mother replied. "Trust me, I've been there. But don't give up on your husband. Keep working on it. Get help if you feel like you need it." My mother gave the lady a sincere smile and a hug.

"Thanks, Adrienne. I really appreciate that. I feel at ease talking to you about this stuff. You are just easy to talk to. By the way, did you see the job listing this week? I know you said you're from Chicago. It looks like a position opened up there this week."

"Oh really? I'm gonna have to check it out. And no problem. I'm always here to listen. Thanks again." My mother's sweet, melodic tones put everyone at ease.

The application was due the next day. Right away, my mother marched into her boss's office to ask for permission to apply. She had not yet worked in her position for eighteen months, so she needed his approval to transfer.

He was a Caucasian guy in his late thirties with blue eyes, sandy brown hair, and a slim build. He was sitting at his desk when my mother knocked on the door.

"John. Can I talk to you?"

"Sure, Adrienne. Wassup?"

"I want to apply for that account manager position in Chicago. My husband and I are having a tough time right now. I'm pretty much raising my triplet boys on my own," she said, remembering her coworker's words. "I realize now that I need a support system, and being back home with my parents would provide me that."

Mom was always a striver and a devoted mother.

"Do what you have to do. I understand. Family is important," he nodded.

My mother turned in the application, and two days later, she received a call from the Chicago office. They were interested.

"We reviewed your package and would like for you to come to Chicago for an interview. You will give a presentation on your thirty, sixty, and ninety-day strategy for managing accounts."

The next day, my mother took a flight from Detroit to Chicago. She parked her rental car at the building and sat there for several minutes, trying to control her nerves.

At FedEx, my mother had a good reputation for being successful and always well prepared for her presentations. She was a hard worker. But this time, everything felt rushed. Still, something within her said to go in and do the interview anyway. She had already made it this far. What did she have to lose? She might as well try.

The meeting lasted an hour and a half.

My mother was driving back to the airport when her manager, John, called.

"Hey, Adrienne. How was it?"

"Oh. I think I did okay. I don't know."

"Well, I think it went more than okay. Because they loved you! The interviewers called me the moment you walked out the office. They want you to start right away."

My mother immediately hung up with her boss and called Papa.

"Hey, honey, how's it going?" Papa answered.

"I'm alright. Dad, I'm moving back to Chicago. I found out Tony had issues dealing with drugs and alcohol. I feel like I'm raising the boys all by myself. I was just offered an account manager position at FedEx in Chicago. They want me to start immediately. Can I come back home?"

"No problem. Sure. We got you. Come on back home. Junior and I will drive up to help you pack. When do you want us to come?"

"Can we do tomorrow?"

"Yeah, sure that works. See you tomorrow, honey."

My mother said she hung up the phone and let out a sigh of relief.

She had had enough. She knew Tony was not reliable, and she needed help raising us. The last thing she wanted to do was leave, but given the current circumstances, she knew she needed a support system.

The only problem was that the area she was used to had changed dramatically since her childhood. Shit was different now.

As promised, Junior and Papa arrived early in the morning the next day. Our four- or five-hour trip from Detroit to Chicago was mostly a blur for us kids. My mother told us about how once we'd gotten in the house and moved our stuff upstairs, she took a moment to stand in front of the bathroom mirror and look at herself. Staring back at her own reflection, she said she felt like someone had just taken an anchor off her shoulder. She thought about how glad she was that she had asked for help. She didn't truly realize the level of tension this entire experience had brought her until then. She gathered herself and exited the bathroom.

"Where's Mom?" she asked Junior.

"She's downstairs."

When my mother opened the basement door, she could smell something burning.

She walked down the creaky, red-brown wooden stairs to find my grandmother standing over one of her girlfriends, doing her hair. Throughout my childhood, my grandmother had a beauty salon set up in her basement. The smell of burnt hair from the hot curling iron, and the sound of loud laughter and women gossiping, greeted us the moment we opened the door to walk downstairs. At home, Grandma was like a hybrid drill sergeant. She kept things around the house in order. Three home-cooked meals a day. Church every Sunday. No excuses.

A diva at heart, we would call her; my mother obtained her strong sense for fashion from Mildred. As a kid, I recall how my grandmother's dark brown maple closet failed to hold the abundance of clothes stored within it. A multitude of rainbow-colored shoe boxes hugged the white shelves. And when she dressed, she did so to captivate.

"Hey, honey!" Grandma put down the hot curling iron and walked over to hug my mother.

"Hey, Mom. How are you?"

"I'm good. I can't complain. How you holdin' up?"

"I'm doing alright. Things get better every day. I feel like so much has changed since I left."

"Yeah, baby. A lot has changed. Especially the neighborhood."

CHAPTER 3

A RUDE AWAKENING

WHAT WOULD YOU DO IF YOU MOVED TO A PLACE YOU THOUGHT WAS A FRESH START, YET YOU ENDED UP FIGHTING FOR SURVIVAL EVERY DAY?

When my mother moved back in with her parents in 1995, she was still married to Tony. A couple of years went by. My mother gave him a chance to step up, but Tony refused to put in much effort. I only saw my biological father twice after we moved from Detroit. On both occasions, my mother took us there to visit. On the first trip, she took my brothers and me to our Grandma Martha's house, where he stopped by to visit briefly.

Martha was a simple Catholic woman with pale skin and a soft, raspy voice. She was over thirty-five years old when she gave birth to Tony, her only child. She idolized him—spoiled him, even—and as a result, my biological father failed to learn the values and morals he should have learned. Despite the fact that Tony didn't have a relationship with my brothers and me, Martha did. She loved us dearly and was dedicated to calling us frequently. As a child, I remember the joy my brothers and

I had the many times she caught the train to visit Chicago. She even kept in contact with my other grandmother, Mildred. They talked on the phone at least once a month.

The second time I saw Tony was at his apartment.

It was a small, two-bedroom place. I spent most of my time at his black dining room table. On the table and all along the couch were piles of *MAD Magazines*. Most of them had this kid on the front, with big elf-like ears, freckles, and chubby cheeks. Right next to the magazines was a sketch pad and multiple sheets of paper that depicted drawings of characters and scenes from the publication that Tony had completed. It was clear he was a fan.

"Andre. Here, see if you can try and draw something out of the magazine," my biological father said.

He handed me his sketch pad and a pencil. I can't recall what my brothers were doing at that moment, probably watching TV or playing with action figures. But Tony didn't ask them to come and draw at the table.

A part of me felt more connected to him than my brothers because I was light-skinned and looked just like him. Plus, we were both artists. I never took an art class in my life, but I inherited my father's gift to draw. It came naturally for me to produce great works of art with various mediums at a young age. I could pick up a pencil, marker, paint brush, and without thinking—almost instinctively—create artwork that blew people's minds.

I completed the sketch and brought it back to Tony.

"That's pretty good, Andre. Now, look, you see the ears? Try adding some shading here to make them look more developed and real. And on the lips, round them out a little bit more at the bottom."

I went back to the table and followed his tips. While I sat there drawing away, I had this warm fuzzy feeling inside. Like the feeling you get when you first start dating a lady you really like. I'd never had this type of experience with Tony before, and I loved being able to discuss art with him.

"Andre, I want to show you something."

Tony went into his bedroom and emerged with a big brown portfolio. He opened it up and showed me all these large pieces of artwork and drawings he had done. One in particular stood out to me.

"What's that?" I asked, pointing at the 2D rendering.

"That's an architectural blueprint of a mall I designed."

The moment he uttered those words, I decided I wanted to be an architect as well.

Tony spent a short time with us that day, only a couple hours, before he finally called our mother.

"Adrienne, I'm ready for you to come pick the boys up."

"What? Tony. Are you serious? I just dropped them off to you not that long ago. You've barely seen them. I brought them all the way to Detroit just to see you."

My mother came by the house and went into the second bedroom and exchanged some words with Tony.

"Come on, guys, it's time to go," she said, emerging from the room after a few minutes.

Before I left, Tony stopped me.

"Andre, take my portfolio. I want you to have it."

I smiled.

I grabbed one of Tony's *MAD Magazines* and a couple pieces of sketch pad paper, and placed them inside the large brown portfolio as well. Then I walked out the front door with my mother and brothers.

That was the last time I saw my father.

Despite my biological father's flaws, my mother never tried to portray him negatively to us. She let us ask questions and form our own opinions instead. I've always appreciated her for that. Tony could call or visit as much as he liked.

But he never did.

* * * *

WHEN MY GRANDPARENTS first bought their home at West 61st Street, Englewood was peaceful. For hours, Papa would sit out on the front porch in his foldable red chair and watch kids play in the streets while he drank a cold Heineken beer or two. It was the beer all the men in my family drank. The sweet smell of delectable foods filled the nostrils of passersby while my grandma threw down cooking in the kitchen. Blue-collar, hardworking African Americans occupied all the homes. For my grandparents, this was their taste of the American Dream.

Every now and then, when we were old enough, my mother or grandparents would send us on a mission to the corner store to fetch some milk, bread, or whatever other small items they needed. We were allowed to use the extra change to buy Hostess honey buns, gummy snacks, and pop. This sounds like a normal childhood, but as the years progressed, home vacancies grew, drugs and gangs swallowed up the blocks, and violence plagued Englewood. There were so many vacant lots where weeds had grown so tall you could barely see the pavement. The row of houses cast a dark shadow of depression and neglect over the neighborhood. Like a rose sprouting out of the concrete, Grandma's house, with its tidy flowers, vegetable garden, and clean-cut grass, stood out among the sea of gray, broken-windowed houses full of prostitutes, thieves, and drug activity.

It was another humid Chicago summer. Cracked alcohol bottles, burnt cigarettes and blunt tips, and pieces of trash covered the ground as my brothers and I made our way to the brown brick corner store. There was a group of guys playing basketball in the street. They created their own makeshift hoop by using a red crate they'd cut a hole in and a wood panel to create their rim and backboard. Black steel gates surrounded all the store windows, another sign that the neighborhood had turned rough.

When we came out of the store with our bags, there was a group of guys playing street craps (shooting dice) against the side of the store. Sometimes you would see guys out there for hours, addicted to gambling or any way they could earn a fast buck. Right next to them was another fella scratching off a lottery ticket. I remember seeing a man standing on his porch across the street. He wore a black hat, red T-shirt, and baggy blue jeans. Like a hawk observing its prey, he stared us down.

Staring down people as they walk by or drive past is an unspoken rite of passage in Chicago. It is a measure of your strength and the fight of the dog in you. When I noticed another man passing by, with a firm face, I stared hard, and my head followed him until he went by me. In most cases, if you looked away during a stare down, you were considered weak. Some people would use that as an opportunity to stop and confront you.

I got this weird feeling in my stomach when I felt the man's stare. My heartbeat sped up.

Something was wrong.

I'd gained some type of sixth sense. Call it intuition, or in my words, "following my gut." Maybe it was another gift God put inside me. Like second nature, I quickly became very obser-vant of how people conducted themselves, which allowed me to know what to say or do in the heat of the moment. I watched the pace of their footsteps. Did the contour of their face change when they noticed me? Did their eyes wander, or were they fixed in a gaze? What story did they tell? How were their hands positioned? What about the tone and elevation of their voices? All these questions poured into my head within seconds of observing someone, and I was still just a little kid.

Three older guys walking toward us blocked our path on the sidewalk.

"Look at these three. What you got in those bags?" one of the big kids said.

He had dark chocolate skin and an oval head. His fake sparkling earrings hung on the edges of his large earlobes, screaming for attention. All three of them were dressed in black: plain 2XL T-shirts, baggy pants, and low top Nike Air Force 1s. They could see our soda cans and some of the snack wrappers protruding from the black plastic bags.

"Give it to us now before we make you."

The leader of the group curled his fists into a ball. The other two accomplices followed suit.

All three of us stared back at our aggressors with blank faces. We'd never been robbed before. We didn't know how to respond.

"Yo, let's fuck these little dudes up, cuz."

The leader of the crew stepped closer toward my face.

I kept looking around, hoping that someone would walk by or that a car would stop and help us. But no one did. Cars just kept cruising down the streets with their large twenty-two-inch rims and trunk speakers blasting rap music. The entire car would vibrate. Parked cars and surrounding houses shook as they drove by. We could feel the sound vibrating through our bodies.

I realized right then that my brothers and I were on our own. No one gave a fuck. This was normal. The South Side was the lost outlet of Chicago and the streets fed off evil. This was what I called home. I thought moving here was supposed to mean a better life for us. I wanted everything to be perfect, especially after everything Mom had been through with Tony.

I hesitated for a moment and glanced at my brothers. But after looking at their faces, I knew this wasn't a fight worth fighting, especially not over some food. They were much bigger than we were, and my brothers were not in the mood to fight.

I slowly stretched out my hand. My brothers did the same.

The three goons snatched our bags and took off running down the street.

"Ah ha. They got yo ass," I heard someone yell. Three shirtless young African American boys rode past on bikes, their jeans hanging so low below their butts I could see the color and texture of their boxers.

What in the world? What type of place is this?

Although a minor situation at best, that day was my first hard wake-up call to life on the South Side. And it wouldn't be my last.

We had failed to blend into our environment to avoid attention, which was a critical tool for survival. Like a job, half the battle of making it day-to-day on the South Side was just looking the part. In the eyes of the hood, we were potential prey. Individuals who looked out of place could be taken advantage of.

After staying at my grandmother's for a few years, my mother managed to save enough money to move us to a three-bedroom, two-bathroom single-family home on the South Side. The roughly one-thousand-square-foot bungalow had a maroon-brown shingle roof and was constructed out of light brown brick. A small patch of lawn directly in front stretched out to the sidewalk, and a large driveway ran from the curb to a two-car garage at the back of the house. When my mother returned from work or running errands, my brothers and I would peek through the wide rectangular windows out front just to see her old mud green Jeep Wrangler pull up in the driveway. This was our first home together as a family without a man present, and the start to a new chapter of beginnings.

Then, we got robbed. Again.

Someone broke into our home. It was 1999, Richard M. Daley was the mayor of Chicago, Black civil unrest was rampant across the country, and Bobby Rush was running for mayoral office, capturing most of the African American vote. A woman my mother grew up with referred her to a guy she knew who was now in the business of installing security systems. He was a former police officer. A few days later, the gentleman made a visit to our home to observe the layout of the windows and doors and provide an estimate. During the visit, he intentionally unlocked one of the side windows in the dining room area without my mother's knowledge. What I remember was what I saw when we came home from the store a few days later.

I was the first one to enter the house. Initially, everything looked normal. There was no damage in the kitchen, and nothing looked out of place. In order to walk up the carpet-covered stairs to the bedroom my brothers and I shared, we had to pass by the dining room. The house had an open floor plan that connected it to the living room. As I walked in the dining room, I could see the silhouette of what appeared to be something lying on the floor.

I flipped the white light switch on the wall next to me.

On the floor, opened and torn into pieces, was my mother's long, light brown wooden jewelry box.

"Mom! Your jewelry box is on the floor," I said in a concerned and elevated tone of voice.

My mother burst into the room.

"Oh my God!"

She reached down and started fumbling through the box.

"Somebody robbed us."

Ten or fifteen minutes later, there were cops walking around our home.

"I believe he sat outside and waited for an opportunity for us to leave one day. My sons and I took a short trip to the grocery store. He was in the house when we pulled up. He had to be. As we came in the door, he probably ran out the window," my mother told the police.

The thief went into my mother's bedroom and stole her one-and-a-half carat wedding ring from Tony and a thousand-dollar Raymond Weil watch my mom bought for herself as a gift. After the police finally left, my mom walked over and took a seat at the edge of the stairs. I remember how quiet the house was. It was an eerie feeling. Then, my mother buried her face in her hands and lap, and the only sound we could hear was her crying. I sat at the kitchen table and watched her. And I began to cry hard, too. Right then, I realized how dark the world truly was. And I realized how much of an impact my mother had on me.

"Are you okay, Mean Person?" I said, walking up to her.

When I was a child, I started to call her the "Mean Person" as a joke. Truthfully, she never was mean, but it's an inside joke that constantly reminds the two of us to be nice to others. In return, she would respond by calling me the "Meaner." I found joy playing little shenanigans on her, such as throwing snowballs or sprinkling water on her, whatever silly little thing I could do to make her smile. That was our version of "mean." We still poke and play-punch each other all the time.

"I feel violated. Someone invaded our space and stole my personal belongings. Growing up, that watch was something I really wanted, and I saved and saved and saved until I could afford it," she said to me in reflection.

"Come here, honey." She pulled me in and gave me a big bear hug.

Despite my stubbornness when I was a kid, I hung on her every word, even when she thought I wasn't listening. It would kill me inside if I disappointed her. She has always been the source of my authority, and even today I seek her guidance. I wish I could repay the sacrifices she made for my brothers and me, raising triplet boys on her own. I wish there were more things I could do to show her how much I admire her and how thankful I am for her.

And then Mom did something extreme.

She seldom made mistakes or did anything out of the ordinary. But she made one mistake so drastic that it would change my childhood forever and even cause me to doubt her at times.

She married an angry, abusive man.

CHAPTER 4

GROCERY STORE STALKER

I HATE VIDEO GAMES.

My mother was in the video game section of Sam's Club when a five foot ten, dark-skinned man walked up to her. He had a thick black mustache and coarse hair. His black gym shoe sneakers and faded blue jeans suggested he preferred a more laid-back, dress-down style. "You like playing video games?" the man asked. My mother looked at him with a shrewd face and blew him off. She grabbed a game and moved to another aisle in the store. The blue cursive letters on the yellow Bisquick box caught my mother's eyes as she grabbed a box from the shelf. Like a ritual, every Saturday or Sunday morning, my mother would make chocolate chip pancakes for my brothers and me. She was an amazing cook.

With three growing boys to feed, Sam's allowed my mother to shop for groceries in bulk at an affordable price. The moment customers walk into the warehouse-like store, their eyes are bombarded with an army of multicolored display items

51

advertised for sale. One week the display could be computers, another week clothes. On that particular week, it was video games. Avid gamers, Anthony and Alex would sit at home and play for hours. I never found playing video games as exciting. After an hour or two, I was done. I spent most of my time drawing or playing in the streets instead.

"You're following me."

It was the man from the video game aisle again.

"Excuse me?" my mother blurted out with a hint of attitude as she looked up. Her gaze was intense as she told him, "In your dreams."

"You love making pancakes?"

My mother made a twisted face. She was not trying to act like a snob, but this dude was acting like a creep.

"I'm sorry, I have to go."

My mom excused herself and expediently pushed her cart toward the register for checkout. The man walked up behind her and started another conversation as they waited in line.

"Hey, I promise I'm not following you or trying to be weird. My name is Dwayne." He extended his hand.

"Adrienne."

"I would like to get to know you more."

"Look, I don't have time to waste. I have triplet boys at home I have to raise."

"Oh, okay. That's fine. I own a barbershop on the South Side called Franklin's. Here's my card. You should bring the boys by one day."

One thing led to another, and they exchanged numbers before leaving the store.

My mother never took us to that barber shop. I'm not sure why.

Dwayne spent a considerable amount of time cutting hair and managing the barbershop, was passionate about radio broadcasting, and loved to drive. On the surface, he wasn't like the rest of the men my mother was used to (her brothers and Tony). He was simple. He had some of those same hard working principles Papa had, and for my Mom, that meant stability and assurance. Plus it was hard to find a man on the South Side who wanted to be with a woman who had triplet boys.

* * * *

IT WAS A sunny December day, and the South Side was coated with about four or five inches of fresh, fluffy white snow. At this point my mother and Dwayne had been dating for a few months, and she wanted to see how we would respond after meeting him and vice versa. I was seven years old. We all met at Dan Ryan Woods Forest Preserve on 87th and Western Avenue. They had huge hills and slopes that my brothers and I enjoyed riding down with our sleds. I was dressed in my poofy forest green coat with snow pants. My brothers and I were standing at the top of the hill when Dwayne walked up and gave my mother a hug. Like a loud record being scratched in a room, my brothers and I stopped what we were doing and stared.

We looked at one another and shared the same expression. *Who was this guy? And how did he know our mother?*

I shrugged my shoulders at Alex, slightly tilted my head, and pointed my thumb at Dwayne.

"You know this guy?" I asked.

"Nah. I don't know that guy," Alex responded.

Alex did the same. He shrugged his shoulders at Anthony and pointed his thumb toward Dwayne.

"You know this guy, Atna?"

"No, I don't know him," he responded.

Mind you, my brothers and I spent a lot of time with our mother. We took trips together, went to the park, went on plane rides, everything. The relationship my mother had with my brothers and me was tight. We were like our own little gang. And now we had this foreign person trying to come around and join.

I went to the top of a hill and got in my red sled. Alex pushed me down. I was almost at the bottom of the hill when, *wham*, my sled toppled over and my face plummeted into the cold snow. I jumped up to my feet. My mother stayed at the top to watch as we went down. Dwayne was at the bottom of the hill and walked over to try and wipe the snow off my face.

"No!" I responded and swiped his hand away with an attitude. Dwayne's neck jerked back in surprise. His facial expression turned serious.

"Oh. You think you're a hard guy, huh? Alright, get it yourself," he commented back in an aggressive tone.

We obviously didn't get off to the best start. My mother didn't notice our tense, awkward interaction.

Dwayne grew up on the South Side of Chicago and became a ward of the state at the age of six. Unfortunately, Dwayne didn't know who his biological father was.

Whether he and I acknowledged it or not, from the moment we first met, the absence of biological fathers was a commonality we shared.

Dwayne was a foster kid for a few months before he was adopted by the Franklin family. Willie and Lubertha Franklin came to Chicago from West Point, Mississippi. They migrated to the South Side by riding in the back of an old pickup truck eating nothing but cold chicken and bread. Mind you, back then, it took them four to five days to arrive because the max speed limit was only forty miles per hour.

Dwayne said the Franklins didn't treat him any differently from their own blood children, yet in reality, his acceptance into the family wasn't unconditional.

"Is that your son?" people would randomly ask on the street.

"Yeah, that's my stepson," Mr. Franklin would respond. Dwayne hated when Mr. Franklin made comments like that because it made him feel unloved. Much of the stress and anger issues he incurred over the years were a reaction to the pain and insecurities he developed as a child. He simply had a strong desire to belong. But he never joined any gangs, clubs, or groups to help him cope. Thinking back, I now understand why it upset him so much when I just called him Dwayne or introduced him to others as my stepfather.

Adding to the pressure was Dwayne's mother, Barbara. She abandoned him at birth but later gave him the impression that she wanted to make amends.

Or did she make things worse in the end by attempting to come back around? Dwayne told us the stories of stunts his mother pulled.

Like how one day Barbara showed up at the house. She shut the door of her green sedan and kept the engine running to make her escape that much more expeditious. Then she quietly climbed the steps of the Franklins' maroon brick bungalow in Chatham. It was a roughly sixteen-hundred-square-foot, single-family home built in the 1900s. There was a square-shaped lawn out front that extended from the small flower garden near the house to the curb of the street. A sidewalk split the front lawn in half, and a long walkway ran along the left side of the house toward the backyard and garage.

Barbara pressed the yellow doorbell a few times and quickly dropped off a wrapped gift on the Franklins' front porch. She then swiftly ran back to the car. The four large concrete steps and sidewalk from the front porch to the curb of the street wasn't a quick sprint. By the time Barbara made it to the car, Mrs. Franklin was already at the large square front window of her home and looked through the blinds to see Barbara driving off hurriedly. Dwayne said this pattern of behavior continued for a few years and later bled into Barbara periodically calling to harass the Franklins.

"Hello?" Mrs. Franklin would answer.

"Is this the Franklin residence?"

"Yes. Who's speaking?"

"You need to give me my son back. You don't deserve him."

"Excuse me? Who the hell is this?"

Click. Barbara would hang up.

Tired of all the drama, Mrs. Franklin called the state and told them to come get Dwayne when he was a freshman in high school.

And they did.

That's when Dwayne moved away and started living with his mother. He said it was total chaos. He stayed with Barbara his freshman and sophomore year before he couldn't take it anymore. Having been taught how to do things one way and then being told something different at her place drove my stepfather crazy. Desperate for change, he packed up his things and left his mother to stay at the YMCA until he graduated.

Dwayne told us so many stories of how hard he had it in high school. He told us how his business teacher, Mr. Reynolds, noticed in class that Dwayne was homeless and not getting any rest. Dwayne just didn't look like a kid who went to a decent, stable home every night.

"What's going on, Mr. Johnson?" Mr. Reynolds asked Dwayne after class one day.

"Nothing is going on, sir. I'm fine." Dwayne said he tried to play it off and didn't tell the teacher anything. Mr. Reynolds continued to approach him a couple more times, but still nothing. Until one of his classmates mentioned to Mr. Reynolds that he was staying at the YMCA.

"Which YMCA are you staying at?" Mr. Reynolds came back to ask another day.

My stepfather said he still tried to fool his teacher. "I'm not staying at the YMCA. I don't know why you would think that."

Mr. Reynolds wanted to help Dwayne. He told Dwayne there was no need to be ashamed and that he was going to get him a job at Jewel's bagging groceries. That way, Dwayne could earn money and take care of himself.

Dwayne held that job at Jewel's until he graduated from high school and joined the Army at eighteen.

* * * *

WHEN MY BROTHERS and I were in sixth grade, Dwayne Corey Johnson married my mother in sunny Las Vegas. That probably worked out for the best because if I had been present, there's a good chance I would have interfered in the ceremony. I wasn't ready to trust another man as my father just yet, nor was I convinced that he was the best fit for my mother.

Isn't that what any overprotective son would do?

But it was too late. Once my parents got married, Dwayne felt he had full rein to discipline and say whatever he wanted to my brothers and me.

If it wasn't tearing our behinds apart, he had us touch our toes for hours until we could barely lean over and began to fall. Our legs would ache and cramp. Or he'd take pleasure in burning our toys and valuables on a grill. Just imagine it: the image of Dwayne filling our black circular bottom grill with charcoal, lighting it with a box of matches, and tossing our electronics and toys into an abyss of smoke and flames. The toys emitted a *hiss, crackle, pop, scream* while they burned under the intense heat. You would think they had a life of their own and that they were pleading for help.

But one of the worst punishments was the manual labor.

At our bungalow home, we had a long patch of red rocks that ran alongside the house. To punish us, Dwayne would have my brothers and I pick up the rocks individually with our hands and place them in large black trash cans. Our hands would be bruised and cramped up from the action. The memory of the way the red residue from the rocks would get on my clothes and hands and take forever to scrub out, or the pain my body would feel from the endless hours of bending over really stuck with me. It wasn't unusual for us to spend the entire day—sometimes multiple days in a row depending on the severity of the punishment—picking up rocks. It's crazy how hours of manual labor has a way of making you go to another place mentally. If I look at things holistically, I bet that's what my stepdad was trying to achieve. He wanted us to realize our faults and in turn change our behavior. I took those moments instead to daydream about being the cool kid everyone liked. And it hardened my disdain for him. Yes, it made my brain ponder deeply—I'll give him that—but it didn't change the way I acted. I was still a hardheaded kid.

Dwayne was also good at combining physical and emotional abuse.

My mother was a churchgoing woman. We went to service every Sunday, and she demanded Dwayne do the same. We were supposed to prepare our church clothes on Saturday nights. It was a household rule.

Of course, I didn't do it that one weekend. I came out of the bedroom Sunday morning, and the moment I walked into the living room area, Dwayne saw that my plain blue long-sleeved shirt was wrinkled.

"What the fuck are you wearing? Why didn't you iron your shirt? Aren't you supposed to prepare your church clothes the night before?"

"I forgot."

His face grew even more intense.

"Go downstairs right now and iron that shirt, boy. We'll talk about this when we get back from church."

I ironed my shirt, and we all loaded up into the van to drive to Apostolic Faith Church. We walked down the red carpeted aisle. Right before entering the pew, Anthony pretended he had to tie his shoe. Alex started walking slow.

Fuck.

The three of us knew you always wanted to be the farthest away toward the end of the pew. That way, if you did nod off or sleep in church, it wasn't as noticeable. Plus that kept you safe from being hit.

I sat right next to Dwayne. When the minister got up to start preaching, I felt a cloud of drowsiness overtake my body. It was like someone instantly put a spell on me. The large sanctuary became hot. I tried grinding my teeth, playing with my fingers, and tapping my toes, but nothing worked. Off and on, my eyes began to open and shut slowly.

Dwayne caught wind of my eye movement and the way my head began to drop and looked over at me. My brothers noticed me too. They looked up and locked eyes with Dwayne. In fear and in an attempt to save me, Anthony started nudging me in the side. I popped back up awake. But a couple minutes later, I started to drift again.

Dwayne looked over again and caught me. Before Anthony could nudge and warn me, Dwayne lifted his hand and *wham!* Right there in the middle of church, he slapped the back of my head. I swear, it felt like he hit me so hard the whole congregation heard it and the bishop stopped preaching.

I grabbed the back of my head and gave him an evil "what the fuck" look.

"You better wake up," he whispered in response. "Just wait till we get home."

I was downstairs in the basement drawing when Dwayne came stomping down the stairs after church.

"Get up! You didn't iron your shirt this morning, and you were falling asleep in church. You shouldn't even be tired. It's not like you work or do anything around the house."

"Yeah, whatever," I said and rolled my eyes.

He scrunched his face up and balled his fists.

"You think you're so hard, don't you?! You think you a man."

Dwayne punched me in the chest, and I flew back, crashing into the wall. He was so much bigger than me. Even if I did try

and fight him back, I knew I would surely get my ass beat. And
he knew it too.

"You're not good at art, you're not good at playing trombone,
you're not smart. You ain't shit." Spit flew from his mouth as he
shouted at me.

I'll never forget my stepfather's words. They cut me emotionally and mentally. What he said stabbed my spirit with
conviction. He probably thought he was doing me some type
of service by challenging me. Yet what made it hurt the most
was that he was supposed to act like my parent, not like an
enemy.

"Art is worthless. It will not make you any money," he
proclaimed. "You barely even draw anyway. You not finna be
nobody's architect. If you was really serious about that shit,
you would be doing it every day."

"What about my music then?" I said in defense.

"Stop it, Andre. You don't even take music seriously. You barely
practice, and you're not even that good."

I didn't study that much in school either, and my grades were
not the best. Man, I felt like a failure.

In the far left corner of the basement was a square insert in the
wall where my mud brown art desk was located.

Dwayne walked over and grabbed the portfolio that held my
father's drawings and some of my own and began to tear them

apart. He threw some of the pieces on the floor and put the rest in the black trash can next to my studio desk.

I was shocked.

I don't think Dwayne realized how much he wounded me that night. That artwork was the only thing I had left connecting me to my biological father. Despite how I felt about him and the complexity of that relationship, that portfolio still had a lot of sentimental value for me.

Now, it was gone.

I sat there in the chair and cried hard, painful tears as he walked back upstairs from the basement. My anger gave me a head-ache. Sitting there in the empty basement by myself, I tried not to think about what had just happened, but it was hard not to. For years to come, that night would haunt my memories. And for several more years, Dwayne would continue to say mean and degrading words about my worthiness and ability to succeed in life as a man. But the anger and pain from my step-father's words lit a fire in me. It was some of the most valuable advice I could have ever received. I learned to live in the fire and harshness of his words. I used that pain to motivate me for years to come.

The only thing on my mind from that moment on was *I'll prove you wrong*.

CHAPTER 5

THE HALLWAYS OF SURVIVAL

WE ALMOST LOST ALEX THAT DAY. HE ESCAPED DEATH BY A FEW SECONDS.

Our family later moved from our bungalow home into the Franklins' old house in Chatham after they passed away. My brothers and I transferred to John Marshall Harlan Community Academy, a public high school located in the Roseland neighborhood. We participated in their middle school program for seventh and eighth grade. The curriculum was supposed to enhance students academically before they entered high school. The high school kids would still pick on the middle schoolers despite their older age and bigger size. But life in Chicago taught me to be hard edged. I had just joined the street gang around this time. On multiple occasions, I found myself sparring away, defending myself as well as my brothers. Word got out that I could handle myself, and I was deemed cool. Come to find out, it made being a thug even more attractive to me. It placed a shield of protection around the three of us, and people left us alone.

Harlan was a one-level, muddy brown school. It was full of dysfunctional metal detectors and was known for its infestation of gangs and drugs. On my first day, there was crack spilled across the bathroom floor. Cops were everywhere. Even teachers were affiliated with gangs. I was walking through the hallway to class when a tall Black woman wearing a red blouse, a black blazer, and black pants walked up to three older guys pressed against the school's baby blue colored lockers. "What up, fellas," she said. "Was gud." The instructor extended her hand and began to shake up *Vice Lord* with all three boys. "Shaking up" or "stacking" is a way members or so-called gang affiliates communicate or identify with one another. Each sect of Vice Lords has different forms of handshakes, but the formation of the Vice Lord symbol at some point within the shake is universal. The most recognized Vice Lord symbol is the *VL*, which involves an upraised hand with the thumb, middle finger, and index finger extended outward. The other two fingers are curled down. The three older guys were dressed in black and red and had maroon bandanas hanging from their pockets.

My classmates and I attended most of our courses in another building separate from the main high school. A rough, gray, zigzag paved road ran down to another murky brown, one-level building where we were taught a curriculum of Spanish, English, math, and history. Our "easy" courses, music and art, were taught in the main school building. Art was the only class in which I truly excelled. In my eyes, school wasn't a priority because I was never really a great student. I only went because I knew my mother would kill me if I tried to drop out. My focus was girls and being cool.

Then I met a young lady named Brittany. She had Hershey brown chocolate skin, a curvy frame, a bright smile, and a silly personality. We hit it off, and she became my girlfriend. After class on sunny days, my classmates and I would gather outside our school building and just chill. Everyone formed their own little cliques. The biggest and tallest kid in our class was a guy named Chris. He was light-skinned, had big, round Dumbo ears, and loved to play basketball.

Word got out that Brittany was my girl.

"That's why yo girl is a bitch," Chris said. He was bitter about an argument we had previously had about who was better on the basketball court.

Look, I was not passionate about the sport, but for whatever reason, Chris always tried to challenge me to see who was better or to boast about how good he was. At the time, Chris and I both played for the middle school varsity team where I walked on and took his starting spot as center. I'm willing to bet that's where his discontent toward me stemmed from. Although I did play ball for a year or two, sports never really became a thing for me. And then there was the added bonus that aside from my two brothers, Chris and I were the two tallest kids in class, and being typical teenage boys, we competed for dominance. It was only a matter of time before we butted heads.

"What the fuck did you say about my girl?" I answered back aggressively.

I was done talking. I pushed Chris with all my strength at the base of his chest and watched him stumble back. Like a swarm of bees attracted to honey, it didn't take long before a crowd surrounded us in a circle. Yelling. Cheering. Like any fight. But I blocked it out. I put my fists up and pranced around the pavement like it was my natural habitat. I was a concrete ballerina.

Jab. Jab.

Move to the right.

Jab. Jab.

Move to the left. Lean back.

In one final combo move, Chris surged toward me with a fury of powerful punches that could have possibly knocked me out, but luckily missed. Like Michael B. Jordan in *Creed*, I landed my own combination of serious blows to Chris's face, giving him a black eye. I was in the heat of battle when our primary middle school instructor and disciplinarian, Ms. Arrington, swooped in and broke up the fight.

"Hey, hey, hey. Stop this. Cut it out," she screamed in her raspy voice.

"*I see you, Dre!*" Girls screamed and shouted my name.

The fight was over. I had won. And all I had to show for it was my pride. I was happy because I was building my credibility around school that I was not to be fucked with. The best part about it was the rush I'd felt course through my veins while

I was in the middle of the ring. I loved the exciting bad boy, risk-taker high, combined with feeling nervous that I might get hurt or end up in trouble.

That type of risk-taker mentality got me in a lot of trouble growing up, but it was also the force I needed that, when harnessed the right way, would later allow me to defy statistics and accomplish the goals I prioritized for myself in life.

* * * *

THE WALK FROM Harlan to our Chatham home took roughly forty minutes. Humid summer, fall, or bitter cold, the Evans trio walked to and from school every day. In my stepfather's mind, he reasoned that the three of us walking to school saved him gas money. When the last bell rang, a sea of students surrounded the front courtyard. From the outside looking in, it had the buzz and appearance of any high school. However, it was the walking home that made me nervous. To this day I can't figure out where hangin' on the corner came from. Throughout the South Side, you could always find people posted up on the corner, like planted trees. Walking home was no different. I would spot a large group of guys standing on the edge of the block dressed in all blue. On another day, a posse of ten to twenty guys would be dressed in red or yellow. Throughout the South Side and West Side of Chicago, there are more than 600 gang factions. This is a big reason why it has been hard to control the violence. With so many crews, and no central leadership like there used to be back in the 1950s, many of the gangs are small cliques that just do whatever they please without answering to anyone. The most notable include the

Gangster Disciples, Black Disciples, Mickey Cobras, Black P. Stones, Latin Kings, and Vice Lords—to name just a few. On more occasions than I can count, my brothers and I found ourselves taking various longer routes home to avoid the gangs or any troublemakers. It would be foolish to attempt to walk past them; you were basically asking for trouble if you did so. Not only that, but I had to continue to protect my own secret identity as a member of one of the street gangs. "Anthony, Alex, walk across the street," "Go through that alley," or "Cut through that backyard" were common phrases I would say to my brothers to avoid crossing paths with other gangs. A walk that should have taken forty minutes ended up being an hour or longer. No discredit to my brothers, but they just weren't street smart. My sixth sense was always tugging at my gut, alerting me where to move to avoid danger and protect my brothers.

The breeze from the humid summer air was just enough to cool us along our walk. Birds chirped in the trees. There were numerous "DON'T SHOOT" signs posted on street corners and buildings. The hustle and bustle of the CTA bus, people yelling, and garbage trucks immersed our ears with a symphony of sounds.

Then my heart started to speed up. My gut started screaming.

Something was wrong.

I turned around quickly.

Two men dressed in all black approached us.

Somehow, they managed to pick us out and followed us home.

Damn. We were literally down the street from the house. The two guys ran up on us. "Run dem pockets, cuz. Give me everything you got. You better not run. I got a gun." One guy lifted up a piece of his extra-large black T-shirt to reveal the butt stock of a forty cal.

Alex took off running.

"Alex, stop!!! Alex, come back!" I screamed. I couldn't believe it.

In that split second, three thoughts went through my head.

One, was this it? Would Anthony and I be shot or jumped?

Two, would they shoot Alex?

The thought of my little brother being gunned down in front of me stirred a quick feeling of sadness, fear, and pain all at once in my stomach.

Three, anger. Frustration toward Alex that he had abandoned us in a critical moment. The men in black never drew their guns. The key was to play it cool and not escalate the situation. I've known people who have lost their lives due to pride or anger. One of the critical keys to surviving on the South Side was remaining calm and not feeling like you have to prove yourself and react to every situation. "Anthony, give them whatever money you have," I barked. I did the same. We handed over the little cash we had without letting them run through our pockets. I never carried valuables with me when I walked to and from school because I knew it would make me a potential target. If we ever did get jumped, they would search our pants and book bags and find nothing. The mysterious men in black took off running in the opposite direction. I turned and looked at Anthony. "This some bull."

Growing up, Alex and I always seemed to butt heads. For this reason, my parents made us share a room. Anthony had his own. We would bicker over the most random topics. Alex seemed to get upset at every little thing I did. But I was still pissed at him for running away.

Growing up, my mother always taught my brothers and me the importance of forgiveness as Christians, and to never harbor anger in our hearts when we went to bed at night. I would later go on to use this advice as a guiding principle whenever I found myself in disagreement with others. We don't have to like each other or be cool, but I would forgive you and remove any bitterness I had toward you from my heart. Life is too short to be bitter or envious toward others. The next day, Alex apologized for running from the robbery, and from that moment forward we built a stronger bond as brothers. He and I both tried hard to work together more and learn what each other liked and did not like. In the end, the event brought us together.

CHAPTER 6

NO FORGIVENESS

HIS FACE WAS BLEEDING.

My fists had blood on them.

I knew the actions I had just committed would put us at war and cause me to have to watch my back.

But I had no other choice but to hurt him.

I'd never hated...been so angry...wanted to punish someone as much as I did that cool August night in Chicago.

Here's how it went down.

It was Saturday. My brothers and I were upstairs playing video games on our handheld devices when we heard the shouts. The yelling grew louder, and feet stomped hard on the square kitchen tiles. I heard banging and the loud shuffle of furniture.

My mother and stepfather argued often when we were growing up. When it happened, my brothers and I would try to leave the house or go upstairs to our rooms to separate ourselves as much as we could. Things always ended the same way. Mom would back down and quiet herself because she knew Dwayne would always keep going until he proved he was right. His stubbornness was extreme. To make matters worse, their arguments occurred sporadically from the smallest, most random things. Some days Dwayne would come home smiling from a good day. He'd be in a silly mood joking with my mother. Then five minutes later, like he was bipolar, he'd be upset about something and raise hell. It was so rare to experience him in a continuous state of happiness that when he was, we cherished it because it meant peace.

But the yelling was different this time.

"Yo, they seem to be arguing a lot louder than usual. If I hear any more loud noises again, Imma go check it out," I said to my brothers. "I just wanna make sure everything is straight wit' Mom."

Minutes later, I heard what appeared to be chairs and other pieces of furniture slamming to the ground again.

The shuffle of feet stomping hard made the house shake.

Both my brothers turned to look at me to see how I would react.

"Alright, I'm gonna go check it out," I said, breaking the stiff silence in the room. I quickly walked down the creaky brown steps and opened the door. The house's main floor had a living room in the front. My parents' bedroom was next door, separated by a wall. The master bathroom was off to the left, and the guest room was in the back, adjacent to the stairs.

I looked into the guest room.

What I saw next broke me.

Streams of wet tears rolled down my mother's rosy brown cheeks.

I knew something was wrong, but out of default I blurted out, "Mom, are you okay?" I was her protector.

"Help me, Andre. I'm so tired of all this," my mother said in a voice so eerie it gave me goosebumps and sent a bitter chill down my spine.

"Let go, Dwayne!" I ran over and pushed him.

"Get the fuck outta here, Andre."

He pushed me back.

I stepped back into the living room.

My mind flashed back to the first time my fists touched the edge of someone's jaw. I was in the fourth grade. There was a boy in my class who found great pleasure in bullying me. My classmates and I could be at the gym, playing basketball, or doing whatever kids did at that age when *wham*, he would come from behind and slap me in the back of the neck. Or we could be in line for lunch when *wham*, he'd come running past after landing another full-forced slap. None of my teachers ever caught him, and I was afraid to fight him back for, well, two reasons. At the time, I had never fought before, and my mother raised my brothers and me to avoid violence and fights at school.

I was sitting at my desk one day, deep in focus working on an assignment, when out of nowhere I got slapped so hard in the back of the neck that I dropped my pencil and my head hit the desk. I don't know what came over me, but I was so furious that I got up, grabbed the boy by his white collared shirt, and proceeded to punch him in the face until my classmates forced me away from him. I got tired of being bullied. I remember the anger in my eyes, my skin hot and my eyes shot with tears from everything that had just happened.

As an African American boy coming of age on the South Side, not fighting was not an option. Raise those hands up, clench both fists as hard as you can, and never stop swinging. If your opponent is substantially bigger than you, pick up an object. But always stand your ground. If you take a blow to the face or lose a fight, get back up, dust yourself off, and press forward.

Like in my first fight, I got tired of dealing with Dwayne's anger and the way he treated everyone. I got tired of having to walk around the house on egg shells just because he was in a bad mood. We all feared him.

Mom didn't want to show it around us, but I could see the toll all the arguments and fights were taking on her. Like when she shrank into herself, not talking. Crying. It was unlike her because she was always a cheerful person.

I thought, in that moment, of everything my mother had taught me. I had a devil and an angel on each shoulder: *respect and obey your elders* on the left, and *punch him in the face* on the right. On that day everything bottled up within me concerning my stepdad came to the surface. I now had a critical decision to make.

Would I take a stand and finally be the man of the house or fold?

I had been in multiple fights at this point and had joined a street gang. I wasn't afraid of Dwayne anymore. I felt like I had the courage and resources to finally fight back and protect Mom.

Fuck it.

I lunged forward and swung my right fist out at Dwayne's face with everything I had. All the hurtful things he said and did to me, it would all end with this punch right here.

I'd been waiting for an opportunity like this for years.

Seeing my mother in fear like that was the last straw. She needed my help. I was taking a stand.

The impact rocked him. He steadied back, blinking his eyes at me in shock.

When he finally realized what happened, he turned his body ninety degrees and threw out a curved punch toward my outstretched jaw.

It was on now.

I jumped back to evade the blow and threw my forearms up.

Swing. Smack. Smack. Smack.

I threw more blows at his temple.

Dwayne's head dropped, and his body hit the cream tile floor with a heavy *thump*. In an aggravated manner, he got back up with a black and purple right eye. He was like a furious gorilla. I could see the rage in his dark brown eyes. His pupils were blood red as he breathed heavily in and out. I felt the huff and puff of his violent breaths on the hair follicles of my skin. My mother rushed in between us. She extended her arms wide like Christ the Redeemer, the colossal statue of Jesus Christ at the summit of Mount Corcovado in Brazil.

"Andre, go downstairs."

I did as I was told and went downstairs to the basement. I could hear my stepdad following, stomping madly down the gray wooden stairs. He was shouting, "Fuck you, Andre. You ain't shit. This isn't over."

I was walking to the back of the basement when a shoe whirled past my head and hit the floor. Dwayne started picking up random objects to throw at me.

"Andre, don't you fight back," my mother asserted, still maintaining a barrier between us.

"Why not? I'm not gonna keep letting this dude throw stuff at me," I responded.

My mother grabbed my stepdad by the arms to stop him. With a quick dash, I blew past them and ran out the basement door, exiting the house. As I made my way from the backyard to the alley gate, the same thought kept replaying in my mind.

What the fuck just happened?

My thoughts were interrupted by Dwayne's vicious screams.

"Let him leave, Adrienne! Don't you fuckin' come back!"

"Andre! Honey. Please come back. Come back in the house!"

I turned around. My mind began to race again as I started to think of my friends and where I could go for the night. At the same time, I also thought about my safety. It was nighttime on the South Side of Chicago, and it wasn't wise for me to wander alone. I later had many stash places around the city where I kept firearms, or I obtained one from one of the guys. This helped keep my parents from finding anything in the house. But that night, I had nothing to protect me. I was on my own.

I felt so much bitterness and anger in my heart. This grown man put his hands on my mother—my queen—and I hated him for it. That night, seeing Dwayne pin my mother down while she kicked and screamed was incredibly scary. It still pains me today to see it in my mind. *What if he seriously hurt her had I not stepped in? Or worse, killed her?* That night only further weakened his stature to me as a man and was the climax to the divide in our relationship.

* * * *

FOR THE NEXT three days, Dwayne and I avoided one another. Everyone could be present in the house, but the atmosphere felt empty and abandoned. The silence was finally broken one afternoon when my mother yelled from the kitchen, "Everyone in the living room now! I don't care what you're doing. We are having a family meeting."

We all did as we were told and went to the front of the house. I sat on the right closest to the end of the table, Dwayne across from me, and my mother and brothers at the left end.

"Look, I know a lot has happened these past few days. And tensions have been high in this house. But as a family we need to resolve this issue. Everyone is walking around on edge. We can't continue to live like this," my mother said.

Mom never let the anger, stress, or sadness she felt toward Dwayne affect how she treated my brothers and me. She was so enduring and loving toward us you would have thought everything was okay. She always wanted the best for us.

"I'm not going to forgive him until he apologizes to you in front of my face," I said with a snarl. I looked Dwayne dead in his eye. It was still red and bruised from the other night.

My mother's words played within the back of my head. "Never go to sleep holding a grudge against someone. Always forgive." But this was the first time in my life I made a vow not to forgive someone.

"Dwayne," my mother said, calling him to attention. He folded his hands and looked down at the table.

"Dwayne," she repeated but more assertive this time. "What do you have to say?" The room was silent. Everyone just stared at Dwayne, waiting for him to answer.

"I'm sorry," he finally muttered out under his breath after a long pause.

Right after we finished talking at the table, Dwayne held back and waited for my brothers and mother to leave. Just when I thought there was a resolution and some form of peace moving forward, he pulled me to the side.

"Don't you ask me for a damn thing. You think you're a fucking man. Do what you want. I don't care about you anymore. Do whatever you want, Andre. Fuck you. I'm not gonna say shit."

He was serious. I could see it in his eyes.

I didn't say anything back. I just walked away.

Although my mother knows this story is included in this memoir, I can imagine that it's still embarrassing and brings up hurtful emotions. My hope is that her dark experience will provide a light others can learn from and that God uses it for his glory.

Despite everything that Dwayne did to her, my mother still did not divorce him. I was sure that night she would. Instead, she did something not many people would do.

She prayed for him.

CHAPTER 7

A CANDY MAN THAT MARCHES

IT STARTED WITH SINGING.

At a young age, my mother noticed that my brothers and I could naturally harmonize with one another, so she made us start taking piano lessons around third grade. But none of us retained any interest. Placing my hands on the sea of black and white keys felt unnatural. But everything changed in fifth grade when I took a band class and started playing trombone. Both my brothers took an interest in the saxophone. Sometime later, Anthony switched to specialize in the tenor sax while Alex remained committed to the alto.

For years, I stuck with playing trombone and later joined my high school marching band at King College Prep, a school widely recognized around the South Side for its performances at the Bud Billiken Parade, Chicago Football Classic at SoldierField, football halftime shows, and for traveling to other cities to perform in battle of the bands competitions.

One of my most memorable experiences was when we traveled to New Orleans to perform.

TWEEEEEEET!

TWEET, TWEET, TWEET.

My brother Anthony, the six-foot-eight drum major in his white paladin uniform, blew his thundering whistle to alert us of the next song as we rounded the upcoming corner. Our band director, Benjamin Washington, walked alongside him, providing song recommendations and instruction in his gold and black sweatshirt (our school colors). He was a short bald-headed man with a slim frame, and he kept a well-maintained goatee. A masterful trumpet player, he was respected among faculty and students for his love and outreach to youth through music.

We marched four abreast down the busy New Orleans parade route that stretched for miles. I was the section leader for the trombone and baritone sections, while Alex was the section leader for the saxophones. "Aye! Get ready. Everyone at attention," I said to my section in a booming voice, signaling them to prepare for another horn flash.

And it began. The drum major raised both his hands in the air and twirled his long silver baton. Without time to conduct our horn movement, our instruments were up at our mouths.

Click.

Click.

Click, click, click, click.

The snare drum players beat their sticks, reinforced with black and gold tape, to count off the song. The mouthpiece from my trombone touched my sore, tender lips. I could feel the ice cold, gold-reinforced metal. My steps felt swift but shallow as my white shoes hit the warm, smooth pavement. In and out, in and out. I took deep breaths to resonate the air through the massive gold bell, playing my heart out as loudly as I could. Playing trombone and baritone gave me a free, aggressive, sensational feeling. I was tired, but the energy from the Super-dome-like crowd propelled me forward.

The breeze of the night sky was sensational and calm. It cooled the perspiration my body produced within the hot, long-sleeved uniform. The moon radiated in the night sky; its grace-ful light shone down upon us, almost as if it acknowledged our musical excellence. On a parallel level, the crowd was far from dull. Both sides of the blocks were occupied by a safari of people. The excitement and noise level was like the Super Bowl itself, with thousands of rainbow colored beads flying through the air, on the pavement, and around people's necks. The wide variety of bead colors in the crowd created a spectacle of light. Hundreds of blue, green, and red fluorescent signs were glow-ing intensely in the dark, bringing the block to life.

"AND DOWN!" The band yelled in sync to signal that we all brought our horns down at the same time. The song was finished. The ecstatic New Orleans crowd went buck wild. Sporadic and spontaneous, a group of women screamed "bari-tones" at the top of their lungs as they came over and looped beads around my neck.

We continued to march through the never-ending maze of streets until we finally hit downtown New Orleans. We turned a corner. The enormity of the crowd doubled!

"CUPID SHUFFLE!" my brother called off the next song in great confidence. He was hoping to select a song that would engage the crowd. And right he was.

Tatatatatatatatat.

Tat, tat, tat, tat.

Like he was commanding a lion, Dexter, the drumline section leader, drove his sticks into the brim of his snare. The entire band snapped our horns to our mouths in response. Immediately the crowd joined in around us, jubilant to hear the hot, up-tempo beat of "Cupid Shuffle." We played the intro, started the tuba break, and began to dance. The vibe we experienced from the crowd made it seem like the entire city of New Orleans was present. We marched through a tunnel, and our sound vibrated off the gray, muddy, concrete walls. The atmosphere doubled in intensity. My brother's high-pitched fox whistle commanded the band to a sharp halt once again. We were done. I looked around to marvel at the gripping beauty of New Orleans.

I also thought about the opportunities that being in the marching band had provided me.

Of all the extracurricular activities present at King, the marching band produced the most revenue for the school and allowed students to travel and experience life outside the harsh dynamics of Chicago. It also brought in the most scholarships every year. Schools such as UAPB, Florida A&M, Tuskegee University, Southern University, Norfolk State, and Prairie View A&M, to name a few, would send recruiters from their marching bands to offer scholarships to students on the spot. For many students, this was the dream. The program Mr. Washington created with the marching band gave students an outlet to escape the South Side and attend college.

The next day, we cruised through the city on our coach bus. The catastrophic damage Katrina had caused in New Orleans gave it a murky look. The black, cracked streets were illuminated in a green, tarnished glow. From last night's experience, one would think Mardi Gras was New Orleans's escape from it all—a dilapidated city's chance for revival.

I reached in my bag and pulled out one of the many packages of Sour Patch Kids I had and shared it with my section. It was common for me to have candy with me everywhere I went. At King, I was known as the "candy man."

Selling candy and drinks at school was actually sparked by my stepfather. On his way to work each morning, he noticed that there was a brand-new Coke machine sitting on a demolished construction site. He pulled up to the curb and stopped to speak to one of the workers.

"Hey, my man. I've driven past this whole week, and that soda machine is still there. Do you know what they are going to do with it?"

"No idea, sir. No one has claimed it yet. But I'm sure they will soon, or we'll have to throw it away. We are almost done with the demolition of this site," the man in the yellow hat and bright orange reflective vest said.

Three days later, Dwayne drove by again. The pop machine was still there. He pulled over once more to speak to the gentleman.

"Did you guys find out whose machine it is yet?"

"No, sir. If you can get someone to help you move it, you can have it." One hour later my brothers and I helped Dwayne lift the Coke machine into the back of his truck. He went on to establish a vending business with a network of machines at several locations throughout the city over the years. Almost every Saturday morning, my brothers and I would help our stepdad move heavy vending machines and pick up candy and drinks from either Sam's Club or his storage unit. He taught us how to understand and capitalize on what consumers liked, how to introduce new products effectively, and how to calculate profit margins. Months after finding the Coke machine at the site, we took his blueprint and used it to sell candy and drinks at school.

Just like we saw Dwayne do, on weekends we would run to Sam's Club and buy an assortment of candies, Flamin' Hot chips, honey buns, and juices. To buy our initial inventory, we used the money we earned from shoveling snow or whatever cash we had from savings. Then, based on how much we bought each item for at cost price, we'd mark it up 10 to 15 percent and sell it to students at that new retail price. The actual routine of the gig came to be pretty simple. We would each dump our entire product into separate black duffle bags and carry those around with us all day in school to sell. We kept our "re-up" stash in our lockers.

"Wassup, fellas! It's my favorite guys in the house, y'all!" Mr. O'Brien, the school's police officer, said as we came through the front doors. He was a thick guy—but not in a fat way—and usually wore blue jeans and a black or blue shirt. His gold Chicago PD badge always flashed brightly. He kept it clipped to his black belt buckle on the left side. I wouldn't say we were popular, but, because we were triplets, my brothers and I were pretty well known among the faculty and student body. We were just cool with everyone. Plus, our mother was an active participant in the school board meetings, so naturally, most of the school staff knew who we were as well.

"What's going on, Mr. O'Brien?" I said, shaking his hand as I threw my bag on the metal detector belt and walked through.

BEEP, BEEP, BEEP, BEEP. The detector screamed like it was on fire. Because violence was common on the South Side, it was normal to see metal detectors placed at the entrance of all the schools.

"You good, Evans, come on through." When Mr. O'Brien looked at the monitor screen to examine the contents within my bag, I could see his eyebrows raise and his face change. Selling candy in school was forbidden, but I'd figured out a way around that.

Just before he could say anything, I reached in my bag and pulled out a Snickers bar, Mr. O'Brien's kryptonite. His face lit up. I could see his gold bottom tooth wave back at me when I handed him the bar and he fumbled the black packaging in his hand. As long as I gave him a Snickers bar every day, he let my brothers and me sell within the school. Naturally, it placed a cap on the campus economy and anyone's ability to compete with us because we were a monopoly. So of course everyone came to us when they wanted snacks.

To expand my business and make more money, I would ask the sexiest girls at the school to work for me. Taking the bait as planned, guys would be more willing to buy from them because they found them attractive. Girls got to walk around and look cute and enjoy being flirted with. The guys enjoyed their company, and students had access to purchasing their favorite snacks more readily and at a reasonable price. It was a win-win for everyone. I would count how much inventory I gave them each day, so I knew how much money I should receive. I compensated the ladies by paying them in candy. My business expanded. Next thing I knew I was making a couple hundred dollars a day. It felt good making money for the first time in my life.

But that good feeling was whipped away fast. The gang was not supportive of me being in the marching band.

I was hanging out with the guys at the park when they confronted me. One of the members in particular, Flame, was a hot-head.

"Yo, folks is not down with us anymore. He stay gone. I seen him the other day playing in some lame-ass marching band. We can't trust him anymore," Flame said, pointing at me.

The air became thick. I felt my skin start to heat up in nervousness. All the other guys looked at me intensely.

Smoke stepped forward. "Is this true, Dre?" he said while squinting his eyes and leaning forward. He gave me the stare of death.

I looked at Flame like, *Are you serious? Did you just really snitch on me?* Like a master puppeteer, Flame stood in the background with a wide smirk spread across his face. Since the first day I joined the gang, Flame always gave me a difficult time. He was jealous and was always out to get me for reasons I'm unaware of. Even in some close-knit families and gangs, there are enemies that lurk in the shadows.

I took a strong gulp and said, "Yes." I didn't know what would happen next.

There was no book or script on how Smoke would react.

Before Smoke could utter another word I blattered out, "I know I haven't been around much. But what if I can still support you all in a different way?" The guys looked back and forth at one another and exchanged curious looks.

"Like how?" Smoke asked.

"I have a candy business. I make great money. I can give you all a portion of the proceeds every month. That will show I am still committed despite being away a lot. Plus I ain't done anything to ever betray you guys' trust. So why accuse me of that now?"

The guys agreed.

Flame was pissed. "You can't be serious," he mouthed under his breath while throwing his hands up in dismay.

I walked past Flame and brushed hard against his shoulder.

"Fuck you, Dre," Flame hissed.

"No, fuck you. You snitched on me and tried to turn everyone against me," I shot back aggressively, dead in his face.

Like a volcano, Flame's temper erupted. What he did next was one of the most disrespectful things I'd ever had anyone do to me.

He spit in my face.

It happened so fast I didn't have time to react. Some of it went in my eyes, and the rest dripped down my face. I was honestly shocked. No one was ballsy enough to dare spit at me. I quickly wiped the saliva from my face and swung at Flame, knocking him to the ground. He quickly jumped to his feet, and I saw him pull a knife from his pocket.

It gleamed in the sun.

"I never liked you," he said, lunging toward me with the blade.

My eyes grew wide, and I grabbed his hand. At that point it was self defense. Flame thrust the blade toward my torso, and I gripped his hand to prevent the metal from piercing my flesh. I kicked Flame hard, which caused him to lose his balance. Then I used my body weight to lean forward and turned the knife around.

With all my might, I thrust the blade into Flame's flesh.

The blade pierced his leg.

"AAAHHH!" Flame let out an anguished cry of pain.

He hit the pavement hard and balled up like a Rolie Polie Olie.

It felt like the whole encounter happened within a matter of seconds. By the time it was over, the guys separated us. I remember seeing the handle of the blade, still lodged in Flame's leg, waving back at me as the guys picked him up. A stain of blood protruded from his denim jeans.

"This ain't over, motha fucka," Flame yelled as he was carried away.

Little did he know that it was going to be over for him real quick.

* * * *

JUST LIKE WE agreed, I gave some of my profits to Boogie and the guys to help with buying unmarked guns, ammo, or whatever else they needed. Since I had moved to a different neighborhood, I didn't see the guys as much. All I could do was hope that they continued to see that I was still playing my part and believed in me.

Each money drop was a simple exchange between Boogie and me. They always used him for the pickup, which allowed us to talk further and get to know each other better. Those recurring encounters helped us develop a solid friendship over the years. I learned that Boogie was just a regular young man like many others. He loved art and basketball, and had a knack for reading and learning about politics and war history.

But one drop off in particular was different. It was two months after Flame had attempted to kill me.

"Yo, Dre, hold up for a second, homie. I gotta tell you somethin', man," Boogie said with his head down. He looked sad.

"What's wrong, man? You're scaring me a little. I never seen you like this."

He slowly raised his head, put one hand on my shoulder, and looked me cold in the eye.

"Flame is dead."

I squished my face up in confusion. Like *how?*

On the South Side, you had to be cautious about riding in a car with more than two people. It created unnecessary attention from the cops, or other gangs would target your car if they saw a chance to take out a group of guys.

Boogie said Flame was in the car with a few other people waiting at the light when another car pulled up and shot up his vehicle. He died on the scene.

* * * *

THE BAND BUS pulled up on a side street blocked by massive traffic and thousands of people. I grabbed my gear and instrument, gave my section a motivational speech, and hopped out of the bus like a kid who had arrived at a playground. The stifling humidity slapped me in the face as I struggled to gather myself from the rapid change in temperature. I was still jittery from the huge bag of Sour Patch Kids I'd eaten on the two-hour bus ride from the hotel. "Line up," yelled the drum major. "Let's go, start a cadence." My brother's convocation started the procession in full force as we marched in intense ninety-degree steps, driving our knees into our chests.

The parade seemed to be passing quickly when all of a sudden it started to rain. The rigid, cold, and uncomfortable Chicago rain was different from the baby soft, warm New Orleans rain. With great vigor, the entire band mustered enough strength to push through. Everyone's faces were full of jovial smiles, entangled in the heated moment of fun and band unity.

Unlike the typical stereotypes that band members are nerds or lame, participating in any of the various marching band programs on the South Side was deemed cool. We played mainstream hip-hop and R&B music while also incorporating challenging dance routines.

With a bold procession, we came to a halt. I walked my section over to a large gloomy building on a corner street. The air was loud and intense. We turned around and were surprised to find another band playing behind us. I glanced down at the creamy, bright yellow swirl on my baritone bell, awaiting the song count off from percussion. The clear rain drops established a camp around the rim of my bell, and some dripped vigorously from the inside—no, wait, that was my spit from playing so hard.

We played right back at the other band, reaffirming the point that we were the best. What unfolded was a band battle—an experience that's hard to describe. You have to experience it to believe it. Back and forth, we shot bullets of songs to play louder and with more intensity than the other. In a last attempt, the drum major called off one last song: "I'd Rather Be With You." Everyone went crazy, and with great excitement I gave it my all, pressing my wet mouthpiece as firmly as I could against my parched lips. When we finished the song, the crowd cheered and chanted "King." They declared us as the winners.

I realized that I was a member of another gang: a marching band.

This was the first time I had joined another gang as a young man. I'd come to find that being in the marching band had the same unity, family feeling, working together toward common goals, mentors and people I looked up to, and identified uniform colors and symbols similar to the street gang. That's when it hit me that groups, clubs, colleges, tribes, and sports teams are all gang factions as well. The only difference is the symbols, colors, customs, and values they adhere to.

CHAPTER 8

WIPE THAT SMIRK OFF YOUR FACE

Nothing stops a bullet like an opportunity.

—COLLEEN DALEY

I MADE IT TO MY JUNIOR YEAR AND STILL HAD NO IDEA WHERE I WANTED TO GO FOR COLLEGE. What I do know is the day my stepfather yelled for my brothers and me to come upstairs from the basement, he opened a door that would change our lives forever.

"ANDRE, ANTHONY, ALEX, ADRIENNE," Dwayne called our names to come into the dining room. In the center stood a brown table where we ate dinner together as a family every night. It also used to hold us captive when my parents, particularly my stepfather, would sit us down and lecture us for hours. Toward the left and directly facing the table was a small, black cube-shaped TV that we used to watch *The Bernie Mac Show*, CNN, and *Jeopardy!* during meals. In the morning, it was common for us to hear a mother screaming in the middle of the street, "My baby. They shot my baby," on the morning news. Every day there were reports of multiple shootings and murders. Many parents didn't even have the money to bury their own kids. My mother was in the kitchen cooking her famous gumbo and listening to Earth, Wind, and Fire.

"What is it? What's so urgent that you had to call all of us up here?" my mother responded. We all stared down at him with curious faces while he sat at the table with his rectangular glasses on.

"Come look at this," Dwayne said. He turned the laptop screen to show us the website of a school called West Point.

"My sons ain't going to war," my mother blurted out after seeing the words "Military Academy" and photos of cadets in military fatigues. She didn't want us to join the Armed Forces for fear we would go to Iraq or Afghanistan. In reality, none of us really knew anything about the military. All we knew was what we read about and saw on TV: the killings of thousands of soldiers in the Middle East. I'd never even considered the possibility of joining the military until that day, largely in part because I hated taking orders from others.

"Noooo, Adrienne, it's not what you think. It's a military college. They pay for the boys' school and even give them a monthly stipend."

"I don't care what they pay. I said no, Dwayne. They're going to a normal college."

"Look, I got out of the Army because I was bitter about the experiences I went through, and I listened to the wrong people who were also cynical about their time in the service as well. It's one of my biggest regrets in life. This is a really good school, guys. I wish I knew back then what I know now," Dwayne explained. "Just watch this video."

He clicked on the screen and made us watch the four-minute video. We still weren't impressed.

Two weeks later, Dwayne brought it up again at dinner. I was mid-chew into my mother's tasty lasagna when he put down his fork and said, "West Point is having a prospective student and parent information session in two days. I want us to go. Let's just check it out. If you don't like it after that, I won't bring it up again. I promise."

"Dwayne, really?" my mother said.

"Adrienne. I want us to go. Let's just go. There's no harm in going and listening to what they have to say."

Two days later we drove an hour to Palatine, Illinois, in the suburbs of Chicago. That's where I met my first Black Commissioned Officer.

Colonel Bernard Banks was the first man I'd ever met who held five master's degrees and a PhD. He was dark-skinned, with low cut black hair and a stocky build. That day he wore his black Army dress uniform, glittered with various colorful ribbons and shiny metals. Without saying a word, the way he walked with his head held high, his back straight, and his shoulders rolled back, he gave off this confident, authoritative vibe. At the time, he was the deputy for the Department of Behavioral Sciences and Leadership at West Point.

There were a handful of other West Point cadets present as well, dressed in one of their many school uniforms: a tucked in white, short-sleeved blouse with soft shoulder boards that portrayed their rank, creased gray pants with a solid black stripe down the middle of each side, and a maroon shawl wrapped around their waists. The presentation that Colonel Banks briefed to open up the meeting addressed many of the concerns my family and I had about West Point. His Power-Point detailed the history of the United States Military Academy (USMA), the admission process, life at the Academy, and any further questions parents had.

"At this time, we will break to allow your children to walk around and engage with the cadets," Banks said. I walked up to one of the Black cadets. He was a tall, light-skinned guy with a bald fade haircut and brown eyes.

"Hey, wassup, man? I got a question for you," I said while extending my hand for a shake.

"Yeah, wassup?"

"Is it true that all of you guys go out and fight in the war like on TV?"

"Nah, bro. Not all of us. Only those who select the combat jobs do," he said with a chuckle.

"The Army is like the civilian world. We have a bunch of different jobs you can do like engineering, medical service, police, being a judge, human resources, and aviation, to name a few."

"Aight, cool. What about the ladies? I heard all the girls that join the military damn near look like dudes. Don't they gotta be all tough and stuff, too?"

"Hahahaha," the cadet burst out laughing. "No, man. There are plenty of beautiful women in the military. So that's nothing you'll have to worry about."

At the other end of the room, my parents spoke to Colonel Banks. My mother relayed the conversation to me later.

"Colonel Banks, great presentation, sir. We appreciated that. I'm Dwayne, and this is my wife, Adrienne," he said while extending his hand.

"Nice meeting you. I'm glad you found the brief informative. What can I do for you?"

"Imma be straight with you, sir. What is it gonna take to get triplet boys from the South Side of Chicago accepted into West Point?" my stepfather said sternly.

My mom gave Dwayne a look. She had found the information session informative and was impressed with Colonel Banks's accolades, but she still wasn't sold on the idea of her triplet boys attending a military academy.

"I recommend your sons attend the Summer Leadership Seminar (SLS) to get a feel for life at West Point first. It's a week long. They'll live and eat with cadets, attend classes, engage in physical training, everything. Have them go to that first. Then we'll talk."

That summer my brothers and I attended SLS.

My transition from thug to the military started the moment I walked out of that West Point information brief.

* * * *

ORIGINALLY A FORT during the Revolutionary War, Army West Point was founded in 1801 and is a national landmark that overlooks the Hudson River in New York. Our large, black coach bus made a stop at what appeared to be a checkpoint or gate. Like guardian angels, two military police dressed in Army fatigues and armed with shotguns and 9mm pistols blocked our entry into the base. "Good morning, sir. I need to see your ID," he told the bus driver. The soldier brought the ID up to his face, examined it, flipped it over and scanned the back, and then handed it back. "Okay, you're good to go." He motioned us to proceed forward.

Like entering a new world, the scenery changed not even five minutes down the road. The grass, trees, and shrubs gave off an elegant, healthy, green glow. Everything looked so perfect and was quiet—peaceful and calming even. I thought I was in *Alice in Wonderland* or some shit. Most of the buildings on base had the medieval style of neo-gothic architecture and were constructed from gray and black granite. Lancet and rose windows with stained glass decorated them. At the heart of the campus were the mess hall, barracks, and parade field. Various statues, cannons, and artifacts dating from the Revolutionary War to World War II were also sprinkled throughout the grounds. I'd never been to a place so rich in history and tradition. Already I felt like the school survived on the ingredients of blood, sweat, and tears.

SQUEEEEEAK. The brakes from the bus made an abrupt shrill sound when it stopped in front of an open square.

I grabbed my bag and hopped out of the bus, excited for the new adventure that was to come.

"GET OVER HERE RIGHT NOW!! GET OVER HERE RIGHT NOW, AND STEP UP TO MY LINE. NOT ON MY LINE. NOT OVER MY LINE. STEP UP TO MY LINE!!"

What the hell?

My eyebrows rose. My face froze. I made sure to look him in the eyes to show I wasn't intimidated or scared.

Did this dude just point and yell at me? Who the flying fuck does he think he is?

Instinctively, I got in a defensive stance and reached for my waist as if attempting to grab hold of the butt stock of a weapon. In a split second I realized where I was and that I had no protection.

I thought SLS was supposed to be a smooth introduction into the life of West Point. It hadn't even been thirty seconds since I arrived, and I already had the feeling that this was no summer camp. But I did as I was told and lethargically placed the tips of my toes at the edge of his red line in the central area.

"WHY ARE YOUR HANDS IN YOUR POCKETS?!" the senior cadet screamed at me, standing inches from my face. Sweat dripped off his pale Caucasian face from the humid New York summer. He was dressed in his summer uniform, a white combination cover (hat) with the gold Army Knight insignia in the center resting on top of his bright blond hair, a firmly pressed and creased white blouse with soft gray shoulder boards, gray pants, a red shawl, and black shoes polished so shiny I could see myself in them.

"I ASKED YOU A QUESTION! WHY ARE YOUR HANDS IN YOUR POCKETS?!"

"Because I always have my hands in my pockets if I'm just standing around. I'm just chillin'," I responded.

"STAND AT ATTENTION WHEN YOU SPEAK TO ME. HANDS TO YOUR SIDES. THAT IS NOT ONE OF YOUR FIVE BASIC RESPONSES! YOUR FIVE BASIC RESPONSES ARE YES SIR/ MA'AM, NO SIR/MA'AM, NO EXCUSE SIR/MA'AM, AYE AYE SIR/ MA'AM, AND I'LL FIND OUT SIR/MA'AM. "

At West Point, you are only allowed to respond in those five basic ways, and anything else is deemed unacceptable. The cadet stared at me intently, waiting for another response. Sluggishly and with hesitation, I responded, "No excuse, sir."

"WHAT! I CAN'T HEAR YOU! SAY IT LOUDER!" the experienced cadet echoed.

"NO EXCUSE, SIR!"

Talk about a wake-up call.

Two days later, we were required to take a physical readiness test (PRT) to measure our fitness aptitude. Candidates had two minutes to complete as many sit-ups as possible and two minutes for max push-ups, followed by a two mile run on flat terrain. Your score was determined by how many reps you could do within the allotted time. After completing the strength portion in a green grassy field (I passed in case you're wondering), the cadets escorted us onto a long gray pavement. Each way down the long strip was one mile. I could see the distorting effects of the hot New York sun on the gray road. When I looked down at the asphalt, it looked wavy and blurry from the heat. There was a portable black clock with red numbers set up to the right of the starting line. All of the candidates placed their feet behind the yellow spray paint.

"Everyone ready?" We nodded our heads.

"THREE. TWO. ONE. GO!"

I took off running. I ran through the thick humid air at full sprint. I laughed and smiled as I flew by my brothers and the rest of the candidates.

"GO ARMY, BEAT NAVY!" I screamed at one of the cadets who was at the end of the road with a small stopwatch. He smirked at me and then smiled.

"I recommend you slow down. You're going to burn out. It's not a sprint the whole way."

Whatever, dude. You're just trying to kill my vibe.

I turned around and proceeded to run the last mile at a full sprint. I held my head high, full of confidence. Then my energy gave out. My legs grew tired, and I realized I wouldn't be able to make it the whole way at that level of intensity. I slowed down and started to jog. But at that point I had no energy left in the tank. I was exhausted.

"Not so fast now, are you?" Anthony and Alex joked at me as they passed me after a minute or two. Next, the majority of the other candidates zoomed past me as well.

I crossed the finished line in time, but I barely passed. I was damn near at the bottom of the pack. I should have listened to the upper class cadet and jogged most of the run and sprinted at the finish. The cadet walked up to me while I sat in the grass trying to catch my breath.

"You don't listen. I see you like to learn from the school of hard knocks," he said, standing over me, and then walked away. *Sigh.* I put my head down and thought about the conversation my parents had with me one day in the living room. I was sitting on the couch, and both my mother and stepfather were standing up in front of me.

"Andre. You like to learn from the school of hard knocks. You're not applying yourself in school, and you're constantly in trouble. You don't listen to us. We don't know what to do with you anymore. So your mother and I are strongly considering sending you to see a doctor for a psychiatric evaluation. We think there may be something wrong with you. We have given and done everything for you we possibly can. We can't force you to listen. I personally give up," Dwayne said.

No one had stopped to finally point out how much of a savage I'd been. When Dwayne said those words, I thought, *Damn. Am I really that bad?* I thought school was pointless and felt I wasn't good at it. I enjoyed the gang fights, vandalizing cars and properties, the respect I had earned, the way girls thought I was cool, and how powerful I felt when I wielded guns in my hands. Being in trouble gave me a rush inside, similar to the feeling you get jumping out of a plane or being on a fast roller coaster. Everything my parents would say to me would go in one ear and out the other. I just wanted to do what I wanted to do.

My mother was silent the entire time.

That scared me even more.

I couldn't bear to look her in the eyes. It seemed that even the person I thought would always see the light and good in me frowned upon my behavior and couldn't see my potential.

I didn't say much in response to Dwayne's words. I could tell from his face and body language that my few words frustrated him even more.

"Come on, let's take a trip. Get in the car," my mother said, breaking the silence.

For the entire fifteen-minute car ride, my mother didn't make a sound. I didn't know where she was taking me. *Was she so upset that I didn't say much that she was driving me to see the doctor now, right away?*

Then we pulled up to my grandmother's house.

I gave her a confused face. *Why were we here?* When we walked in the house, my grandmother was busy in the kitchen, cooking. She looked so peaceful and sweet as usual. "Sit down. I want you to explain to your grandmother why you can't act right," my mother said. My mother knew how much respect I had for my granny, so she figured maybe an intervention with her would change things.

Dwayne looked into any solution possible to find a way to explain the madness in my behavior. Eventually, he landed on the music I listened to. He decided that hip-hop was the root cause for my "do what I want" and "act like a thug" mentality. Yes, a lot of hip-hop does glorify violence and portray African Americans in a negative limelight. But for me, hip-hop gave me confidence, and it helped me focus. The way T.I. and Young Jeezy would spit fire over bars and their insane work ethic resonated with me. Listen, I didn't have any dreams of being a rapper. I just wanted the same hustle that was inside them.

Little did my family know that it had nothing to do with music.

I was a part of a street gang.

The entire time I hid my gang life from my family. I knew that if they found out, especially my mother, they'd be incredibly disappointed and would keep me on lockdown. Keeping them in the dark was also my way of protecting them. If they knew about my affiliation, I knew they would worry about me every time I left the house. It was easy to hide my gang activities from my brothers because they spent most of their free time inside playing video games.

"What's going on, Andre? Why is your mother telling me you can't act right?" my grandmother said. "Look at me." Her face was red and full of tears. I could see it in her eyes that she was disappointed in me.

And her disappointment crushed me.

Of all the evil in the world, my grandmother represented everything that was good. She had such a nurturing, enduring heart that it was hard not to like her. I'd never seen her upset or emotional before. I'd never met anyone who had a disagreement with her. She always held in the emotions that bothered her and addressed them quietly within herself. Her heart was so big that she would do whatever it took to help someone out and never asked for anything in return, even if sometimes helping came at an inconvenience to her.

My eyes turned bloodshot, and I burst out crying right there in the middle of the kitchen. Seldom did I show much weakness, but in that moment, I broke down so badly in tears that I lost my words and any confidence to speak.

Imagine someone so profound and good in your life, that when you let them down, it's a different type of pain. A pain that cuts deep and haunts you to the core. A pain that makes you feel insignificant and worthless.

I had let down the two most important people in my life.

* * * *

I GOT UP from the grass and ran back to the barracks. *I was gonna make this shit at West Point count.* The rest of the week at SLS was filled with obstacle courses, intramural sports, marching to drill cadences, military training, and academic classes. In particular, I attended a physics workshop, along with a brief presentation of the nuclear engineering major at West Point. This led to my participation in two lab exercises: determine an unknown radioactive source by using a sodium iodide (NaI) detector and a multi-channel analyzer (MICA) and determine the absorption coefficient for lead and aluminum. There was something about the nuclear world that seemed dope to me. Maybe because it was a rare career field to pursue. All I know is that my academic bug was unlocked at SLS. At some point, I developed a mentor relationship with the assistant director of physics and nuclear engineering at West Point, Lieutenant Colonel Gillich. We had many discussions beyond the lab, exploring ideas on the type of materials that could be used to hold and store radioactive waste.

At the end of SLS, an award ceremony was held to recognize individuals the cadets and staff felt stood out that week. "ANDRE EVANS." I heard my name called loudly on the black microphone positioned on the center stage. The announcement caught me off guard and by surprise. I got up slowly and walked down toward the wooden stage. Dr. Gillich was waiting for me at the center of the stage, holding what appeared to be an award. It was a Certificate of Excellence in Nuclear Engineering.

"Congratulations, Andre. You deserve this. In all my years of teaching, it's rare for me to come across a student like you who showed that much curiosity and enthusiasm for nuclear physics. You should be proud of yourself."

And I was. I had to make my granny and mother proud of me.

* * * *

BACK IN CHICAGO, my brothers and I briefed our parents about our SLS experience. Despite the fact that I never thought I would join the Armed Forces, I actually enjoyed it. I felt free at West Point. I didn't have to walk around and watch my back, and I didn't have to worry about being shot. The environment was all positive. The instructors at West Point had a strong desire to see cadets succeed and would do whatever they could to find the appropriate resources and tools to assist them. The feeling itself was so foreign. I wasn't used to being at a place where my education and personal development were deemed important.

In short, Army West Point was a breeding farm for developing leaders. If my brothers and I were accepted, my mother's worries of trying to figure out a way to pay to send triplet boys to college would end. In addition, we would receive a monthly stipend. I could pay my own bills and not bother my mom for a single cent. Not everyone can rap or play a sport for a living.

Attending a Service Academy was my ticket out of the hood.

And most importantly, I felt "safe" being there. I got a taste of what life *could* be like if I continued to work hard and focus.

But I wasn't out of the trenches yet.

I had the physical ability, I had the ambition, and I had the opportunity. Only one thing stood between me and attending a Service Academy: my gang affiliation.

CHAPTER 9

LEAVING THE GANG

When you are at war you have to have a heightened sense of vigilance. In some ways, what some of these young people are experiencing—particularly young African-American and Latino males—is they have to be hyper vigilant at all times. They don't know when they can let their guard down. Even soldiers and military people get some type of rest and a time to step out of that. For these young people, they are (constantly) in spaces that serve as a threat or they perceive as a threat.

—WALDO E. JOHNSON, Associate Professor, University of Chicago

(CHICAGO TRIBUNE, 2013)

"MEET ME ON THE CORNER," THE TEXT MESSAGE FROM BOOGIE READ.

I was still in my last class of the day at King. When the school bell finally rang, I hopped out of my seat, sprinted down the red spiral stairs, and briskly walked out the large, black front doors. I met Boogie on the corner and got in his car. We drove to a food spot in another neighborhood on the South Side.

"Yo, was gud? Wassup wit' the text?"

"Wassup, G," Boogie responded while we stacked up. Then his face turned cold and serious, and he got straight to the point.

"Yo. We need to talk to you about your loyalty and involvement. You know you my guy, and I always got your back. But Imma be real wit' you. You ain't been around like you used to, bro. Giving us money from you selling candy and shit ain't enough anymore. N*ggas is starting to really question whether you still down wit' us or not, especially after that incident with Flame."

Stop. Something isn't right, my instincts screamed.

I knew that feeling. Something bad was about to pop off.

Those instincts were my guardian angels. They had saved me many times before: nudging me when to duck, when to avoid a certain street, when not to trust someone, and when to fight and shoot back.

We were standing outside talking when it happened.

"Yo, hold up, bro," I extended my hand and touched Boogie's chest. I cut him off from talking. "You see that car right there? Don't make it obvious when you look, too. But that's the third time they don' circled the block and drove down dis street."

Living in the hood, it was common knowledge that if you saw a mysterious car approaching or something that looked out of place, it was best to take cover or find a way to escape.

Boogie discreetly looked over his shoulder and noticed the car from the corner of his eye behind him.

"Yeah, I see it."

"Yo. You got another strap on you?"

"Dre, is that even a question? You know I stay ready." Boogie lifted up his shirt and handed me a piece. I stuffed it in the waistline behind my back and prepared for battle.

"Get ready, bro. When these folks come back around, we finna' blast they ass."

Five minutes passed. The car never came back around.

Was I being paranoid?

Was my visit to West Point and my lack of time on the streets causing me to lose my edge? Maybe the mysterious car saw that we noticed it and decided not to come back. Or maybe they really were just lost.

Boogie and I continued walking and turned into a parking lot.

I had that feeling in my stomach again.

Thump, thump, thump, thump.

I whipped my head around and scanned my surroundings. The buildings. People. Cars. Everything.

Then I saw him.

A Black man wearing a hoodie and driving a beat up red Honda came screeching around the corner. The back windows of the car rolled down, and two additional male figures emerged from both sides with guns pointed at us.

Fuck.

My heart dropped to the bottom of my stomach.

Pop. Pop. Pop. Pop. Pop. Pop. Pop. Pop.

Multiple gunshots rang out.

I can't believe this, I thought. I just got back from West Point and I'm only eighteen years old. I barely just started living life, and now it is over.

"Get the fuck down!" I screamed at Boogie.

We were standing wide open on the sidewalk with no cover or protection. We took off running.

Like the robotic toy whack-a-moles that pop their heads up and down in the arcade game, Boogie and I quickly ducked and zigzagged within the nearby parking lot. We returned shots back. I moved around sporadically to make each gunman's job harder. Maybe those assassins, those young men hiding under the cover of their dark hoods, had just joined a gang, and this was their first time wielding a gun. Maybe they were just like me, trying to figure out their place in this complex world as young men.

Was this karma?

Then, I tripped and fell.

Gang members are sixty times more likely to die than the general public.

I could hear the sound of glass shattering and objects denting from the impact of the bullets. A picture of my mother and brothers standing above my casket flashed before me.

I scrambled back to my feet and kept running.

Like a baseball player sliding into first base, I swiftly slid on my right side behind a black Chevy truck. My heavy sporadic breaths fogged up the paint of the car.

I didn't feel any pain.

I don't think I was hit.

I patted myself up and down the chest just to double check. A sigh of relief came over me.

But what about Boogie? Was he okay?

I spun my head around left and right but didn't see him.

"Boogie, you straight?! Boogie, you good?!" I yelled.

The only response I got back was the loud siren of an ambulance zooming down the street and a dog barking in the distance.

"Boogie!!" I yelled again.

I peeped around the corner to see if the coast was clear. It looked like the assassins who tried to shoot us up were long gone.

"Yo, Boogie!"

I got up and started searching around the row of parked cars. I ducked down to the ground to see if I could spot Boogie's legs. At least then I'd know where he was located.

The next row over, two cars down, I saw a pair of straight legs in a horizontal position pressed together. They weren't moving. It looked like his body was just lying there.

"Boogie! You good?!"

Still no answer.

Fear crept in. I think Boogie got hit while running and sat down on the pavement because he was probably bleeding out.

I rushed over to the pair of legs and found Boogie lying there against a yellow Hummer. My heart started to beat fast.

"Boogie, you okay?"

His eyes were shut. He opened them, and I could see tears rolling down his face. I was crying too. I'm not ashamed to say that. I believe everyone does at the brink of death when your life is about to be snatched away from you by force, especially when you have so much to lose. I had people counting on me.

"I'm sorry, man. I heard you. My bad I ain't yell back. I was just having a moment. Just the other day my moms had told me that I needed to get out the gang life. That I needed to do more wit' my life before I ended up dead or in prison. This shit just made me think about it again, yo."

"I feel you, bro. Trust me, I do. Das why I been distant. I wanna get out this life too. Das what I was trying to tell you. Come on, man, let's get the fuck outta here."

I helped Boogie up to his feet. We got in his Mustang and took off. He dropped me back off at King.

* * * *

I DIDN'T SLEEP that night.

My eyes watered and burned with exhaustion. As I laid my head on the pillow and stared at the dark ceiling, the events that transpired that day haunted my thoughts. One o'clock bled into three o'clock in the morning. My head was full of the sound of gunshots. Every car I heard zoom down the street made my body jerk and jump in fear. The PTSD would instantly make my mind flash back to the car and the two gunmen. What was once a black ceiling now turned into an animated horror movie. Although I had been in a shootout before, this was different. It felt more personal.

Every time I went outside, I felt like I was going to get killed or that stray bullets would hit my parents' bedroom. I was constantly in fear of karma.

They say that everything in life happens for a reason. But I couldn't help but wonder what if God set this up? What if God wanted me to be shot at? Maybe this was his plan all along. And I survived that day because God wanted me to. It wasn't my time to go yet because he had more in store for me with my life.

So what was I gonna say to Smoke and the rest of the guys?

"Stop!! Chicago police! Stop where you are!"

My thoughts were interrupted by shouting.

I jumped out of my bed to the sound of police sirens and loud yells.

My brothers and I slept with the windows open upstairs to save money from using the air conditioning when the weather was warm—our stepfather's idea. He used every tactic possible to save money. Alex and I shared a room with three windows that opened up toward the front of the house. Easily awakened by the late night activity of the South Side, Alex and I became light sleepers. We would lie awake stressed out about the orchestra of distressed sounds that came from those windows. It was the chorus of the streets, Chicago's theme song.

I bolted toward the window and looked out to see two suspects running in front of my neighbor's house across the street. The third suspect jumped the fence to hide in the backyard. I could see a handful of cops with flashlights. A police chopper with a search light could be seen and heard above.

After about fifteen minutes, the police emerged from around the corner with three suspects in hand. "They got 'em, bro," I told Alex. But when I turned around to look out my bedroom window again, all I saw in handcuffs was my future self. That is, if I continued to travel along the path I was on.

There was a one in a million chance the gang would let me walk away.

But was attempting to leave the gang to turn my life around worth the risk of death or being seriously injured?

Derrick Rose found a way and used basketball to escape the hood.

Barack Obama found a way and rose out of the South Side and became president.

There were also Common, Bernie Mac, Chance the Rapper, Kanye West, and many others.

These are stories of people who came from my environment and looked like me. Although difficult, their success is proof that opportunity was within reach. Even for me.

Why couldn't I find a way to escape?

* * * *

THE NEXT DAY, I met up with the gang. I was in the basement of some house that Smoke texted me to come to. When he arrived, he walked right up to my face. The rest of the nine guys stood around me. Light protruded from the windows and shined on the floor, allowing me to see everyone clearly this time. Both of the ceiling lights were on.

"Boogie told me you got something you need to say to us."

"Yeah, I want out. I can't do this no more."

"Oh, yeah? And why is that?"

"I feel like I belong somewhere else now. I got an opportunity to go to a really good college. Shit, plus the other day these dudes tried to pull a drill on Boogie and me. I took that as a sign. I got people counting on me, yo."

"Pull a drill" was slang for drive-by.

"Then you know what you gotta do to blood out. Let's hope you wake up this time."

The group surrounded me in a circle, and my mind flashed back to my initiation process.

Last time I was in this position, I was willing to die to join a street gang. But was I willing to die today to leave a street gang to join a new gang, a Service Academy?

"Aight, let's get it over with. I'm ready."

When you have a true WHY in life, you can handle any pain.

Someone pushed me to the ground, and the group proceeded to beat me. It wasn't even thirty seconds later before Smoke interrupted.

"Stop. Dre, get up."

I rose to my feet slowly. The guys exchanged perplexed faces at Smoke. Even I was confused.

Then Smoke leaned in close and said something to me that I'll never forget. There was a deep chill in his voice.

"I saw from the beginning that you was a different type of n*gga. You a smart-ass dude, and you got hella folks that support you. I just wanted to see if you had the balls to man up and say it to us and was willing to do what you had to do to get out. This shit ain't for you, yo. The folks and I had already been talking, and we think you got a good shot at makin' something of yo'self. We live through you. Plus, Boogie told us what happened. What you said to him and that you went to check on him. You a leader, G. You can go. You good wit' us."

In the light, nine figures all nodded in agreement.

"I appreciate that, Smoke," I responded and shook his hand. I went around the group and stacked up with everyone one last time.

When I made it to Boogie, I stopped and looked him in the eye. "You better be right after me, bro. I'll see you on the other side."

"Let's hope so," he said with a smirk.

I walked out of the front of the house and let the screen door *slam*. I lifted my head and took a moment to look at the clouds in the sky. They were a majestic blue and danced in the heavens with valor.

"Thank you, Lord," I said under my breath.

Once again God was at work in the trenches of my life. There's no way I could have walked away like that unscarred without his grace.

I was supposed to be another statistic.

What's still crazy is that during my gangbang days, no one in my family knew. It wasn't until I reached college that I decided to open up to them about it.

In the end, I made the choice that one day I wanted to be a great father, an author, a mentor, and a man who provided for his family and took care of his responsibilities the legal way. I made the choice to be a better version of myself.

If I didn't face my fears and look my demons in the eye, there was no way I would have gotten out. And that's a 100 percent guarantee. We as people need to take this same approach to other events in our lives.

I'm humbled to say that people have always seemed to gravitate to me for some reason, and the gang was no different.

If I could get a group of street thugs to believe in me, who else could I inspire?

What I don't understand is why we don't do that for more youth who come from urban environments. The hood will protect and support a kid who plays football and basketball to see them escape and "put on" for the city. Yet we can't do the same thing for kids who are serious about education, politics, or any other discipline that would bring a positive light to the community. That's crazy to me, and I wanted to change it.

Less than 1 percent of people receive the chance I was given to walk away.

I know my mother has always prayed over me, and I do believe I am blessed. But what's also clear to me is that I was extremely lucky. I was lucky to have the relationship I had with Smoke and for the type of leader he was. I was lucky that I survived. I was lucky I had parents who still cared for me. I know many people who have it so much worse, and for that I'm thankful.

I left the street gang and didn't look back.

CHAPTER 10

APPLYING TO A SERVICE ACADEMY

MY MOTHER WAS A SAVAGE. I'D NEVER SEEN HER FIGHT THE WAY SHE DID DURING THE APPLICATION PROCESS. She refused to let us stay in Chicago after high school.

There were multiple components to the Service Academy application: physical fitness, health, academics, and a nomination.[1] My mother knew we needed all the support we could get to make our goal happen, so she sat everyone in the family down in the morning and made us pray together. She started it off: "Dear heavenly Father, we thank you for everything you have brought this family through. We praise you for all the blessings and opportunities you have given us, and we thank you in advance for the ones in the future. Guide our steps in this rigorous application process. No matter what people say or what the statistics dictate, we stand in agreement right now, Lord, united in prayer that Andre, Anthony, and Alexander will attend the Academy together. Give them wisdom as they

---

1 See Addendum "My Advice for Applying to a Service Academy."

complete their application. Guide every step they take, Father God. It's in your precious and holy name we pray. Amen."

Being close to my brothers wasn't a necessity. We always knew that we had different interests and would later move on to separate career fields, but for college, we wanted to experience that together. What we didn't realize was that the Academy's secret goal was to separate us.

It was 2010, and leaves were just beginning to hit the ground that brisk August night when Dwayne walked up Judge Steele's concrete stone steps and rang the front doorbell of his home. He was an African American man with light skin, square gray glasses, and a bald head. He lived across the street from us on the corner. In general, most of the neighbors on our block knew Dwayne from when he lived with the Franklins.

Dwayne asked Judge Steele what it would take to get all three of us accepted into West Point. The judge said the application required us to receive a nomination from a senator or congressman, and Bobby Rush—the local United States Representative at the time—was the best shot we had at receiving one. Dwayne asked Judge Steele if he could get us in touch with his office.

"I'll have to get back to you," Judge Steele answered while swiftly motioning to close the door.

He gave Dwayne a generic answer—probably because he thought the request was impossible. Determined, Dwayne went to visit the judge several more times over the course of the next two weeks. But his response was always the same: "I'll let you know. I need some time."

In the meantime, my mother was facing another battle in helping us. Throughout the application process, my family and I had the most resistance completing the medical portion. Depending on your residence, applicants were prescribed certain medical facilities they could visit to complete their examination. I think back on the many trips my mother made to the North Side, suburbs, or far West Side of Chicago to ensure the three of us made our appointments on time. The Service Academies set strict standards for the medical examination process. The applications had to be damn near perfect. The smallest health-related issue would disqualify you.

In our case, there were multiple episodes when West Point attempted to exclude us for minute items on our medical records. For example, Anthony had eczema as a kid. Despite his condition, which was nothing severe, he never had to see a dermatologist or experienced major skin problems. If anything, it was more of a dryness to his skin or a small irritation. Unfortunately, Anthony's honesty came to haunt us in the end when he mentioned eczema on his application. After a few days, we received a letter from USMA. The beige envelope was placed on top of the other mail as it sat on the concrete gray porch. My mother opened the brown screen door and picked it up.

Rip.

She broke it open.

"DISQUALIFIED."

My mother thought the reasoning of the rejection was ridiculous, so she challenged them. Without hesitation, that very

same day she wrote USMA a thorough response letter specifying that Anthony had never had major skin issues. Days later,
we received a second response letter: Anthony was recom-
mended to see a dermatologist. The appointment only lasted
five to ten minutes, and the doctor already had an update for
us. "I think your son might have an allergic reaction to nickel
because his necklace irritated his skin around the neckline,"
the dermatologist told my mother. *Seriously?* You would think
for how important this medical check was to the application
process that the doctor would provide a more thorough examination. Still, we submitted the results and waited for the next
response from West Point.

A few days passed before another letter rested on our front
porch.

"DISQUALIFIED."

Persistent, my mother wrote a counter letter back indicating it
was unfair to reject Anthony medically just because the dermatologist said he "thought" he was allergic; there was no solid
evidence presented to make a conclusion.

The next letter we obtained read differently.

"WAIVER."

Anthony was cleared by the medical board.

The rollercoaster started again when Alex mentioned that he
occasionally experienced slight headaches on his application.
Like clockwork, West Point sent their favorite letter to initially

disqualify him. Following her gut once again, my mother drafted an immediate response specifying that Alex had not had any major medical problems or long-term issues with head-aches. "Have the candidate complete several tests, including a CT scan," West Point replied back. The results from viewing my brother's brain came back clear. Alex had no issues of concern. Just like Anthony, another "*WAIVER*" letter was obtained.

"I feel like God moved me to write those letters," my mother said in reflection some time later. Many people would have given up after the initial response from Army West Point. They might have given up and thought, *there's nothing I can do about it if they disqualified my child.*

Wrong.

My mother's refusal to take "no" for an answer is a testament to what it takes to accomplish what you want in life. No one will care about and see your vision more clearly than you do. It takes courage to be exceptional. It takes courage to tap into what you see inwardly and apply it outwardly to accom-plish your dreams, no matter what people say or the statistics dictate. Speaking of numbers, that's another thing. We didn't let the admissions acceptance rates intimidate us. The day you start letting statistics and the opinions of others determine how you move in life is the day you fail to exist.

Finally, after multiple attempts, Judge Steele rang our doorbell late one evening.

"Hey, Judge Steele, what's going on?" Dwayne said when he opened up the front door.

"Here's the contact information for Congressman Bobby Rush's office."

The next day, my family and I climbed into the car and made a visit to his compact office on East 79th Street. Ms. Thyatiria Towns, his secretary, was sitting behind a black desk when we walked in.

"Hi, can I help you?"

"Yes, we wanted to know how we go about the process of receiving a nomination from Mr. Rush for West Point," Dwayne responded.

Totally ignoring his question, Ms. Towns cut in: "Wait. Are they triplets?"

"Yes. They are."

"That's so cool! Ohhh my goodness, ohhh my goodness. I'm so excited about any opportunity to get Black males accepted to a Service Academy! And triplets!" She made a soft clapping motion with her dark hands near her face while she spoke. "Don't worry about the nomination. We got you."

Each year, every congressman and senator is issued a certain quota of nominations. Because competition for the nominations is stiff, most offices have their own interview process to select candidates. Sadly, because African American students fail to apply from the South and West sides, many of the nominations from Chicago come from the White districts. Over the span of the next few weeks, Ms. Towns worked with my brothers and me to make sure we had everything we needed to submit a complete application.

* * * *

DURING THE APPLICATION process, my brothers and I received a call from the Naval Academy to fly to Annapolis for a visit, all expenses paid. In excitement, we left on a Thursday to come back on Sunday. My time visiting USNA was a blur. I found that the structure of the institution was similar to West Point except that it had its own unique naval traditions and culture.

Back in Chicago, three letters labeled "Naval Academy" awaited us on the living room table. My family and I stood around the table, eager to open them. We gathered our hands in a circle, and my mother said a quick prayer. I could feel the squeeze from the hands next to me tighten in anticipation as my mother said her final closing words. Our lives had the potential to be changed forever based on the contents of a mail package.

The envelopes were small. There had to only be a few sheets of paper inside based on how slim they were.

The three of us leaped forward and tore open the mail.

They were rejection letters.

What the hell?

The Naval Academy's misstep shocked us. We all exchanged disgusted yet confused faces with one another. I closed my eyes and shook my head slowly in disbelief. *How could this be? Why would the Naval Academy pay for us to come visit just to reject us right when we got back home?* We glanced at the date the letters were prepared—they were written the day we arrived on campus. Something wasn't right. From my parents' perspective, they felt like the reason for rejection lay in the issue of our skin tone: once the admissions board saw that we were Black, they sent the letters to deny us. I can't personally speak to whether that was exactly true or not. But the situation itself was odd.

That same day, my mother went to Congressman Bobby Rush's office and showed Ms. Towns the letters. Without delay, Ms. Towns sent a copy of the letter, in addition to attaching her own personal note, to the office in Annapolis and in DC. A day or two later, Ms. Towns received a call from the Naval Academy. It was the Dean of Admissions, Andrew Phillips. He apologized to Ms. Towns and asked what he could do to fix the problem. She told him, "Offer them an appointment. They deserve it."

Two days later, my brothers and I received our tickets out of the hood—acceptance letters to the Naval Academy Prep School.

We called Ms. Towns to thank her the same day.

"I'm so proud of you three. And thank your mother too. She's been a trooper. She was the one who reached out. Now go make Chicago proud." I wasn't surprised to hear that. Everyone always loved Mom. People respected the way she carried herself: she was a beautiful, spiritual, hardworking, good-hearted woman.

When you submit an application to any of the Service Academies, selecting to go to the prep school first is not an option. Candidates must still receive a nomination even if the admission board asks if you're interested in attending. If I could offer any advice to prospective candidates, I would encourage them to attend the prep school. It takes away the "shock" many people experience from transitioning directly from high school into the Naval Academy, and it provides them the freedom to make mistakes early. So don't be discouraged if the admission board throws the words "prep school" your way; it's actually a blessing in disguise.

At the end of it all, West Point decided to offer a direct acceptance to Anthony, a civilian prep school for one year to me, and West Point prep school for one year to Alex. They wanted to split us up. We said no.

By the time my brothers and I emerged from the foggy application process, USNA had billeted all its direct spots. In return, they offered us the prep school option. Among the three Service Academies that my brothers and I applied to, we encountered the least drama from the Air Force. Right away they offered to place us in three quotas at their prep school in Colorado. My brothers and I now had a decision to make: Air Force or Navy? For whatever reason, Anthony always leaned more toward West Point; Alex favored the Air Force because of their cyber and computer programs; myself, Navy. I believed it offered the best majors and set us up for the most successful post-military life.

One night, to make a unified decision, we locked ourselves in the basement and mapped out the advantages and disadvantages of attending USNA versus USAFA. We went all over the place, discussing topics such as quality of life, majors, location, jobs available after graduation, and post-military opportunities. After debating for an hour, we picked the Navy.

Months later, after receiving an admission offer from the Naval Academy, Judge Steele admitted that he thought my stepdad was joking. That he was crazy because it was hard enough to get one child accepted in the Naval Academy. Three at the same time seemed impossible to him.

Some may argue that three Black triplet boys were accepted to the Naval and Air Force Academies under the shadow of affirmative action. That could possibly be true—we may never know—but we were actually rejected on our first try. Luckily, my family never took "no" for an answer. My mother could have accepted defeat the moment she received the first medical denial letter. Yet, she didn't. She fought back. Every step of the way, we believed in ourselves. Through the whole process, not one day went by where we let off the gas. We wrote down our goal, prayed about it, and reflected on it every single day.

I truly believe we deserved a chance. That was all I wanted. To show the entire city of Chicago that three Black boys from the hood could attend the Naval Academy, still remember where they came from, not act differently after leaving, and graduate. I didn't dodge bullets, bloody my fists from fighting, join a gang, and wake up every day in the ghetto just to fail and not have a chance. My parents didn't go through what they went through just for me not to have the courage to try. No matter what I went through at the Naval Academy, I still paid my dues. Those are the reasons I worked as hard as I did. I would later graduate from the Naval Academy at the top of my class. I valued my opportunity.

Only 50 percent of youth with prior gang affiliations actually graduate from high school.

Less than 5 percent graduate from college.

Less than 1 percent attend an Ivy League or top-tier institution.

It was time to show everyone what my name meant.

★ ★ ★ ★

My brothers and me in our adolescent days dressed in the same clothing, something my mother was notorious for when we were younger. Oh, how much we hated it. From left to right: Me, Alex, and Anthony.

My mother Adrienne (middle), and her parents, Mildred (right) and Clarence (left) Johnson, posing for a picture in front of their home in Englewood.

Visiting my grandmother Martha Evans, my biological father's mother, when she lived with Caulet and Billy in Bowie, Maryland.

Anthony stands tall at the center of the King College Prep Marching Band directing as the lead Drum Major during the Chicago Classic Battle of the Bands. Our band director, Mr. Benjamin Washington, is shown standing next to Anthony on the right.

My brothers and me standing outside the main entrance of our NAPS barracks, Ripley Hall, in Navy Working Uniform (NWU Type I) fatigues. This was the first picture we ever took in uniform together. All three of us sported three bar "stripers" as indicated by the collar devices on the right of our uniforms.

Here I am again, climbing the slippery, several feet long Herndon statue located near Stribling Walk. Most midshipmen took their shirts off to wipe off the gooey gunk from the monument in order to make it easier to climb to the top. Traditionally, climbing Herndon marked the end of plebe year. Rumor has it that whoever acquires the plebe cover placed at the top will become an Admiral one day.

Here I am depicted sitting across the table and having lunch with the First Lady, the beautiful Michelle Obama, inside King Hall during my plebe year.

This was my first time meeting the Superintendent of the Naval Academy face to face, Vice Admiral Ted Carter, let alone visiting the SUPE's house. I was invited during my youngster year by Ms. Janie Mines, depicted in the center of the photo.

Singing in the gospel choir allowed me to stay in tune with my church-going roots from the South Side. Every Sunday morning, whether we liked it or not, my mother made sure my brothers and I attended service. I believe being a member of GC added to the diversity of my experiences while attending Annapolis. In this photo is Dr. Karla Scott, directing us during a performance within the Naval Academy Chapel for Black History Month.

This is me, sometime during my youngster year, after speaking to a promising group of students in Chicago at the Air Force Academy High School.

Just like gaining muscle from lifting heavy weights in the gym, Sea Perch gave me the reps I needed to practice the effectiveness of STEM programs within the Black community, particularly at-risk neighborhoods.

I walked into that gymnasium with a speaking agenda in mind, only to be persuaded by the eyes and faces of the South Side—our youth. I heard a voice whisper in my head, and in that moment, I spoke something completely different. From this angle, you would think that the kids here at Bronzeville High School learned something or were inspired. And I hope so. But I also realized something about myself: I personally chose to wear the uniform not only to engage in battle if necessary for our country, but to go to war for every child in Chicago.

What a great photo taken by Miriam Stanicic, the community relations director at the Naval Academy! I believe it captures my love for outreach in action the most, especially with the powerful words captioned in the back. This photo was taken while I conducted a tour of the Naval Academy Museum for a bright group of African American kids from a school in Washington, DC.

It was a hot, humid Annapolis day as I stood there at attention before my plebes and detailers as the 2019 Plebe Summer Regimental Commander. My staff is shown behind me in typical "wedge" formation. Our hands were still raised at a ninety-degree angle as we waited for the Commandant to finish reciting our Oath of Office and duty as detailers.

"EYES RIGHT!!!" I yelled, to command my Regimental staff to salute with our swords as we marched past the Superintendent, the Commandant, and their guests. This was one of many formal parades midshipmen participated in during their time at Annapolis.

A silly picture with my entire Regimental and Battalion staff at the front entrance and steps of Bancroft Hall. This was taken after another one of our long "drill" practices in T-Court.

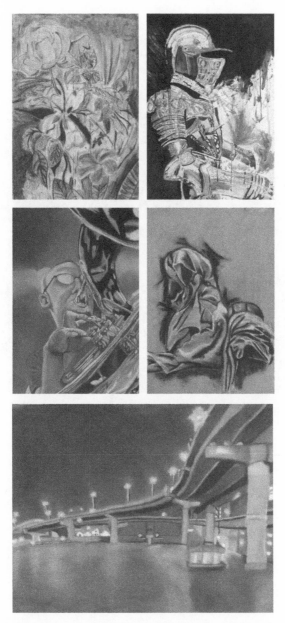

A few of the artwork pieces I have done in ink, acrylic paint, and pastel.

After another grueling morning workout during Plebe Summer, Colonel Liszewski stood before the class of 2019 and its detailers to offer a few words of wisdom. A motivated Marine at heart, seldom did he miss the opportunity to stand before his troops and offer words of encouragement.

After thirty-six years of service, Admiral Michelle Howard became the first Black Officer and first woman to ever hold the position as Vice Chief of Naval Operations. She was also the first female admiral to command operational forces. Here we are on stage, as I humbly accept my BEYA student engineering leadership award from her.

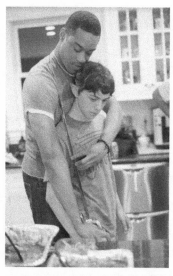

Hayden's passion for military history and the Naval Academy, for me, was always refreshing. Here I am showing Hayden how to correctly wield a naval officer's sword. The night before graduation, the Bandes hosted a large dinner for Alex and me at their lovely home, with our family from Chicago.

I knew early on that God had a plan for my life. More often than not, he's placed me in the most difficult leadership positions, where I have to go in and fix things. And he's given me a heart full of passion, always seeking to help others. My ultimate goal in life is to see the people I inspire add value and uplift others. Here I am with Ms. Mines and members of the Midshipman Black Studies Club (MBSC) standing outside of the Pentagon.

If there's one thing I've learned in life, it's how to deal with pain. There's the pain we dislike the most that's forced upon us from the pressures of life. Then there's the pain of hard work. It produces certain things complacency can't. Service selecting submarines was a big exciting moment. For me, it took an undying amount of faith in God and relentless effort. Service selection night was one of my fondest memories at Annapolis.

The 10th Company Logo. It depicts a muscular King Neptune in the center surrounded by an Naval jet, helicopter, and surface ship.

My 10th Company mates and I walked into the stadium with a mix of emotions: anxiousness, excitement, and fear of the unknown to come. We made it though. It was our time to become a part of the long Blue and Gold line.

Screaming ecstatically at the top of my lungs while our covers are thrown in the air: the day every midshipman longs for. Like making a wish or final statement, I threw my cover in the air and said, "This one's for Chicago."

A graduation day photo of the Evans/Johnson family after Alex and I were commissioned from the United States Naval Academy.

Dwyane in his younger days when he was enlisted in the Army.

I've always loved this picture for some reason. Maybe because I can't think of a picture more suitable to depict his journey as a man. When Anthony left USNA, he kept running. When he moved to DC and worked three different jobs, he kept running. He never stopped running no matter how difficult life got. And Alex and I were right there next to him, running along the way in support. Here is Anthony in action, running the physical fitness test (PRT) on the track as a midshipmen candidate at the Naval Academy Prep School in Newport, Rhode Island.

Standing outside MIT Lincoln Laboratory. Unfortunately, I wasn't able to get a photo in front of the main building, due to now updated security reasons.

Here is Anthony on graduation day after earning his badge as a secret service agent. I'll never forget how special that day was for our family. He opened a door our family never thought was possible. With God's help, he shattered decades of negative African American stereotypes and shined a positive light over the city of Chicago. It hurt me deeply not being able to see and support him on his big day. I was answering our nation's call to duty, serving underway out in the middle of the ocean on a ballistic missile destroyer naval ship. Nonetheless, I was even more honored to call him my big bro.

It's amazing how much you can accomplish with a solid support system—the entire Bandes family was nothing short of that. Alex and I would not have been able to succeed at the Naval Academy without their hospitality, love, and guidance. We celebrated holidays, birthdays, and other joyous milestones with the family. When Hayden and Brooke had stage plays, art shows, sporting events, or conferences at school, we went to those too. What was important to them was important to us.

In such a demanding place as Annapolis, midshipmen always find a creative way to have fun. Depicted here is a tradition we like to call "carrier landings." Plebes coat the floors with copious amounts of water and soap and, using an old bed mattress, run and hop on top of it to enjoy a fast glide down the long p-way (hallway) to the end. It's a game that brings the entire company together with the addition of music, pictures, and laughter. As you can guess, the name is derived from what one would see with jets landing onboard a US Naval aircraft carrier.

My baby: a 2015 Dodge Challenger SRT Hellcat who I nicknamed "Louie." ABOVE is a picture of him out in the wild after receiving a fresh bath and coat of wax. The second I saw him, I fell in love with the orange-peanut-butter-colored laguna leather interior. BELOW (sad face) is Louie at the tow yard a few days after the crash. Whenever I look at that picture, it reminds me yet again of how blessed I am.

Since birth, my mother raised the three of us to look out for each other no matter what. Like any family, we have had our ups and downs. Despite our separation among different states and the curveballs life throws at us, one thing has remained constant: our bond and love for one another.

The first time I met Eric Thomas, one of my favorite leaders and motivational speakers, was on the basketball court with my brother Alex at Annapolis. The second time I got to see him was at his conference in the suburbs of Maryland. His speeches have always been a source of inspiration for me.

A picture of me testing a futuristic double hull submarine within the Naval Architecture tow tank. The tank allowed us to test and see vessel hydrostatics and performance under various conditions. This project was my independent research project that I started in my junior year at the Naval Academy.

ACT II: THE UNITED STATES NAVAL ACADEMY

One of the reasons you are suffering right now is precisely because the purpose of your struggle is unclear. What are you working toward? What are you fighting for? Who are you going to be?

—ERIC GREITENS, *Resilience: Hard-Won Wisdom for Living a Better Life*

CHAPTER 11

A FRESH START

"WHERE THE HELL DO YOU THINK YOU'RE GOING?! GET OVER HERE RIGHT NOW!"

My brothers and I were dropped off at the Naval Academy Preparatory School (NAPS) in Newport, Rhode Island, a day before check-in. It was 2011 and a nice summer day. My mother and stepfather left us early that morning because they both had to work in Chicago the next day. We walked into the admin building for Officer Candidate School (OCS), the place where our professors' offices were located, and turned in our registration paperwork. It was an old, dingy brown building. The air inside was stale, and the mood was awkward. The time had come for us to officially say goodbye to our parents.

"You're not gonna miss anything in Chicago. The same people will be hangin' on the block. The trees will get taller. Don't worry about us. Just stay focused," my mother said as she gave each of us a big, warm hug. My parents wanted us to leave the South Side for college and never come back. The fact is they knew that cutting off our negative blood relatives and escaping the bullets was crucial if we had any chance of being successful and making something of ourselves. Many of our friends—and even family—discouraged us from attending the prep school. A great deal of people in Chicago even took bets that we would fail to graduate.

We all refrained from being sentimental. My mother was strong-willed about it and didn't shed any tears. Deep down, I think she knew we would get emotional if she did. "If you could do only one thing for me, one thing: just graduate from the Academy. Please," Dwayne said while shaking each of our hands and giving us a hug.

The next day, like a flood of ants bunched together, the rest of our NAPSTER classmates stood outside in line while they waited to check in at the gym. The shape of the building itself resembled a cylinder cut in half, a common architectural form seen on military bases, particularly for aviation hangar bays. On Naval Station Newport, the small gym was used for a variety of activities: promotion ceremonies, drill practice, medical vaccines, physical training, and graduations.

"AT THIS TIME, YOU NOW HAVE FIVE MINUTES TO SAY GOODBYE TO YOUR LOVED ONES!" a Lieutenant Naval Officer shouted from the center of the wooden basketball court floor. He was wearing a peanut butter khaki uniform.

"Ughhh." A mother erupted into tears at the sound of his words. Like dominos falling, her cry started an emotional chain reaction among other families. More people started crying and gripped their midshipman candidates in death-like hugs, like they would never see them again.

Shit was about to get real, soon. There was no turning back now. I remember the awkward loneliness my brothers and I felt as we stood there in the gym by ourselves, looking around as everyone said their final goodbyes. I was ready for the journey to start.

"Are you here with anyone?" a voice said out of nowhere. A gentleman with a lean build who appeared to be in his fifties emerged from the crowd behind us. His thin, rectangular-framed glasses complemented his gray-streaked brown hair. His first words and the way he approached us creeped us out.

"No. We are here alone." I guarded myself and looked at the mysterious man with suspicion.

"Hi, I'm Chaplain Doug Rosander. I'm the head Chaplain here at the Naval War College." His slender lips formed a warm smile, and he reached out his hand to shake each of ours. His palms were soft. The grip of his hand was subtle. He wasn't in uniform.

"Nice to meet you, sir," I responded warily.

"I noticed you all looked lonely over here. Everyone wants to feel like they belong. So I wanted to come over and keep you guys company. We can form our own group and talk in the meantime. I hope that's okay."

"Yea, that's fine, sir." We engaged in small talk about Newport and why my brothers and I had joined the Navy.

"LET'S GO! THAT'S IT! YOUR FIVE MINUTES ARE UP! I NEED ALL MIDSHIPMEN CANDIDATES TO MOVE TO THE LEFT SIDE OF THE GYM, AND I NEED ALL LOVED ONES TO EXIT OUT ON THE RIGHT!" the Lieutenant yelled and directed everyone with the palms of his hands.

"Good luck, Evans triplets. I'll see you three around," the Chaplain said and walked away.

* * * *

IT WAS 0400 in the morning the next day when I was awakened by violent screams and banging on my door.

"GET UP! EVERYONE UP! MUSTER[2] OUTSIDE FOR MORNING PT!" It was the first day of the indoctrination phase, or INDOC for short: a four-week boot camp designed to break and destroy everything candidates knew about civilian life and build them back up to transition into a military lifestyle. I scrambled out of bed, threw on my issued gear—a white cotton shirt and blue mesh shorts—and followed my classmates running out the two black front doors of Ripley Hall barracks. We lined up in platoon formation on the football field. Let me definitely take the time to point out how much I hated those NAPS and USNA shorts. For anyone tall, they were extremely uncomfortable and hugged the thighs of your legs to make you look like you were wearing booty shorts. *They were evil.*

Two square metal platforms stood on either side of the field, the structural integrity of the podiums held together with an

---

2 Muster is another way to say roll call.

"X" shape insert. These podiums are common in the armed forces to demonstrate military exercises to a large audience from a high vantage point. Depending on who led the workout that morning, exercises varied from planks, mountain climbers, and sit-ups to squats, flutter kicks, and more. At that moment, another figure emerged from the front doors of Ripley Hall. The lights above the field were out, and since it was still nighttime, all I could see was the outline of a muscular man. The mysterious guy climbed on top of the podium.

Then, like he was some movie star who'd timed his entry, the large field lights came on and beamed down on him.

The man who stood before us was Marine Gunnery Sergeant (GYSGT) Paul Ford. He wore a snug red T-shirt with thigh-squeezing forest green shorts. He was bald with dark skin and had a slim athletic build. His demeanor was stern-cold. He looked mean as hell.

We all stared at him in silence on the field. *Who is that?*

"Everybody, take your left hand and raise it up in the air like this." He demonstrated by lifting his own arm toward the sky. Veins protruded through his thick forearms. He had a powerful, demanding voice.

He paused and waited for all of us to comply exactly as instructed. "Now take your right hand and put it up like this."

Another long pause.

"Now put them together like this." He placed his hands together to make the shape of a diamond.

Pause.

"Now place them on the ground like this." He put his hands directly on the base of the podium and got in a leaning push-up position.

We all did the same.

And then in a blood curdling scream, he shouted, "NOW PUSH dammit! One, two, three. One, two, three. One, two, three."

This man started calling out cadence for push-up repetitions.

That was my introduction to GYSGT Ford.

Over time, I'd learned that people feared to look him in the eyes because of the death stare he would give back, like he wanted to kill you just for looking at him. His pupils spoke of pain and violence: a result of the time he'd spent in combat commanding M1A1 Abrams tanks. Ford was a thoroughbred Marine who specialized in discipline and instruction. He dreamed about it. Like a lion rising in the morning to hunt, whenever he saw a recruit, his bodily instincts and mind would automatically yell, "TRAIN."

The football field was also where Gunny made us "drill" once a week. Plain and simple, drill was marching. It's argued to be the foundation of instilling discipline within trainees and requires focus, sharp movements, and attention to detail.

And oddly enough, I fucking loved it.

It reminded me a little bit of the marching we did in the marching band at King and all the practice and precision that went into preparing for halftime shows. What I also loved about drill was that it taught me how to be resilient, a quality that can be applied to multiple areas of life to overcome adversity. I wanted to master it. Oftentimes, participants are required to stand completely still at attention for a considerable amount of time. Drill forces you to focus your mind and ignore all distractions in order to execute each task you do with the best of your ability. Today, drill is mostly used for ceremonies and parades within the military.

And GYSGT made sure we took it seriously. One of my classmates learned that the hard way on our first day on the field.

I'm not joking. Ford made a grown-ass man crawl around on the turf like a dog for hours.

Here's what happened. It was nighttime, and we were all dressed in our Navy camo fatigues marching around, when all of sudden I heard yelling.

"COME HERE, GODDAMMIT. WHAT THE HELL ARE YOU LOOKING AT?"

Apparently, there was a guy who was looking around while marching. Precision drill required everyone to look forward and be still at all times.

It didn't matter if a wasp stung you or a bug was crawling on your face. You couldn't move unless you were executing a drill movement that was ordered to you.

Now that's resilience.

"I wasn't looking at anything, GYSGT."

"GET IT BACK. I WANNA KNOW WHAT THE HELL IS SO GODDAMN INTERESTING OUT THERE!"

"Nothing, GYSGT."

"NO. TELL ME WHAT THE FUCK YOU WERE LOOKING AT. YOU DREAMING OF MAMA'S COOKING? DO YOU SEE A FAT, CUTE ASS BUNNY OUT THERE OR SOMETHIN'? I WANNA KNOW!"

"It was nothing, GYSGT. I swear. I'm sorry," he said in a trembling voice.

"COME HERE RIGHT NOW. GET ON ALL FOURS RIGHT NOW," he yelled while pointing and motioning for the man to get on the ground right next to him.

The guy did as he was told. He looked crazy, bent over like an animal.

"NOW I WANT YOU TO CRAWL AROUND AND COME FIND ME."

The man made a confused face, like "What do you mean?"

"I WANT YOU TO FOLLOW ME WHEREVER I GO. SINCE YOU WANNA LOOK AROUND, I'LL GIVE YOU A BUNCH OF SHIT TO LOOK AT."

The large man crawled around on his hands and knees. While shaking his head back and forth left and right to pretend he was looking for something, he followed GYSGT around the drill field and yelled, "WHERE ARE YOU, GYSGT!?"

"I'M OVER HERE. I CAN'T HEAR YOU."

"WHERE ARE YOU GYSGT!? WHERE ARE YOU GYSGT!? WHERE ARE YOU GYSGT!?"

Over and over, he repeated those words all night.

My classmates and I fought with all our might not to laugh. But no one dared. We didn't want to be next.

When NAPSTERS failed to pay attention on the drill field or participate fully in PT, we were sent to something called the "sand pit," a large rectangular or square box filled with, you guessed it, sand. Forest green colored sand bags surrounded the box to create its border, and depending on the real estate available at a particular location, pits could be constructed to hold as few as ten or up to roughly forty people. A common tactic used by Marine training sergeants to humble, fatigue, and discipline units, the sand pit is known to torment the memories of thousands. Drill instructors (DIs) loved playing in the sand pit. In a froggy, hoarse voice, Gunny made us perform group push-ups, sit-ups, mountain climbers, jumping jacks, planks, and other exercises within the pit. With group push-ups, my classmates and I formed a circle or square, and each person placed their legs in the air on the shoulders of the person behind them. The only thing that touched the ground was your individual hands. Everyone supported one another. If someone failed to pull their weight and complete a "down" or "up" rep, we all suffered. It made us trust each other and operate as a team. Teamwork and learning to accomplish tasks with others are crucial for success as a leader in any environment, but especially in a high-stakes environment like the armed forces. The density of the sand made performing the exercises even harder. Working in the sand pit was called "making sugar cookies," because we would emerge from the pit coated in sand.

I knew the miserable and intense physical requirements were a part of military training, but it seemed like my platoon or squad was there all the time, more than most. I couldn't help but wonder if some of it was payback for some of the acts I'd committed in the past.

Like the time I beat this guy with a gun.

Most people refer to this as pistol-whipping. It was another gloomy Chicago day. I was fourteen, meeting up with a group of guys who were also members of the gang. We met in a parking lot. We were just chilling and shooting the breeze. Then we saw this guy who was affiliated with another gang walking past us across the street. He appeared to be alone.

My friend Benzo said to me, "Yo, Dre, that's that dude that was talking crap and threatened to go after your brothers. You should go over there and show him what's up. Go handle your business, bro."

At this, Benzo slid a pistol into my hands. I quickly grabbed the gun and stuffed it behind the back of my waistline, covering it up with my long Academics brand T-shirt.

I knew this guy, the "enemy," would notice me walking over and immediately be on guard. Like a chameleon, I changed up my entire body language and demeanor. I gave him a friendly wave and a slight smile as I approached him. Halfway across the street, I said something to myself along the lines of, "I'm gonna be fine. I'll mess this dude up and walk away scratch free. You got this, Dre."

Even before I knew what I was doing, I was applying the power of affirmation into manifestation, even if it was in the name of a quarrel, machismo, and ultimately street credibility. Little did I know that these key qualities would allow me to become successful at the Naval Academy years later.

Back to the action, mano a mano, man to man. He already knew who I was and whom I was affiliated with, so I had to be careful. When he first noticed me jogging across the street, I saw his face harden, and his whole body plumped up in a defensive stance. I remember seeing his hand move toward his waistline, to grip and draw his gun for protection. "It's all good, yo," I said and lifted my hands up. "I just wanna talk." When I finally reached his face, I gave him a handshake to throw him off guard. Just as he reached his hand out to mine, I grabbed his arm, pulled him toward me with one hard jerk, and gave him a solid right hook to the face.

Animal survivalism took over, and what I saw next was mostly RED. I took the gun tucked in the back of my sagging pants and proceeded to beat him viciously with it.

"WAIT!!! STOP. PLEASE STOP!" my opponent said. My arm was up in the air, ready to strike another blow. He raised his arm up to attempt to block any further impacts to his face. With all his might, he gave me the best vulnerable face he could put on, hoping I would take pity and stop.

And for a brief moment—I did.

But then I had to be real with myself. If the roles were reversed, he wouldn't have hesitated with me.

"Nah, homie," I responded with a deathly whisper, and I kept thrusting my energy into the butt of the gun to pound into his flesh. It was so visceral—dreamlike in many ways. It was fall in Chicago, and as if I were outside of my body, I watched the autumn leaves splatter with his blood.

In the gang, we had values. As a man, I have values. The ethics of the streets are complicated, and the line between right and wrong can be easily blurred. I knew that if I didn't set the tone on how I wanted to be perceived and what I would tolerate from others, I would forever be perceived as a target or as weak. This guy threatened my brothers and family, so it had to be addressed.

I didn't kill him, but he left that day with a black and blue face covered in red and a broken jaw. Today, I know what I did was wrong, and I'm sorry for it. But at that age on those streets, I felt like I had no other choice. It was me or them, and I did what I had to do to protect my family and survive. I felt like I deserved every single sand pit session I endured at NAPS.

★ ★ ★ ★

BEING PUNISHED AND trained by GYSGT was INDOC in a nutshell. Yet, it was also an amalgamation of learning military knowledge and terminology, teamwork, and becoming physically fit.

At the end of INDOC and the start of the academic year, an email appeared in my inbox stating that the three of us were selected for the sponsorship program even though we hadn't signed up for it.

When my brothers and I underwent the check-in process at NAPS, we were asked if we would like to participate in the sponsorship program. It allowed members of the Newport community, usually military, to connect with midshipmen candidates and provide a "home away from home." The three of us said "no" right away—not because we didn't think it would be beneficial but because we really didn't know much about the program itself.

Chaplain Rosander and his family sponsored us.

They challenged a lot of the stereotypes we had about White people. Growing up on the South Side, most of my social and professional interactions involved Black people. At the time, I honestly believed what I experienced in Chicago, which was that most White people are racist and selfish. It's what my family experienced firsthand for years with the police and politicians within the city. Today, I know that's not true.

The Rosanders truly defied those stereotypes we believed about Caucasians on Thanksgiving. Violence in Chicago had continued to surge at unprecedented levels, and included multiple shootings around our house. Seventy-five to eighty percent of African American men between the ages of seventeen and twenty-four are at risk of being fatally shot on the South Side. In an effort to keep us safe and protect our opportunity to attend the Naval Academy, my mother insisted that we stay in Newport for the holidays. My mother recalls that a week or two before Turkey Day, she received a random phone call from Mrs. Rosander.

"The boys told us about their situation, and we would love to have them at the house for Thanksgiving. I want to make this special for them. Could you tell me what their favorite dishes are and provide me with the recipes?" Mrs. Rosander was sweet. She had straight brown hair down to her neck and dressed in a casual wardrobe. Her big bear hugs and genuine high-pitched voice would make us feel loved. She led worship services on the weekends, where she played piano every Sunday. Their oldest daughter, Kimberly, was around six feet tall with straight blonde hair that descended down to her shoulders, complementing her bright smile. Most of her time was spent working in the chapel, singing praise and worship during the weekends, or teaching middle school children during the week.

"Macaroni and cheese. And I make a sweet potato casserole they really love," my mother responded.

She later reflected that it meant a lot to her that Mrs. Rosander cared enough to want to make sure that our first Thanksgiving away from home was enjoyable. That phone call changed my parents' perception. The Rosanders were the first to challenge that childhood belief based on the way they treated my brothers and me. On the weekends, they would pick us up from base and take us to their home, where we could do homework, relax, and have a nice home-cooked meal. The experience actually did feel like a home away from home because the Rosanders had a genuine, vested interest in the three of us. They would go out of their way to help us and just make sure that we were doing okay.

We continue to keep in contact with them to this day.

* * * *

I WOKE UP at 0630 to prepare for morning formation at 0700. Our Battalion Commander, a four-striper whose overall responsibility was for the oversight and organization of the entire NAPSTER class, stood directly before us as the three companies under him arranged themselves in ranks. A single solid gold collar device encompassing four slim rectangular bars attached together formed the insignia he wore on each side. "BATTALION! ATTENTION! REPORT!" he would yell, indicating the unit was to snap to attention. Company Commanders would report the accountability of their people. "ALL PRESENT" or "ALL PRESENT AND OR ACCOUNTED FOR" was usually heard as each commander saluted. After accountability was received, the Battalion Commander would address the unit and pass out any relevant information for the day. At the end of morning formation, NAPSTERS gathered in packs to march down the street in unison to Nimitz Hall Galley, the building where chow was served.[3] We had to eat fast because at 0800 morning classes started, and they lasted until 1145. At 1205, noon meal

---

3 "Chow" is another way of saying food in the military.

formation occurred. The half hour between 1250 and 1320 was considered training time. Midshipmen candidates could use that time to study, receive extra instruction from professors, and take care of administrative or medical appointments. The remaining afternoon classes took place from 1330 to 1530. Those recruited for varsity athletics would attend their respective practices from 1545 to 1800. NAPSTERS not employed in sports either participated in intramural athletics or worked out on their own. Lastly, evening meal formation took place at 1815. Study period was scheduled from 2000 to 2300. Like a clock, we operated on this battle rhythm every single day. Even after graduation from NAPS, I would later continue this same schedule during my time at the Naval Academy.

In the end, I'm thankful for my opportunity to attend NAPS before the Naval Academy. There were multiple benefits. My academic struggles and learning how to effectively study would later serve me well during my time at Annapolis. Gunny Ford's intense training, plus NAPS INDOC, took away the initial shock most incoming plebes fear adjusting to military standards from civilian life. I stepped foot on the yard with a group of friends and credible relationships that supported me all the way to graduation.

I also learned the value of saving money. Seeing nine hundred dollars post to your checking account every month would make most kids who recently graduated from high school feel rich. It was the most money I had ever seen in my bank account. With an infant mentality about money management, I did what most of my classmates did and spent it. Any night of the week, the corridors of Ripley Hall were filled with Domino's pizza boxes, Chinese food, or boxes of goods ordered online. At the end of my year, I had nothing to show for money I received on the fifteenth and thirtieth of every month. Looking back, I wish I knew then what I know now about money. I could have graduated from NAPS with a decent amount of savings, especially since my only bill at the time was my phone. I wish someone had sat me down and forced me to create a budget and save smartly. Even though I failed to manage my finances properly, I never asked my parents for money. That was one thing I promised not to do. When I left home, my parents would always ask if I needed anything, but I never said yes. I paid my phone bill, and that was it. I knew we didn't come from money. However, we weren't poor either. I didn't ask for money not out of pride, but because I tried to take care of my responsibilities as a man.

CHAPTER 12

EMBRACE THE SUCK

He who will not risk cannot win.

—JOHN PAUL JONES

"Welcome to Baltimore/Washington International Airport," the flight attendant said in a cheery voice over the intercom. Her announcement and the sudden impact of the aircraft wheels against the runway woke me up from my sleep. My brothers and I grabbed our green sea bags and made our way to the arrivals terminal. There was a blue, white, and gray coach bus with "U.S. NAVAL ACADEMY" printed in white on both sides waiting along the curb to pick up candidates. As NAPSTERS, we were required to report a few days earlier than the rest of the candidates.

The drive took us thirty minutes.

Annapolis, Maryland, has played an instrumental part in the historical relationship between the military and African Americans. Often described as a microcosm of African

American heritage, Annapolis is the birthplace of several civil rights movements and maritime traditions. In 1864, Maryland outlawed slavery an entire year before Congress signed the 13th Amendment. And here I was, just a young Black man from the Midwest, hoping that the legacy of Frederick and Thurgood still resonated with the city.

I'd come to find that in Annapolis, with all its liberties, I would have to build my own legacy.

We exited the Maryland Route 450 highway and drove across the Naval Academy Bridge, a long lime green and gray structure that crossed the Severn River and provided entry onto "The Yard." At the center of the campus, and a common navigational aid for many sailors at sea, lies the Naval Academy Chapel, with its large bright gold dome. Like a skyscraper, it towered over all the other monuments and buildings and was the first thing that caught my eye when we drove along the bridge. Tradition has it that if a fourth class could place their cover (hat) at the top of the dome, plebe year would be considered over. [4]

It didn't take long before the bus emerged at the main blue gate. There was a gray brick structure on the right with large gold-brown letters that read:

UNITED STATES NAVAL ACADEMY

FOUNDED 1845

---

[4] The class levels at USNA are described by many different terms. First years are also called fourth class, 4/C, freshman, and plebes. Second years are also called third class, 3/C, sophomores, and youngsters. Third years are also called second class, 2/C, and juniors. Fourth years are also called first class, 1/C, seniors, and firsties.

Military police in blueberry-colored fatigue uniforms and civilian police dressed in black conducted routine ID checks at each vehicle that passed by. Just like West Point, the guards were armed with shotguns and 9mm pistols. Bill the Goat, the school's mascot, seemed to jump out at us when we passed the front gate checkpoint. The black-bronze statue portrayed Bill in an aggressive charge with his yellow horns ready to ram something. To the immediate right of the entry gate was Halsey Field House, a multipurpose building used for gym classes and by various sports teams for practice. A short Black lady wobbled past, walking like a hobbit. Her plain white shirt and black pants stood out from the starched white and khaki uniforms around her. Different from the gloomy world of West Point, the yard at USNA was bright. Most of the buildings were constructed from Jerusalem limestone and had a white or light gray color, while the copper roofs were green with the patina of age. Bancroft Hall (or Mother B), where the entire Brigade of Midshipmen slept every night, was the largest single dormitory in the world. It had one main section and eight connected corridor wings. The academic buildings were located on the far side of campus overlooking the chapel. Overall, USNA was made up of one Brigade of Midshipmen, two Regiments, four Battalions, and thirty Companies.[5] The Naval Academy was an education beacon with a curriculum parallel to an Ivy League, with the added bonus that midshipmen were required to play a sport and hold leadership positions at the same time—no exceptions.

I'd just joined one of the most prestigious gangs in the world.

---

5 See Appendix for organizational chart of the Brigade of Midshipman.

* * * *

I HATED THE wake-up noises.

Clink, clink, clink, clink, clink.

The blue metal baton slapped the hard floor and woke me up in a fury.

I was used to sirens and loud music, yelling, and gunshots while I slept; it was a part of the territory that came with living in Chicago. But metal screeching objects? Hell nah. I woke up swinging, ready to fight.

Bang. Bang. Bang. An upperclassman knocked ferociously on my door. *Swoosh.* Someone swung the door open and yelled inside, "GEEEEEEEEEEET UP! GET UP! FALL OUT NOW!"[6] I jumped out of bed and frantically threw on my uniform. It was still wet from sweat from the constant physical activities we performed under the blazing Annapolis sun. The cold, white-gray infused floor tile shot a chill of adrenaline through my legs to wake me up. Then came the ear-splitting sound of screaming rock music—"Bodies" by Drowning Pool. It rattled the bed frames.

How is this even music? What the fuck am I listening to? It sounds demonic. Bodies hitting the floor, really? I ran to the sink, brushed my teeth in thirty seconds, and ran out of the room. I glanced quickly to the left and right. The music blasted from

---

6 At Annapolis, "fall out" meant to come outside our rooms and line up at attention.

an enormous black rectangular speaker placed at the end of the p-way (hallway). The p-ways were several feet wide and stretched for miles. The music played until everyone scrambled out of their racks (beds) and mustered on the bulkhead (walls) outside our rooms with our bed sheets stuffed in a pillow case. We ran as fast as we could, bumping into one another. As an easy way to show our detailers[7] that everyone had their linens present, we were required to hold out one hand with the pillowcase clenched in our fists. Like canines searching for drugs, the first class went through all the rooms to make sure no one left anything behind.

"WHAT THE FUCK?! WHAT THE FUCK?! WHERE THE HELL ARE YOUR BED SHEETS?!" a detailer screamed at my classmate next to me.

"Sir. Uh...uh...uh...I'm sorry, sir. I forgot them," the plebe responded.

His body trembled in so much fear it almost looked like he was dancing at attention. He licked his lips and swallowed hard.

"IS THAT ONE OF YOUR FIVE BASIC RESPONSES?!"

"Uh...no. No, ma'am," he muttered out.

"DID YOU JUST CALL ME A FUCKING MA'AM?!"

---

7 A detailer is a midshipman that trains incoming plebes on the traditions, discipline, and customs of the military and the Naval Academy. They are in charge of the incoming classes moral, physical, and mental development while executing the Plebe Summer Training Schedule.

The detailer went ape shit.

"Sir, I'm sorry, sir! I'm so sorry, sir!"

"GET THE HELL OUT OF MY FACE! GO GRAB YOUR SHEETS NOW! AND BEFORE YOU GO TO BED TONIGHT, I WANT A ONE-PAGE ESSAY ADDRESSED TO MY MOTHER ON WHY YOU THINK I'M A MA'AM!"

It wasn't even 0600 in the morning yet, and the walls already steamed from our body heat. The p-way stank with the smell of sweat and foul body odor.

The detailer raised his right arm and touched a button on his dual black G-Shock watch.

Beep.

"Alright, you have two minutes to make your racks, get ready for chow, and make it back here on the bulkhead. Annn-nnd...go!" Like race horses out of the gate, we were off. My classmates and I ran back into our rooms to fix our beds to Navy military standards as fast as we could: eighteen inches from the head of the mattress to fold, fold was eight inches wide, four inches from the pillow. I used a binder to make the crisp hospital corners and tuck all the excess bedding under the bed. If we finished early, it was drilled into us to help one another. It's not about you and how fast you can individually make it out. We all had to make it out together. As a unit, we are only as strong as our weakest link. If we failed to make the time, we did it over and over again until we did.

It may sound like a stupid thing to do every morning, but it was one of the many things that taught us how to work together as a team. At the end of your four years at Annapolis, you will be a master at learning how to be a part of and organize various teams/gangs.

My classmates and I would also engage in "uniform races" for hours. Just imagine it. Picture all my classmates and me standing on the bulkhead at attention. In front of us would be a group of upperclassmen, all of them adjusting buttons on their watches in order to time how long it would take us to change into a particular uniform. But that meant we couldn't cheat and "pre-arrange" all the ribbons, nametags, and accessories on the uniform. Just like mustering outside with our bedsheets in a pillow case, upperclassmen would call out a particular uniform such as "service dress blues," "NWUs," or "summer whites," and we had to muster on the bulkhead with just the bare uniform on a hanger to prove that it was not prepped at all. With so many uniforms, the options were endless. Then they would give us a time goal to make as a class, usually starting with five minutes or so. Each time, the goal was to get faster and faster, so if we made ten minutes, then next time it would be five minutes, then three minutes, and so forth. It's hard to even attempt to explain how the sucky feeling of doing uniform races for endless hours would be replaced with joy and pride at everyone completing a very difficult time evolution. Sometimes, it would take a few weeks to reach a certain time goal. You learned to cherish those mini victories. And that's exactly how life is in the pursuit of accomplishing something hard. It may take you hours or days or months, maybe even years. It may suck working at that goal day after day. But inch by inch you get closer to your objective, and one day you will achieve it. The process you went through to get there will make you cherish the opportunity that much more.

Just like making our beds, we were all expected to be mustered outside wearing the uniform with all the correct accessories. If everyone wasn't on the bulkhead at the same time—we failed. If we didn't meet the time hack—we failed. If the uniform was not put together correctly or had discrepancies—we failed.

The punishment?

Anything creative the detailers could think of that would be miserable.

During the rest of your time at Annapolis, you realize that the pain associated with failing to complete certain tasks within a certain period of time trains your brain on how to hyperfocus and complete objectives efficiently. You then apply these same traits into accomplishing your goals or leading people.

We did this routine every day on top of the rest of our military training.

I hated being taken by surprise.

After the third or fourth day being awakened by the sound of batons hitting the floor, I had had enough. *I can't keep waking up like this. I gotta figure out a way to outsmart these folks.* With our watches and cell phones confiscated, there was no accurate way to track the time. Even though there were clocks mounted on the walls in the p-ways, our detailers covered them with white bed sheets. Losing the concept of time made the days feel longer. It was only on Sunday, when the detailers lined us up along the wall, removed our cell phones from a large Ziploc bag, and allotted us thirty minutes to make a phone call, that we had contact with the outside world.

I perfected my wake-up routine to the point that I pre-staged brushing my teeth and getting dressed. My "white works echo" uniform rested on a hanger against the left closet door. The blouse of the uniform had an extension around the neckline that looked like a small superhero cape in the back. The trousers flared toward the bottom leg like bell bottoms. On Sundays, for parades, and during special events, we wore "white works alpha," the only difference being the addition of a black, synthetic fabric neckerchief that was worn around the neckline centered on the chest and tied in a neat square knot. The only task left for the morning was to throw my sheets in a pillowcase and fall out on the bulkhead.

It was another morning before an abrupt wake-up call. As usual, it started with a door opening and small voices.

Squeak.

Click.

Step. Step. Step.

"Let's start on this side," a voice whispered.

The caramel-brown doors always let out a loud whine whenever they were opened or closed. I could hear the tap of the detailers' low-top black shoes as they attempted to lurk around the p-ways. I could hear them whispering loudly to one another. Like I was possessed, my eyes popped wide open.

Reveille was coming soon. The upperclassmen's noises were my alarm clock.

My body lay motionless in the stiff bed for roughly thirty minutes, pondering what I could do to achieve the upper hand and conquer the day. By now, I had adjusted to rising earlier. So I shifted my attention to becoming a nighttime crusader. It didn't matter if I hit the bulkhead first because if my classmates weren't out there with me, what was the point?

I climbed out of bed and, after preparing myself, tiptoed outside my door. I pressed my back against it and used both my hands to make sure it shut quietly. Then I made a run for it. In my socks (to be quiet, of course), I slid across the hall. My soft, white New Balance socks glided smoothly across the tile floors as I crept from door to door like Santa Claus. I woke up my classmates thirty minutes to an hour early. By the time we heard the banging of doors and loud music, a good handful of the tenth company plebes were able to fall out and align the bulkhead in record time. Little did I know that my nightly antics didn't go unnoticed.

★ ★ ★ ★

"IS ANYONE INTERESTED in singing in the gospel choir or glee club?" my detailer randomly asked one day during "Grey Space," a period of dead time when there was nothing scheduled in the plan of the day (POD). Our detailers had plans, though. They either made us stand on the bulkheads and study

Reef Points, polish our shoes, or fix the bad discrepancies they saw within us on a daily basis, whether that meant more physical training, uniform races, or drill practice with our rifles.

In sailing, *reefing* a sail is when you roll and tie up the extra sail material onto the boom for better performance and stability in heavy winds or severe weather. In this same fashion, *Reef Points* is a compass for plebes that helps them navigate the rough seas of their transition into becoming a member of the Brigade of Midshipmen. Considered the Bible of the Naval Academy, *Reef Points* is a small, dark blue book with the USNA crest on the front cover in gold. It has over 250 pages of more than 177 years of naval history in it. If we were not being instructed by our detailers, we were required to always study our *Reef Points*. In order to study, we had to hold the book up in the center of our face with our arm up and bent at a ninety-degree angle. *Reef Points* included topics such as the Sailors Creed, the mission and traditions of the Naval Academy, military rank structure, and more. Plebes were required to remember EVERYTHING within it verbatim. One of my favorite pieces of knowledge within the book was the "Man in the Arena" speech by Theodore Roosevelt:

> It is not the critic who counts; not the man who points out how the strong man stumbles, or where the doer of deeds could have done them better. The credit belongs to the man who is actually in the arena, whose face is marred by dust and sweat and blood; who strives valiantly; who errs, who comes short again and again, because there is no effort without error and shortcoming; but who does actually strive to do the deeds; who knows great enthusiasms, the great devotions; who spends himself in a worthy cause; who

at the best knows in the end the triumph of high achieve-
ment, and who at the worst, if he fails, at least fails while
daring greatly, so that his place shall never be with those
cold and timid souls who neither know victory nor defeat.

For me, it embodied the underdog, make-the-most-of-life
mentality I've always felt and believed in. That quote was a
source of encouragement for me many times at Annapolis.

My long arm protruded from the bulkhead to show my interest
in joining a singing group.

It was Sunday afternoon, and I had survived another week. One
of my detailers walked me to Alumni Hall, an indoor stadium
used for assembly briefs to the Brigade of Midshipmen, and
home to the men's and women's basketball teams. It's also where
the USNA choirs practiced. The space where the gospel choir
held rehearsal every Monday was all white: white tiles combined
with white painted walls, polarized by a single large black piano
on the center of the floor. The room was stiff and the steps of
my feet echoed when I walked up to the choir director, Dr. Karla
Scott. Her round cheek bones were the most unique feature of
her face. The brown-black patterned glasses she wore paired
well with her dark brown eyes and curly black hair.

"Why, hello there, Mr. Evans. Nice to meet you," she said in a
cheerful voice.

"Nice to meet you, too, ma'am. I'm glad to be here."

"Why do you want to join the gospel choir?"

"I grew up in the church, and I also sang in the chapel when I was a student at NAPS. I enjoyed it. I want to be a part of something at Annapolis that makes me feel like I belong, and I heard the choir has a strong family camaraderie," I responded back to Dr. Scott.

"You're absolutely right, Mr. Evans. A lot of people come to find that the choir has a large impact on their mental and emotional stability at USNA. Midshipmen come here and discuss their struggles without the fear of being judged. And we support and pray for one another in addition to having fun singing and traveling on tour."

Dr. Scott placed "Amazing Grace" before me on the piano stand. "Sing the tenor or bass line for me please." As instructed, I let the melodic flow of the song emit from my mouth. My lips and jaw slightly vibrated in an attempt to swing each note or phrase with vibrato. "Very good, Mr. Evans. I think you'll make a nice addition to the choir."

I'd joined yet another new gang.

* * * *

DURING YOUR ENTIRE four years at Annapolis, there will be a few defining moments that you will remember forever. One of those is Hello Night. Or, as some companies called it, "HELL-o Night." At its core, it's an event where plebes are introduced to their Company Officer and the rest of the upperclassmen. The severity of someone's Hello Night is dependent on the culture of each individual company. Some were deemed "chill" while others were intense. Your life as a plebe, as well as the rest of your time at the Naval Academy, could be significantly better or worse based merely on company placement.

It happened the night before reform (when the entire Brigade returns from summer training), and all my classmates and I were dressed in our PT uniforms. Those consisted of a white cotton shirt with a blue stripe that lined the neckline and sleeves and blue shorts (booty shorts for tall guys) with the letters "USNA" printed in yellow-gold. Our New Balance issued socks were motivated[8], and we all wore the same issued light gray New Balance sneakers. I stood with my face inches from the bulkhead, staring at the small cream-colored tiles. Every light in the p-way was turned off. It was pitch black. All I could hear were my classmates' hot breaths as they smacked against the wall.

Fwheeeeeeeeeeeeew...BOOM!

RAT-A-TAT-A-TAT-ATATA!

FRAAAAAAK...FRAAAAKKKK...

The whistling sound and explosion of 60mm mortar rounds broke the silence. It was followed by an incessant firing of machine gun sounds that made it even harder to hear.

What the hell was going on?

---

8 "Motivated" socks: Naval Academy lingo to have your socks pulled all the way up. They were not allowed to scrunch up or sag. If your socks sagged and a detailer told you to "motivate your socks," plebes were required to scream at their socks, "Get up socks, come on, get up socks!" while they were pulled all the way up.

Then it happened.

All at once, over a hundred upper-class midshipmen stampeded down the hallway.

"GET ON YOUR FACE RIGHT NOW! DROP AND GIVE ME TWENTY RIGHT NOW!"

A big, burly looking guy ran up and started screaming at me. He was light-skinned with black hair and had huge dimples.

I jumped down to the ground and started to bang out push-ups.

"YELL THEM OUT. I CAN'T HEAR YOU!"

"One! Two! Three! Four! Five, sir! Six!"

Then another upperclassman leaned down to the ground and got in my face.

"GET UP RIGHT NOW! GO IN THAT ROOM RIGHT NOW!" He pointed.

The next thing I knew, I was running around the p-ways in something called "white works Jesus," a made-up uniform where bed sheets are used as a robe and cape, shower shoes are used as sandals, a T-shirt or sock is wrapped around your head for a crown, and a broom is carried in your hand as a walking stick.

As I ran down the p-way looking ridiculous, I observed that there was so much going on.

"ZOOM, SIR!" one of my classmates yelled. It was a phrase we had to say whenever we changed from one adjacent bulkhead to the next.

One upperclassman would tell you to do something ridiculous. Then another would come behind and confuse you by telling you to do something else. Some of my classmates found themselves in a puddle of sweat because all they did the entire night was engage in physical fitness training. Others stayed on the bulkhead and just talked to upperclassmen. There was screaming, basketballs bouncing, music blasting, gunshot sounds, and people laughing. I didn't know what was happening. It was all a huge clusterfuck.[9]

"Yo! Hit the bulkhead, you fucking plebe!" this guy screamed at me in the dark. He came out of nowhere and walked right into my face. He was average height with a stocky, muscular build and a bulky, round nose. He had tattoos all over. My guess was that he must have been a recruited football player because he had this navy blue Nike dry-fit shirt on with the letters *Navy Football* written on the front.

The football player stared at me with a mean mug face. I stared back at him, waiting for his next set of words.

"Chill out, plebe. Wassup, I'm going to be your squad leader. I'm 1/C Biggs or 'B' for short." He extended his hand for a friendly fist bump.

"Nice to meet you, sir." I fist bumped him back.

---

9 Military lingo for "big mess" or "mass confusion."

"Where you from, kid? You a tall-ass mothafucker."

"I'm from the South Side of Chicago," I said with as much authority and aggression as my deep voice could assert. I held my head up high. I wanted to make the point that I wasn't one of those kids who grew up in the suburbs of Evanston or Juliet who falsely claimed the city. I was proud to be the unconventional kid from the South Side who also earned and deserved to be at the United States Naval Academy. For me, it was the source of my swag. A city that made me grow up fast and gave me an old soul demeanor several years beyond my age. There's something special about being from Chicago.

"Oh shit. Chi-city, huh? Dass wassup, Evans. I'll see you around."

At the end of the night, we got our phones back, and Plebe Summer was considered officially over. My next challenge was learning how to survive the academic school year.

CHAPTER 13

CAN YOU SAY PLEBE?

Plebe (noun): A member of the lowest class at the Naval Academy. Short for plebian, Ancient Rome's lowest class, excluding slaves. Someone of lower mental capacity; trash; scum of the earth.

I WOKE UP AT 0530 EVERY MORNING FOR PT. Like most things at the Academy, the type and severity varied depending on your company. Some would go for a run, work out at the gym, complete a boxing workout, or play a sport. Around the Brigade, "Training Ten" had a reputation for being one of the harshest Companies on the yard. And there was no better person to lead training than 2/C Oxford. He was a moderately statured White man with a square, box-like frame who spoke in a deep baritone voice. He was our 2/C training sergeant, which meant he was overall responsible for our development and ensured that we carried out our required duties as plebes. Right away, I considered him to be a dick, largely in part because he was the ringleader behind our body-draining physical exercises. One day in particular stands out to me.

We were on hospital point, a bulky grass-covered hill and one of the highest vantage points that overlooked the yard on the far end of campus near gate eight. The Naval Health Clinic was located at the very top. Directly in front was the sacred Naval Academy cemetery, where midshipmen, graduates, and famous heroes were buried. He turned right and led us onto an open field. My classmates and I were all out of breath from the fast pace of the run. There were four large, dirty logs lying on the ground.

"Pick up the log," Oxford barked.

I went straight to the back of the log. You always wanted the tallest person at the very end to make it easier to carry for everyone else. But it sucked being in the back because you had to carry more weight than everyone else.

"Everyone good? Aight, one, two, three. Raise," I said after my classmates were in position, bent over with their hands under the log. At the same time, all four of us raised the log up directly above our heads. Specs of dirt-infused snow dripped down on our hair and upper bodies. I could feel small crawling creatures dripping on my neck and scurrying around. I wanted to use my other hand to swat them off, but I couldn't because I knew that if I brought the log down everyone else would suffer.

"Now put it on your left shoulder," Oxford said, beaming at us. He was waiting for us to mess up, hoping even. He had this snickering evil smile etched across his face while he watched us, as if he marveled and took pleasure in our pain and suffering. We all slowly shifted the sturdy log to our left and let it rest against our shoulders and heads.

"Right side, now." We shifted it to the right.

"Above your head. And you better not drop my log." We sluggishly shifted the log from our right shoulders to the middle and then extended our hands all the way into the air.

We'd been holding the log in the air for about fifteen seconds when one of the girls in the front dropped her hands because she couldn't bear to hold it anymore. The log came crashing down on our heads and hit the ground.

"I told you not to drop my log! Everyone get down and bear crawl to the street and back. Now!"

Dammit, man. I hated bear crawls. Like imitating a bear running, I leaned over and got on all fours and proceeded to move as fast as I could to the street. Being tall made the crawls more difficult because the knee caps of my long legs would always hit against the backside of my arms. I made it to the street and back.

"Pick up the log again and put it back over your heads." Using our frail, sore arms, we lifted the log up to the dark night sky like we were presenting an offering. I could feel the thick flakes of the wood bark rubbing against my skin. My hands were a filthy mud-brown color.

"Now follow me." Oxford started jogging.

We took off after him while carrying the log above us in the bitter Annapolis snow. Oxford led us to the end of the field and down a hill that led to a small patch of beach. There were a bunch of black ribs placed around it. As we approached the shore, my mind pounded from exhaustion. My bones shook.

I knew what was about to happen.

We were about to perform what was called "wet and sandy." It's what it sounds like: jump and roll around in the cold murky water of the Severn River while completing exercises in unison, such as push-ups and sit-ups. Then get out of the water and PT in the dirty sand. Repeat. Deriving from US Navy Seal BUD/S training, the purpose was to build mental toughness and team unity. Teach sailors how to be comfortable being uncomfortable.

It fuckin' sucked.

"Drop the log, and everyone lay down facing forward against the edge of the water in the push-up position." At this point my other classmates carrying their logs met up with us, and we all lined up along the edge of the snow-covered sandy beach. A small ripple of water came rushing onto the shore and passed through the center of our bodies.

"OHHHHH! FUCCCK!" everyone moaned and groaned from the bitter cold. It felt like someone took a knife and was stabbing at the inside of my stomach, and all I could do was lay there helplessly.

"Up! One, two, three."

"One!" we shouted. Three push-ups counted as one rep, and we had to do them in unison or start over again.

"One, two, three," Oxford counted.

"Two!"

"One, two, three."

"Three!"

"One, two, three. One, two, three. One, two, three. One, two, three. One, two, three."

By the time we finished, our bodies were covered in snow and sand.

"Everybody in the water. Get on your backs and link up." I twisted my body around and connected my arms tight with my classmates. The only happiness I could reach out and grab hold of was the little warmth I obtained from my peers' body heat next to mine. My joints were red and ached with pain.

It was the same type of feeling I'd had during my three-week basic training phase at NAPS. When our platoon made mistakes as a unit, our detailers would make us conduct a physical exercise called the "tunnel of love." It involved everyone getting on all fours, somewhat like a push-up, while arching our backs so that our butts pointed upward. Each person's arms were positioned directly next to another's. Whoever was at the very end of the line would lie down on the floor and, like a worm, squirm under the tunnel until they reached the end, where they would then reset in the arched position. The tunnel continued until everyone had crawled through. As you can guess, at the end of it all, puddles of sweat lay on the floor from everyone's perspiration.

When I first crawled through, I thought that shit was nasty. People's wet sweat dripped into my hair and rolled down my neck. I could feel the small puddles forming in my ears. I closed my eyes and mouth to prevent any running drops from entering. I breathed heavily through my nose. The tunnel itself was warm and cozy from my classmates' body heat and heavy gasps for air. "Ughhh," they moaned. It sucked. "Damn, I miss being home so much," the guy next to me said. My parents' homesick talks growing up actually helped my brothers and me. One of the biggest mental hurdles for incoming candidates was dealing with the "shock" of missing their former home lives. We learned to deal with the emotions of being homesick, so dwelling on it was not an issue.

On my fourth or fifth time through, something in me clicked. I had this weird feeling of humor in my stomach. What made it even weirder was that my classmates felt it too. They all started looking at each other with these wide grins. Then the next thing I knew, we all started laughing and joking at how ridiculous we looked and the pain that surged through our joints. We encouraged and shouted at one another. "GO, EVANS. ATTA BOY! YOU CAN DO IT, CHI-TOWN!"

My NAPSTER classmates were another gang for me.

The detailers at the end of the hallway looked at us like we were crazy. But after a while, even they couldn't help but laugh. They wore bright yellow shirts and short blue USNA shorts. On the front of the shirt was a colored picture of that class year's eagle crest. On the back, the word "detailer" was printed in solid black.

I believe there comes a point in military training—as well as in life—when shit sucks so much that after a while the pain and turmoil is replaced with humor and grit. Moments like that bring units together in teamwork. I never thought I would have so much fun sliding through a puddle of sweat.

Lying in the cold water of the Severn River, I waited for that same level of humor to rise up in my stomach.

It never did.

"Up! Down! Up! Down! Up! Down!" Like a bunch of monkeys linked together at the joints, we rose in and out of the water together in unison, supporting and helping one another up. Just when my body temperature began to adjust to the cold water, I heard Oxford's watch *beep,* and he stopped to glance down at it. It must be 0630. *That meant workouts were over. Thank God.*

"ON YOUR FEET! RUN BACK TO BANCROFT AND GET READY FOR CHOW CALLS."

By the time I got back to the hall and chopped up the stairs, I was so exhausted I could barely keep my eyes open. Plebes had to "chop" (literally jog in the middle of the hallway) everywhere we went; the only exception was academic buildings. I made it to the top of the fifth floor (yeah, I had to run up and down a flight of long stairs multiple times a day. You were lucky if your company was located on the first or second floor) and pivoted my feet hard—like marching on a drill field—to turn the corner right. I shouted, "GO NAVY, SIR," or "BEAT ARMY, SIR," at the top of my lungs at the same time I rotated my feet: another plebe requirement. My gray issued New Balance shoes made a *squeak, squeak* when my forward momentum suddenly stopped and shifted to another direction. To make matters worse, chopping proved to be even more difficult when upperclassmen removed privileges to rate (have access to) backpacks. When this happened, I had to carry my heavy bag in my hands. The only thing that supported the backpack from touching the ground was its straps wrapped tightly around my forearms.

I took a quick five-minute "plebe" shower, threw on my uniform, chopped out of my room, and stopped on the edge of the tile. Three of my classmates were already there, waiting. They all stared in anticipation at the minute hand on the black clock, which would strike the top of the hour and let us know to start.

A chow call was an event when four plebes stood at attention on each side of a silver metal tile (deck plate) and yelled out the menus for the day. The deck plates were aligned throughout the middle of the p-way. Starting ten minutes before breakfast, lunch, and dinner—and on every minute—my classmates and I conducted chow calls without a second of delay. A correctly completed call lasted about thirty to forty-five seconds.

My classmates started whispering and bickering about how to say one of the menu items for the morning meal. See, during a chow call, everyone had to be in unison. The menu might say that the dessert is "tasty buttermilk waffles," but we all knew from eating downstairs in King Hall that it was just "waffles." That was the easy way to say it anyway. But there was always that one plebe that had to be perfect and make life difficult.

"What are we going to say for describing the waffles?" one of the plebes on the deck plate asked.

"Tasty buttermilk waffles," another responded.

"What? No. Why would we do that? That's so much longer. Just say waffles."

"But they are tasty and buttermilk. Details matter."

"Dude, stop it. Just keep it simple. We gotta be together on this. Just say waffles."

"Okay, got it."

Breakfast was always the easiest meal because the menu items were usually the same.

Then the clock struck 0650.

"TEN MINUTE CHOW CALL, GO!" One of the plebes shouted at the other end of the hallway.

"SIR, YOU NOW HAVE TEN MINUTES UNTIL MORNING QUARTERS FORMATION. FORMATION GOES INSIDE AT 0700. THE UNIFORM FOR MORNING QUARTERS FORMATION IS SUMMER WORKING BLUES. THE MENU FOR MORNING MEAL IS SCRAMBLED EGGS, WAFFLES, ASSORTED CERE-ALS, BACON, FRESH FRUIT, MILK, ORANGE AND APPLE JUICE. THE OFFICERS OF THE WATCH ARE: THE OFFICER OF THE WATCH IS LIEUTENANT MURPHY, SECOND COMPANY OFFICER. THE MIDSHIPMAN OFFICER OF THE WATCH IS

MIDSHIPMAN COMMANDER PEBBLE, SECOND REGIMENT
COMMANDER. THE PROFESSIONAL TOPIC OF THE DAY IS
NAVAL WARFARE PLATFORMS. MAJOR EVENTS ON THE
YARD ARE NONE. YOU NOW HAVE TEN MINUTES, SIR!"

Right when I started shouting the menu, a First Class (1/C or
senior midshipman) walking past stopped dead in his tracks.
With hawk eyes, he zoomed right in on me. He looked me up
and down, checking my uniform for discrepancies and listened
to every word I said. Veins popped in my face while I yelled as
loud and fast as I possibly could. Spit flew while the 1/C now
stood inches from my face.

He continued to stare silently at me. I started to get nervous.

Please don't ask me about another menu.

"What's the menu for evening meal?"

*Fuck. I didn't have time to ask what the rest of the menu was. I had
to make something up.*

The night before, I'd stayed up late studying for a math quiz
and had failed to look over the menu items. That's what made
chow calls tricky at times. You couldn't just study the menu for
the food you were about to eat. You had to know all the meals
for the entire day. Anything was fair game.

"I'm waiting, Evans. What is the menu for evening meal?"

Fuck it.

"THE MENU FOR EVENING MEAL IS BAKED HAM, TURKEY, MACARONI AND CHEESE, SWEET POTATO CASSEROLE, CRANBERRY SAUCE, GREEN BEANS, DINNER ROLLS, AND POUND CAKE, SIR!"

The 1/C let me finish my chow call before he shouted back at me.

"EVANS! WHAT THE FUCK WAS THAT?! THAT IS NOT THE MENU FOR TODAY! WHERE THE HELL DO YOU THINK YOU WILL BE EATING FOOD LIKE THAT?"

He pointed at me.

"SIR, I COULD NOT REMEMBER THE MENU. SO I JUST SAID ALL THE FOOD ITEMS MY MOTHER USED TO COOK BACK AT HOME."

A bunch of other Firsties (another way of saying First Class) in the background erupted in laughter. The upperclassmen in front of me shook his head back and forth with a slight grin.

"You know what, Evans? You completely butchered the menu. But you said that shit with confidence. And I like that. That's the whole point. Maintaining your poise is everything."

I let out a subtle grin. I thought I was in the clear.

"Now drop down and give me twenty," the First Class uttered.

I hit the deck, banged out my twenty push-ups, damn near kissing the floor with each rep, and jumped back to my feet at attention. Regurgitating the menu wasn't the only thing on my mind as my heels stood on the edge of those deck plates.

I still wasn't out of the weeds yet.

Each day, I still needed to read and display knowledge of a world and US news topic, as well as a sport. The purpose was quite obvious: military operators must be aware of current events. *Please don't ask me about the news,* I thought.

Luckily, he didn't. At that point, chow calls were pretty much over. I "shoved off" (chopped away from the deck plate and concluded chow calls) and ran to get in line for morning meal formation at 0700.

At the end of plebe year, I realized that chow calls weren't so stupid after all. What I find remarkable is how, in the end, they enhanced my self-confidence and ability to pursue the unknowns of life with motivation, which are critical aspects of leadership. Oftentimes, leaders are required to manage others and show a level of assuredness even when they don't know themselves. You learn to give out information under intense pressure. You learn how to be stoic and remain calm under the force of a yelling superior. In addition, chow calls taught me how to take a piece of information and memorize it quickly.

I came back into my room and stuffed my backpack with my textbooks and binders for that morning's classes. Right before I chopped out into the p-way to head downstairs to eat, I turned around and double checked to make sure the lock on my brown storage "con" locker was secure.

At USNA, midshipmen left their possessions out in the open. I guess in their minds, because we were in the military and attended a prestigious school, stealing would not occur. During my time at Annapolis, many of my roommates would leave their lockers unlocked. For me, this took some time to get used to. On the South Side, I learned in my adolescent days the importance of quietly safeguarding your personal belongings. Look away for just a moment and you'll find your stuff gone. In my world, I didn't care what school I was at, military or not. I always locked my things up.

Now it was time to eat.

Named after Fleet Admiral Ernest J. King, who served as the Chief of Naval Operations during World War II, King Hall was the place where the entire Brigade of Midshipmen ate together at the exact same time. It was nothing short of a mega colosseum food court filled with long brown rectangular tables. Each company was assigned to a certain area. Food was served family style, and every table seated a squad. Even within a strict company, some squad leaders allowed 4/C to relax at meals while others utilized that time to "rate" (test) plebes on pro quiz knowledge or required reading topics.[10] It was the luck of the draw with what was handed to you.

1/C Biggs was big into working out. One of my assigned tasks each meal was to make sure milk was present at the table. If I didn't, Biggs would curse me out, punish me with push-ups, or rate me so much during "chow" that I wouldn't have a chance

10 Pro Quiz: a professional knowledge test taken once a week, every Friday night, over various Navy and US Marine Corps topics.

to eat. Lord knows I couldn't afford to skip a meal; I needed all the fuel I could get to continue to perform in the classroom and complete the tough mental and physical tasks assigned to me daily as a plebe.

A couple of feet from our table, there was this massive, rectangular stainless-steel cooler that had these little portable jugs of milk in it you could grab. But I wasn't the only plebe assigned the task of milkman. Like flies swarming around the sweet aroma of trash, plebes from other squads zoomed in from all directions. I shot them a determined look. I communicated with my face, like, *"You better not take all the milk and leave me with nothing. I'm willing to fight for this here milk. Are you?"* They shot back their own looks of willpower, like, *"Nah bro. I gotta get this milk, too. You bet your ass I'm willing to fight for it. I gotta do what I gotta do to survive this place just like you."* I abandoned my rushed pace and broke into an all-out sprint. I reached the fridge first and flung the door open. Like an animal eating its first meal after multiple days astray, I greedily grabbed a pile of about ten milks. I caressed the stack of mini jugs in my arms like I was carrying a baby. I was walking back to the table when I noticed this round lady sitting down in a chair against the wall.

It was the same lady I'd seen walking on the yard the first day I arrived. She was an old-school Christian woman in her fifties with brown skin and thick, short black hair.

"Hey there, young man. Come here," she said. She examined my uniform and eyed me up and down. "Evans, is it?"

"Yes, ma'am."

"You're in tenth company?" I nodded my head in a fast motion. "Who's your squad leader?"

"1/C Biggs."

"Oh, you're in good hands, baby. He's a good one. I'll be keeping my eye out for you. Have a blessed day."

"You too, ma'am."

When I made it back to the table, Biggs was already deep into mowing down a plate full of chunky tuna. He ate tuna every day after working out. He looked up at me. "I see you met Ms. Nisey. She's good people. She stay lookin' out. Get to know her, Evans."

"Yes, sir," I responded. Biggs went back to eating his tuna. As a plebe, he taught me the art of being strategic and patient. Learn the game of the Naval Academy while also being true to yourself, and use it to your advantage to get ahead and help others at the same time.

Biggs ran the squad with a more laid-back approach. I was still required to perform my standard plebe duties, but he ran meals like a family would. He asked us about our day, shared with us his experiences as a midshipman, and found unique ways to bring humor to the table. One of those unique ways was through something called plebe dates.

As you can guess, a plebe date was when a 4/C (what plebes or freshman are also known as) asked an upperclassman they had a crush on or found attractive out on a date. By "out," I mean they were invited to your table for lunch or dinner. At Annapolis, 4/C were not allowed to date (fraternize with) more senior ranked midshipmen. To make things interesting, Biggs required us to bring a plebe date every week. My first one was probably the funniest and remains clear in my mind.

Her name was Adriana. She was a tall, slender African American woman and a varsity athlete. She had long, elegant black hair, plump luscious lips, and a huge bright smile. She was bad.

During meals, varsity athletes had their own team tables. Adriana was sitting down at the table with her teammates during lunch when I approached her from the right of her seat.

"Excuse me, ma'am."

"Yes, how can I help you?"

"I don't mean to bother you. But I'll cut straight to the chase and say that I think you are beautiful and have an amazing smile. Will you go out with me?"

And smile she did.

Blushing, her lips spread so far across her face. She didn't know what to say. I might have been a plebe, but I definitely had swag. I was smooth.

"You know what? I like how blunt and sweet you are. You're cute. Sure, I would love to. What day?"

"How's tomorrow sound?"

"Okay, great. And what company are you in?"

"Tenth company, ma'am."

The next day, I escorted Adriana to my table. The moment Biggs looked up and saw her while eating his tuna, his jaw dropped.

"Hell nah. Not her. Ugh ugh. How the fuck did your ass pull that off?"

I looked at Biggs and gave him a devilish grin.

"That's some bullshit, Evans," he said jokingly with a smile.

I pulled out 1/C Adriana's chair to motion her to sit down. Then I pushed it in for her.

I stuck out a "paw" (extending your hand to ask a question or for permission to speak) and asked to join the table to eat.

"Sir, permission to join you for lunch?"

"Yeah. Sit down, motherfucker," Biggs said with a face. His eyebrows were raised.

Plebes did not "rate" (to be allowed to have or utilize) their chairs, so I had to sit on the front three inches of my chair during meal times. The purpose of this, you ask? It was argued that "weakness" leans back in a chair.

I placed my elbows at my sides. Elbows were not allowed on the table either. I reached forward and checked all the condiment bottles in front of me to make sure they were filled and that any old residue from the tips was wiped away (another plebe task).

During the summer, all meal bites had to be "squared." Squaring your meals meant picking up the food with a utensil, passionately raising it up laterally until it was even with your face, and then bringing it forward to your mouth to eat. The robotic pattern individuals made with their arms formed an upside down "L." Eating like that takes forever. Thank God we only had to do that for the summer.

"Introduce us to your date, Evans."

"Squad. This is Midshipman 1/C Adriana. She's a member of the varsity track team, wants to service select Marine Corps, and is from Iowa."

One of my classmates at the end of the table started to laugh while I talked about my date. He had broken his bearing (poise or military discipline).

"And what the hell is so funny down there?" Biggs shouted. "You know what? Get the bearing bear. I want you to stare at the bearing bear for the rest of the meal."

The "bearing bear" was literally just a golden honey bear bottle. Upperclassmen would stack the bear at the top of other items on the table so that it was face level, and 4/C would have to stare at the bear in the eyes for the duration of the meal. It was supposed to be a silly way of correcting your bearing. That shit looked stupid. Imagine someone just staring at a bear-shaped bottle of honey inches from their face. Not moving, not talking, nothing, for several minutes.

I spent the rest of the meal talking to Adriana about what she thought of the Academy. Before leaving the meal, she turned around, touched me on the shoulder, and said, "I'll see you around, Evans. Have a good day."

"Wait, wait, wait! Not so fast. I still can't believe Evans asked you out on a plebe date. I gotta know. How did he do it?" Biggs shouted.

"He was confident and sweet," Adriana responded.

"Confident, huh? Alright, Evans. Before you leave, I got a question for you that I need you to address for the squad table."

"Yes, sir," I responded.

"HOW LONG HAVE YOU BEEN IN THE NAVY?"

I jumped up and stood in my seat, and with a fork in my hand and swinging my arm back and forth, I screamed, *"All me bloomin' life, sir! Me mother was a mermaid, me father was King Neptune. I was born on the crest of a wave and rocked in the cradle of the deep. Seaweed and barnacles are me clothes. Every tooth in me head is a marlinspike; the hair on me head is hemp. Every bone in me body is a spar, and when I spits, I spits tar. I'se hard. I is, I am, I are!"*

This saying was one of the many rates an upperclassman could ask you from *Reef Points*. When asked, you had to say it verbatim and sometimes act it out.

Whistles and claps erupted around me from other midship-men within King Hall. "Alright, mothafucka, get down. You're good," Biggs said.

Like a circus, all around my squad's table, you could hear a bunch of random *pops* and *BEAT ARMY* screams from 4/C slapping mustard or ketchup bottles on their foreheads as hard as they could.

If you took a step back and blocked out the arena of loud voices and yelling with the court, you'd be able to catch the cat-and-mouse-like pranks between 4/C and upperclassmen. On a typical day, but especially during Air Force and Army-Navy week, you might encounter a few common pranks like a pie in the face or a milk jug being poured over someone's head, a jet being moved on the yard (yes, you read that right, an actual military jet), or a sailboat being stolen and placed in the middle of King Hall. I swear, midshipmen are some creative, funny motherfuckers. One of the funniest things I've seen was when a group of plebes moved an upperclassmen's entire bed and set it up outside in the middle of the courtyard. Other midshipmen were walking to class in the morning laughing and taking pictures, and this upperclassman was just lying there asleep with his blanket. You'll see a lot of mixed reactions from these pranks and jokes. Some are so shocked they just sit there while those that get mad put a target on their own backs for future pranks. If the culprits were still around, most upperclassmen took off running after the plebe in full sprint. Typically, if the 4/C successfully makes it back to their room in Bancroft successfully, they are deemed safe. If the plebe gets caught, well, then they are at the mercy of the upperclassmen.

✳ ✳ ✳ ✳

IT WAS THE end of yet another exhausting day.

Knock, knock, knock.

Our brown door swung open, and like a concerned parent, Oxford poked his head in to make sure my roommates and I were in our beds with the lights off. Plebes had a mandatory 2200 bedtime. The moment I heard the door click shut, I set the alarm on my iPhone to 2230.

Chim, chim, chim.

The melodic buzz of the "waves" ringtone pierced through the room's silent darkness. I got back up, crept over to the silver door knob and locked it, and continued to study for the Chemistry II exam I had the next day. It wasn't abnormal for me to regularly study into the late hours of the night, sometimes even two or three in the morning.

The moment I sat down at my desk, I started to nod off. Like a kid slurping a nice cold strawberry Capri Sun during the summer, the rigors of the academic day and my plebe duties sapped all my energy. I looked over at the small corkboard on the side of my desk. The entire panel was full of pictures of my family, motivational quotes, and my goals. I read my goals every day—multiple times a day—which allowed me to visualize them into reality.

It allowed me to mentally "trick" myself into thinking that they were possible, no matter how steep.

cularly on the photo with my mother and thought: picture Mom and Grandmother k them in the eye and tell them they're not they're not worth staying up late and sacri-ficing ... erything they did for me when they raised me, tell them it's not worth fighting for.

I couldn't...

The laziness was shunned from my bones.

Determined, I grabbed my chemistry notes, taped them to the wall, and stood up to study. I know I looked crazy, but this would become a regular pattern for me. It was the only way I could stay awake and keep studying after the long, exhausting plebe days.

I was back on track and in full study mode when I was abruptly interrupted.

"Evans," a voice whispered in the shadows. "What the fuck are you doing staring at the wall?" It was my roommate. "And why do you have a hat on your head?"

"I'm trying to study. Go back to sleep." I had a black Chicago Bulls New Era cap on my head. It helped set the mood. I did whatever I could to center and remind myself of home and what I had come from.

"You look crazy standing there facing the wall like that. Some-thin' is wrong with you. It's not that serious."

But that's the thing—it was that serious for me. I valued this opportunity and had to prove myself.

What was I supposed to do? Go to bed knowing I didn't know the material or have my work not completed and fail?

Failure was not an option.

The next day I chopped up the stairs after completing my morning classes. Plebes had to jog up the latter wells from the outside farthest from the railing. Even when we chopped—and every single place we went to on and off the yard—we had to "plebe" our covers. Basically, that meant placing your hand inside your hat with your fingers spread out, palm facing inward, to keep the hat secure within the cup of your hand at all times. After a while, it became a habit of unconscious thought.

"GOOD MORNING/AFTERNOON/EVENING, SIR/MA'AM" was the necessary command anytime you saw higher ranking midshipmen within the p-way while chopping. I passed by 1/C Fields. She was Caucasian with curly orange hair and a high-pitched, annoying voice.

"GOOD AFTERNOON, MA'AM."

Nothing.

She proceeded to walk down the stairs.

Ah, hell naw. I know she didn't just ignore me.

I stopped and turned around.

"You're not gonna say anything back?"

"Excuse me. Who do you think you're talking to?" she barked.

"It's rude to just walk past someone when they greet you," I responded.

"You're such a disrespectful plebe, Evans. Stand by."[11]

"I don't understand you all. It's mandatory for me to greet every single upperclassman I see, but it's okay for you all to ignore me? Even you used to be a plebe a couple years ago. How did you feel when people treated you that way?"

Her face went blank. But I could see that my comment made her think.

"Whatever, Evans. Shit ain't supposed to be fair here. I outrank you. I paid my dues to get where I am, and you need to learn to do the same."

Fields told Oxford, and the next thing I knew I was on my face doing burpees and push-ups later that evening. "Keep going until I say stop," Oxford commanded. I was approaching rep eighty when he said, "Stay down." I lowered my body to the floor and maintained the "leaning rest" position.

The hallway was empty with no one in sight. Oxford could say or do whatever he wanted. I was at his mercy.

---

11 "Stand by" was lingo for just wait and see, this isn't over.

"What's this I hear about you talking back to upperclassmen?"

"I asked her a question, sir. I wasn't being disrespectful."

"That's not one of your five fucking responses, plebe!"

"You asked me a question, sir, so I answered it."

"I also heard you've been getting up in the middle of the night and studying past your curfew."

I didn't respond. I raised my neck up and glared at him. *How the fuck could he have known that? There's only one possible way: my roommate.*

To make matters worse, on multiple accounts, Oxford proved himself to be a racist, hateful, and demeaning leader.

"You all don't deserve to be here," he'd say. His eyebrows arched, and his face was scrunched up. He'd constantly hurl racist comments at me.

He was just about to spit another insult when two upperclass-women turned the corner at the top of the stairwell.

He paused.

It was that type of awkward silence where you eyeball someone as they pass by because there is so much more you have to say but you can't until they are out of ear range.

I tried to make eye contact with the two ladies and speak with my eyes.

Help, please! Help! This dude is fucking ridiculous. Stop him now.

I'd called predominantly Black schools home for most of my adolescence. Growing up on the South Side, you don't think much about your Blackness. Colors were always reserved for the gangs, not the people. When White people did enter the neighborhood, I could always tell if they were cops or Jehovah's Witnesses. I knew the blocks, the hoods, the community. It wasn't until I attended Annapolis that I realized that the inherent kinship I felt back home wasn't going to be felt here. My Blackness was seen first.

When Oxford wasn't directing his attention toward me, it was toward my own brothers. Yup, you read that right. He'd purposely find my brothers and say degrading things to them, such as, "Your brother is a piece of shit as a plebe," or "He needs to quit and go back home." Mind you, both my brothers lived on the opposite side of Bancroft Hall. I found Oxford's efforts disgusting, and for a while, I even considered reporting him. But I refrained from doing so because I didn't want to draw attention to myself. It was one thing to act that way toward me, but to include my brothers was another. It was a personal move he made to get under my skin, and you better believe that after my brothers told me he came to visit them multiple times, I walked into his room and laid into his ass. He had crossed the line.

"Don't you ever include my brothers in this. What you have against me has nothing to do with them. Your actions are unprofessional and unbecoming of a future Naval Officer. Leave them out of this. If you ever speak to my brothers again, we gonna have a fuckin' problem."

He was on his laptop working when I stormed in. The lights in the room were off. I think the darkness aided in the scary delivery of my message. He jumped up, startled.

After I said my piece, I walked right out.

I never had issues with Oxford again.

I still had one more piece of unfinished business though: my roommate. He was sitting at his desk playing on his phone when I barged in.

"You fucking snitched on me," I said. "Don't nobody like a fucking snitch." I balled my fists up and stepped right into his face.

"You weren't following the rules, Evans. And I'm not going to get in trouble because you want to stay up and study."

I reached forward, gripped his neck, and slammed him against the wall. Like a yellow rubber chicken, his eyes grew and looked like they were about to pop out of his head. I could feel the pulse of his airway circulating within the grip of my hands.

"Don't you ever fucking snitch on me again. I'm not bothering you by studying. I'm doing what I got to do to make it through this place. I have to study and work three times as hard just to get by. The door is locked, so they can't even come in anyway. Is that understood?"

"Yeah, Evans. I'm sorry. It won't happen again," he said calmly.

I released my grip and chopped out of the room.

I know that violence is wrong, and I regret resorting to it with my roommate. At the time, I was still learning to let go of the negative instincts and habits honed on the streets for what I knew was the "proper" behavior at the Naval Academy. I later apologized to my roommate, and we keep in contact and are close today.

CHAPTER 14

LIVING WITH HONOR

ONE SAYING DWAYNE REPEATED TO US FREQUENTLY GROWING UP THAT I'LL NEVER FORGET was "the biggest word in the dictionary is 'if.'" "If" I had done this or not done that, I would be here or at a certain position.

Chances are you too have a few "ifs" in your life. We all make mistakes, and that's a part of life. But how long you splash in your puddle of fears is what matters. You have to believe that there is something greater for you out there and keep pressing on. In Chicago, we have a saying: "Don't get caught lackin'." It means you should always be prepared; never find yourself in a situation without a gun for protection or unaware of your surroundings. The same way street guys on the South Side put in extensive effort not to get caught lackin', put that same amount of effort into your goals. They won't come to you, waiting around for the perfect moment. No one is going to fulfill your destiny or hand you an opportunity.

You're going to have to work extra hours on top of your work schedule in order to place yourself in a position to advance. To give you a personal example, I finished the first manuscript of this very book while serving underway on a US Navy warship on a mission to gather intelligence on Russian ships. With a jam-packed military schedule full of trainings, drills, and helicopter flight operations, the long days blurred together. It was exhausting and difficult to put time into the book every day. But each morning I rose at 0400 to write for an hour or two. Then at the end of the day, starting at around 2100 or 2200, I would write some more into the night. But I was committed to writing a book that would add value and help people. Because that is what I felt God called me to do. One thing I know for sure is that, if you don't try, you'll always be in the same place. You already know what defeat feels like. You won't get any further by just sitting there feeling sorry for yourself. You'll feel much worse knowing you didn't give something your all.

It's a risk not to take a risk.

Essentially, I know my stepdad was attempting to explain to my brothers and me the importance of living a fulfilled life and making wise decisions now to prevent looking back in regret.

For Atna, his first big "if" occurred at the end of plebe year. "I'm not feeling this class, bro. Everything we do is so boring. I'm over the papers and trying to study for it," Anthony reflected to me, describing his English class with a professor by the name of Lieutenant Wright. At the time, I didn't realize his negative perspective would later translate to his school work. Like any close brother, I listened in support and assumed he was venting.

Anthony was later assigned an English paper that he consistently brushed off. I'm not sure how long he was given to complete the assignment, but at the last minute, he searched Google to find related subjects to copy and paste to create the essay. LT Wright immediately confronted him about it.

"The Naval Academy takes plagiarism very seriously, Mr. Evans."

"I don't know what you mean, sir."

"Yes, you do. Your entire paper came from the internet."

What was supposed to be a simple warning turned into more. LT Wright submitted Anthony's name to the Honor Board, a group of midshipmen brought together to weigh in on an ethical action that challenged the morality and Honor Concept of the Naval Academy: "Midshipmen are persons of integrity. They stand for that which is right. They tell the truth and ensure that the truth is known. They do not lie."

The honor treatise expected mids to walk with a hard, unwavering stick of personal integrity. It urged us to follow our hearts and "do what is right" as leaders beyond just not breaking the rules.

The council determines if the person before them should receive immediate remediation or if the case should be forwarded up to the Commandant. Like a dean of students at a civilian university, the Commandant was responsible for the welfare, day-to-day training, and development of the roughly 4,500 Brigade of Midshipmen. Because this was Anthony's first offense, the honor board assigned him a remediator, Captain Bobby, a senior and well-respected Supply Officer on the yard. As part of the remediation process, my brother attended numerous counseling sessions and was required to read a book called *The Speed of Trust* by Steven Covey. At that point, I figured the storm was over.

Until a few classes later. Anthony had a free response quiz on a novel they were currently reading. Because he had failed to study and thus didn't know the answers, my brother copied off of another mid next to him. One of the questions from the book involved identifying the name of an essential character.

LT Wright confronted him again.

"How did you get your answer?"

"I guessed, sir. I couldn't remember the name of the character. But I didn't want to leave the question blank either. So I put the name of an action figure I remembered from a video game."

"I don't think that's true because that's the same name that your classmate next to you has, which is completely wrong."

Anthony stuck to his story.

It didn't help that the fact that he'd cheated on the quiz came out during his remediation process. With a second offense in a matter of days, my brother was assigned more counseling. The final rush of the roller coaster came when Anthony had to submit another essay for English class and he plagiarized that one as well. With three offenses back-to-back, Anthony's case was forwarded to the Commandant for review and ultimately to the Superintendent for separation.

"I gave you a chance, and you blew that. You obviously don't have what it takes to be here," the SUPE (short for Superintendent) said to my brother.

I'll never forget waiting outside the Superintendent's office with Alex. I was sitting on a bench. Around me were a gang of my NAPSTER (Naval Academy prep school) classmates and members of the gospel choir who'd showed up in support. Everything had blown up so fast. Just the other day Anthony was singing right beside me in gospel choir, and now he faced the possibility of being separated. The mood was dark. Ten minutes later, Anthony walked out.

The large door slammed behind him. It was a depressing sight. Anthony had his feet together at a forty-five degree angle like he was standing at attention. His black midshipman uniform had razor sharp creases. His shoes were polished so well they sparkled like glass. He looked like a true military professional. But his back was hunched over. His head was down. He stood before all of us like a preacher in the pulpit. Through the windows on the left of me, I could see the sun was going down.

"Anthony, what is it? What did he say?" I asked.

He lifted his head slowly. My eyes met his. Like a rock thrown in a small pond, the buildup of water around his pupils rippled back and forth.

"What is it, bro? Say it." My eyes, too, began to water.

"They kicked me out of the Naval Academy. I've been separated."

People burst into tears. "Ahhhhhh fuck," someone shouted. Everyone stared at Alex and me with their mouths open in awe. Even they knew the significance of what had just happened.

We were the first set of African American triplets to ever be accepted into the Naval Academy. We would have made history had we been the first to graduate. Until now.

My mind froze.

When we received our acceptance letters, there wasn't a doubt in our minds that we would all make it. Our future was clear. But when Anthony spoke the words, "I've been separated," doubt punched me hard in the face. Truth is, the reality that one of us might fail to graduate was always there. But it was less scary when we had each other for support. Now that happy ending was gone; the three of us would no longer walk across the graduation stage together. Then a new reality set in with an outcome we didn't envision or plan for.

Fear now displaced our hope.

And that still wasn't the hardest pill for me to swallow.

The gang that I was born into and that meant the most to me—being a triplet—had just been ripped away.

And this time I didn't even have a choice or say in the matter.

How was I going to bounce back from this? Was it worth continuing on?

Life did not become any easier knowing that his dismissal came three days before I took my first set of academic finals at the Naval Academy. Like a rotating clock, at the end of each exam, I rushed into my room and sat at my desk. The dark blue cushion on the chair provided no comfort as I leaned back. Tears rolled down my checks at the thought of my brother leaving. As triplets, we did pretty much everything together. It's hard to explain a bond like that to others. My anger began to boil. After everything the Academies put us through during the application process, we promised to graduate together. Where was all that now? What happened to proving people wrong? How could Anthony let Alex and me down like this?

That evening, Alex and I were talking in King Hall when Ms. Nisey approached us. We had sad looks on our faces.

"I heard about Anthony. I know you all are close as triplets, but don't let this get you down. You two need to stick together and finish this thing out," she said, pointing at us. Alex and I didn't say a word. "I'll be praying for you." Without delay, she walked away and continued to clear the tables of food.

But the truth was that I thought I was going to be kicked out next—and over something as stupid as swimming.

On the South Side, my access to a decent pool was limited at best. When I did find one, my time was spent joking around or chillin' with friends and cute girls, not doing laps. When I arrived at Annapolis, I quickly realized it wasn't just a Chicago thing. Most of the African American mids struggled to swim. The perception was stereotypical but true.

Lejeune Hall was a large sports complex home to the USNA swimming and diving team. It was also where swimming classes took place. From the outside, it looked like a regular brown building. The inside, however, was nothing but bright white and blue. The aquatic natatorium was equipped with an Olympic-sized twenty-five by fifty-meter pool and multiple diving platforms. Four large horizontally oriented flags hugged the far wall. From left to right: America, US Marine Corps, US Navy, and the US Naval Academy. Hundreds of rich blue foldable bleacher seats surrounded the complex. When you looked up toward the ceiling, above the center of the natatorium was a large, gold painted USNA "N Star."

Midshipmen were mandated to take and pass three years of swimming instruction in order to graduate. If there was one thing I could pinpoint that I struggled with the most and that could have prevented me from graduating, it was this. After failing the first few swim tests, I began to have doubts on my ability to make it. For plebe year, the course involved learning the various swim strokes, a breathing underwater test, and learning how to inflate your uniform as a flotation device. The culmination of the course was a 200-meter swim test.

I jumped in the water and braced myself for the whistle. *TWEEET!* I took off. Attempting to slice through the water, I extended and placed each hand in front of the other. I focused all my energy at paddling my long brown feet and staying above the water. Fatigue kicked in fast, and I grew exhausted. I began to sink through the water like a rock. With more than six laps to go, I completed one more, stretched, then grabbed the edge to rest.

I thought about a memory of Dwayne to fuel me to push further.

More times than I can count, Dwayne took his temper out on the three of us when he was upset with our mother. This usually resulted in him lecturing my brothers and me about whatever small thing he could find around the house to pin on us. Every sentence that erupted from his mouth involved a curse word of some sort. One of the worst times was when we made Dwayne wait outside in the cold for over an hour.

It was the end of December, and King had just released for winter break. After several months, my brothers and I had discovered that the band had its own internal woodwind and brass fraternities. The alumni that went to marching band powerhouse schools like FAMU, UAPB, and Southern University came back and helped form the fraternities in the high school to breed more serious and dedicated players. So, naturally, we wanted in.

I was joining a fraternity gang.

Grant, a moderate height, light-skinned guy who played trombone at FAMU, pulled up to the front of the school in his blacked-out Nissan Altima. He was one of the alumni assisting with the crossing-the-line process. It was around 3 p.m., and school had just let out when about five of us crammed into his car and sped away. My brothers and I told Dwayne to pick us up at 5 p.m,thinking we would be back before he arrived. The alumni assured us they would have us back before then.

We'd driven three blocks down the street from the school when the car stopped in front of a brick home. I remember a black metal fence out front and a large brown door. The alumni immediately took us down to the basement and blindfolded us. Long story short, we were hazed into the fraternities. We had to memorize a bunch of information about the founders, perform a cluster of silly acts, drink from a bowl of liquid that we were told was someone's piss (but was really a mixture of various liquids like hot sauce, alcohol, syrup, and juice), and were beaten with a wooden fraternity paddle.

When the ceremony finished, it was 6 p.m. Fuck. We were late.

My brothers and I ran out of the house and called Dwayne.

"Where the fuck are you all?!" he answered.

"We are down the street at a friend's house."

Two minutes later, he pulled up in our mother's red van and smacked us across our heads until we got into the car. When we finally made it home, that's when all hell broke loose.

"Drop them draws right now," Dwayne yelled the moment we walked through the basement door. We had to be the only high schoolers receiving whoopings. It was embarrassing. But it was more than just a whooping. It was more like a beating. And Dwayne seemed to enjoy it.

I was the first one up. My stepdad would whoop us with an old leather barbershop straight-razor belt that hung up on the wall near the furnace.

I wasn't even fully bent over when—*CRACK*—the full force of the leather struck my bare ass.

"YAAAAA!"

Dwayne proceeded to beat me until my butt was black, blue, purple, and peeled off skin. It looked much worse than how it actually felt. Shit, some people may have considered that abuse. But that's what they did back in the day. He was old school. Then he had my brothers join in.

"Here, let's go. Hit him." He handed Alex the belt. Alex looked up at him like he was crazy.

"I'm serious. Hit him. I want you to spank him until I get tired and say stop. And you better not go easy. Cause if you do, Imma take it out on you."

Alex and Anthony took turns beating me with the belt. That's right. Sometimes he would make us whoop each other. If my brothers didn't hit me with a considerable enough force that my stepfather deemed appropriate, he would grab the belt and hit them in return. I was like *yo, this man is nuts.* We were being disciplined for things that didn't warrant this level of punishment.

I snapped out of my memory and pushed myself back in the water.

I completed three more laps when *BUZZZZZZ*, the large digital clock went off. My determination to prove Dwayne wrong had given me some energy to keep going—but not enough. I had failed by a long shot. Midshipmen had to pass within a certain period of time. I attempted to breaststroke the 200 meter because it seemed to be the fastest way. From what I observed, that was how everyone passed it. Even my brother Alex passed it. But I found myself falling short continuously.

Although I had failed the 200 meter twice already, I made it to the end of my plebe year. During the summer, the Naval Academy sectors out one corridor of Bancroft Hall to use for transient midshipmen to live in between summer trainings. All mids are required to move out of their rooms at the end of the academic year because different corridors of Bancroft are used for certain functions (such as Plebe Summer, sports camps, STEM, etc.) It was the day before I reported to my next summer training event. I checked in at the registration desk they had set up in the middle of the hall to receive my room for the night.

"Room 312," the midshipman said.

"Got it, thanks."

I grabbed my bags, headed up the stairs, and opened the door.

There was Oxford.

I thought I would have the room all to myself.

He was sitting there watching a TV show on his issued black Lenovo laptop. I immediately reacted defensively and expected him to do the same. Instead, he stood up, faced me, and said,

"I'm sorry. I shouldn't have said those things to you and your brothers. How I acted was wrong."

"It's cool, man. I'm over it now. But I wasn't expecting to run into you or for you to say that. I appreciate it. Means a lot."

"Oh, by the way...I knew about your nightly antics during Plebe Summer when you would go around and wake your classmates up."

"I don't understand. You weren't even a detailer. How would you know?"

"One of my classmates saw you one day. When I became your training sergeant, they told me about it. What I said and did to you was wrong, but one of the reasons I was also harder on you was because I saw you were a natural leader even as a plebe. And I secretly admired that. Despised it, even."

That was not the response I expected.

I'm not sure what motivated Oxford to say what he said to me that night. But whatever it was, I was humbled and thankful.

Years later, after graduating and receiving orders as a Supply Corps Officer in San Diego, I went underway with another ship to receive training for my helicopter control officer qualification (HCO).[12] Guess who was an Officer on board and helped me out?

Oxford.

_____

12 The primary duty of an HCO is to supervise and coordinate the landings of helicopters on the backs of US Naval warships.

✳ ✳ ✳ ✳

THE RIFLEMAN'S CREED resonated with me personally. We were all issued a 7.62mm caliber, M14 service rifle. It was the standard rifle given to all US military personnel in 1959. Today, it's used across the military as a drill purpose rifle, which means the weapon can only be used for training purposes and cannot be fired because the firing pin has been removed. Like many rates, we were required to remember it verbatim. Accredited to expert marksman and author of "My Rifle" Major General Williams H. Rupertus, the creed went like this:

> This is my rifle. There are many like it, but this one is mine.
>
> My rifle is my best friend. It is my life. I must master it as I must master my life.
>
> My rifle, without me, is useless. Without my rifle, I am useless. I must fire my rifle true. I must shoot straighter than my enemy who is trying to kill me. I must shoot him before he shoots me. I will.
>
> My rifle and myself know that what counts in this war is not the rounds we fire, the noise of our burst, nor the smoke we make. We know that it is the hits that count. We will hit.
>
> My rifle is human, even as I, because it is my life. Thus, I will learn it as a brother. I will learn its weaknesses, its strengths, its parts, its accessories, its sights, and its barrel. I will ever guard it against the ravages of weather and damage as I will ever guard my legs, my arms, my eyes,

and my heart against damage. I will keep my rifle clean and ready. We will become part of each other. We will.

Before God, I swear this creed. My rifle and myself are the defenders of my country. We are the masters of our enemy. We are the saviors of my life.

So be it, until victory is America's and there is no enemy, but peace!

Every time I touched the weapon, I would flash back to one particular day.

I was in the alley playing basketball with a few of the guys when the shootout started.

I barely had time to react.

Boogie was going up for a layup shot, and I was defending him. I pumped my chest up and bumped into him to give him some resistance as he drove toward the net. All of a sudden, I heard this loud SCREEEECH as an SUV pulled up out of nowhere in the center of the alley.

I heard glass shatter.

Then the bullets started whirling.

My predatory instincts activated.

This is my rifle. There are many like it, but this one is mine.

Like the Wild West, shots went back and forth. Thank God there were no innocent people around and that we were confined within the tunnel of the alley. Everyone weaved back and forth behind cars and garages for protection.

I must fire my rifle true. I must shoot straighter than my enemy who is trying to kill me. I must shoot him before he shoots me. I will.

The adrenaline rush was insane. My heart was racing. But I was still so present in the moment. We had to end this in some way. We couldn't keep this up for long.

"DRE!" Boogie screamed and tackled me to the ground.

Boogie saw another foe out of the corner of his eye. He had his barrel pointed right in my direction.

My rifle is human, even as I, because it is my life. Thus, I will learn it as a brother.

I exchanged a quick look of appreciation with Boogie. We always had each other's backs. We were losing the fight. There were only four of us against the guys who came from the car. There had to be seven or eight of them.

My rifle and myself are the defenders of my country. We are the masters of our enemy. We are the saviors of my life.

Smoke was our savior. Out of nowhere, another car pulled up from the other end of the alley and started returning fire. I saw Smoke pop out with a group of guys.

The tide of the fight had turned.

Our opponents re-grouped and drove off expeditiously down the street. We searched around to see if anyone was hurt. One of the guys took a bullet to the shoulder, but no one was severely hurt or killed.

Every time I touched my M14 drill rifle, I thought about that moment. And an instant surge of appreciation and motivation would come over me. It was an appreciation for God allowing me to escape my circumstances on the South Side. A motivation to channel my deep passions into everything I did as a midshipman at the Naval Academy.

My detailers would have my classmates and me on the bulkhead practicing rifle movements for hours.

* * * *

I'M STILL IN AWE at my own transformation.

I thank God for sparing me from becoming another nameless statistic. Some people who meet me are surprised to learn about my gang ties from the past. They'll say, "I don't see it. He speaks and expresses himself clearly. He doesn't dress or act like a thug." I've always looked at comments like that with pride. I wouldn't have been able to graduate and excel at Annapolis with the same thug mentality I strived for growing up. There is no "hood" Naval Officer. The Naval Academy beat that right out of me and made me a better, more polished man. I struggled during my plebe year because of it. Like the Marvel movie *Venom*, where the dark parasite and Tom Hardy battle for body dominance, no one knew about the internal war that was commencing inside me. I felt alone during such a big transition. Yes, I recognized that being a midshipman was a great opportunity, and I truly was thankful for it. But I struggled with facing my past head-on and learning how to bottle it up and use it as motivation correctly. When I would lie in my bed at night, I would think about those many emotionally infused conversations my parents and I had back home in Chicago. Everything they said to me—whether it be stern words or loving advice— went in one ear and out the other.

Here I was in a different state, under the roof of a different form of parenthood, and I still refused to listen.

At Annapolis, at the end of the year, your classmates would rank you and submit comments about your performance and behavior using a portal we called the MIDSYSTEM. It was almost like social media, except you didn't know who wrote what.

Reading comments about what people really thought about me was humbling and hurtful. I received words like "not a team player," "not around," and "aggressive."

After being ranked at the bottom of my class my entire plebe year and reading the negative comments my classmates wrote about me, I decided to make a change. I had to swallow my pride and admit my parents were right: I had a problem with learning from the school of hard knocks. If I was going to make it through Annapolis, something had to change. If I really recognized that attending a federal Service Academy was the opportunity of a lifetime, I had to change my attitude and approach how I operated on a daily basis differently. All that change started with me first. I had to move differently next year.

CHAPTER 15

YOUNG "STAR"

I NEVER GREW UP SAYING I WANTED TO BE A SPEAKER, yet I started traveling to speak to schools across the country during my youngster year. I can't recall who, but an Officer within the admissions department asked if I was interested in flying back to Chicago to speak to students on the South Side about my experiences at Annapolis. I spoke to four schools: Bronzeville, Harper, Phillips, and the Air Force Academy High School.

But the first time I shared my story with the outside world was when I was a midshipman candidate at the prep school.

My knowledge of writing grew during my English class at NAPS. My professor, Lieutenant Commander Jason Phillips, was known among my classmates for his gripping naval career stories, most of them about his time serving in Afghanistan. He also took many opportunities to speak to us about his passion for narrative warfare, education, and youth outreach. His desk was placed at the front of the class, overlooking the field of metal chairs arranged in a U-shape.

"The final assignment for the course is to create a portfolio of all your previous works, in addition to writing a personal narrative," Dr. Phillips said.

When he mentioned the project, I knew I wanted to center the portfolio on illustrating life growing up in Chicago. Then fear crept in. The Navy had a zero-tolerance policy on gang involvement. I worried I would be separated if I emerged from the shadows and openly discussed my past.

But at the same time, I knew that telling my story would help. It might inspire other kids on the street to work hard and not give up. It might inspire other minority midshipmen. It might change people's negative perception of Chicago based on what they saw in the news. It would defy the stereotypes placed on Black folks at Annapolis. I mean—wasn't that what I wanted to do after all? I talked it over internally, running the scenario through my head hundreds of times.

My guts squirmed with nervousness about the way ahead. Unsure of how Dr. Phillips would respond, I sought advice from the English writing tutor, Professor Lori Hawks.

"Hi, Mr. Evans, how can I help you?" she said with a hot cup of tea in her hand. She grabbed the purple-brown-orange scarf hanging around her neck and crossed it over her torso in an "x" pattern. She had eggplant purple gel eyeliner. Her warm demeanor felt welcoming.

"I was in a gang in Chicago before I joined the Navy. I need to do well on this final writing assignment to receive an A or B in Dr. Phillips's class. I need the points. I'm barely maintaining the 2.2 GPA I need to graduate. But I can't do any of that without sharing my full story in this portfolio."

During the summer before the start of the academic year, we took Scantron placement exams to determine the difficulty of the courses we would take. I was placed at level one in all three core classes: math, chemistry, and English. It was very apparent that the Chicago Public School system didn't adequately prepare me academically. The classes were a lot faster paced, and I found the material more difficult. Every week, I received individual learning counseling to identify and perfect how I studied best.

"That was in the past. As long as you're not affiliated with the gang anymore, you're fine. I think you should tell your story. Let's arrange a meeting with Dr. Phillips," Professor Hawks said. She ran her pale hands through her black hair. It had purple highlights.

The next day, like animals stuffed in a cage, Professor Hawks and I crowded inside Dr. Phillips's small office. I sat in a black chair, swerving my head in amazement at the hundreds of books on his bookshelves. Souvenirs Dr. Phillips had acquired serving in Asia and the Middle East filled his desk and office walls. The room was awkwardly silent for a moment as Dr. Phillips looked at me with an intense stare, waiting to hear what I had to say. "Go on, Evans, it's okay," Professor Hawks said. Like a running faucet, I unloaded all of my feelings about my upbringing on the South Side.

Would Dr. Phillips report me and have me separated from NAPS? Was telling my story worth the risk? How would I explain something like this to my mother? I would let her down. I would have wasted the opportunity Smoke gave me to escape. Would I ever get another once in a lifetime opportunity like this again?

What Dr. Phillips said next surprised me.

"Evans. God is going to use you. More people need to hear about your story. It's inspiring. I'm excited to read about it."

"I'm shocked, sir. I thought you were going to judge me and not understand." It was in that instant that I felt Dr. Phillips and Professor Hawks had taken a vested interest in me and would become my mentors. Through them, I learned to believe and have faith in my own story. Through them, I got a taste of the impact my story could bring to others. Opening up about my past proved to be a turning point. Instead of judging me, I discovered people wanted to walk my journey with me.

After days of being diligently focused on crafting the best portfolio I could, I turned in my assignment and received an A. What I didn't realize at the time was the impact my writing would have on the generations to come.

* * * *

I PARALLEL PARKED my rented gray Toyota Corolla into a spot near the end of a row of parked cars. Right in front of me was the high school. The school was a long, rectangular building that stretched along the entire block. Dirty brown bricks outlined with degraded cream columns made up its construction. Three large black doors were at the front entrance in addition to a short set of stairs. The outside landscape was neglected with nothing but dead grass and weeds to walk on.

Visiting Chicago allows me to recharge my spirit as a man. The South Side is my roots, and whenever I find myself at a standstill or unsure of myself, I try to make a conscious effort to go back. Driving through the hood, seeing "Don't Shoot" and "Stop the Violence" signs and murals and kids walking in the middle of the street to and from school to avoid the stray bullets, it doesn't take long to gut check myself. It still feels unreal sometimes that I had the chance to escape. I feel so blessed. So lucky. I allow all that energy that comes with the hood to penetrate me, and I reconnect with it. I draw power from it.

I walked into the building and came face-to-face with two tall, gray metal detectors standing at attention. I removed my dress blue jacket and cover and placed them on the black moving belt to the left. I was fastening the gold-plated eagle buttons of my jacket when I saw a man who caught my attention turn down the hallway. He had to be like five foot eight with lean, moderate muscle tone, and he wore a blue button-down shirt with black pants. I glared at him hard, so hard that even the two security guards at the front door began to notice. I could read the baffled expressions on their faces. They started to look in that same direction, too. I leaned my neck forward and squinted. "Is that who I think it is?" I said under my breath.

"Who we talkin' about?" the guard asked. After hearing me mumble to myself, he must have thought I saw a celebrity or something.

"There's no fucking way. That can't be him," I said, raising the volume of my voice.

The security guard now completely stopped what he was doing and looked down the hall.

"BOOGIE! Is that you?"

Like in a horror film when a character freezes in fear right before they are about to be chased or killed, the guy stopped moving.

Then he broke out into an animated dance and spun around.

"Dre? Ohoooo shit. Wassup, baby?!" He extended his arms out wide, walked up, and gave me a big hug.

I burst out laughing. He still had that same stupid sense of humor. "You hilarious, man. I see some things haven't changed. I can't believe it's really you, bro. What the fuck are you doing here?" I responded.

"I got out, Dre. I followed you, G. Seeing you leave and do something better—that shit resonated with me, man. I don't think you realize how much everyone looked up to you, yo."

"I'm so happy for you, man. This is crazy. Never in a lifetime would I think I would run into you, of all people. So what are you doing here?"

"I'm a teacher, bro. And I love it. I don't want these kids to make the same mistakes I did. I try to use my background to relate to them and keep them off the streets."

Boogie had joined a new gang.

"What are you doing here all dressed up and shit?"

"Funny you ask. I'm in the Navy. I'm here to speak to the students. Same thing you're doing, bro, trying to give back, just a different way."

"I don't know who you were supposed to speak to, but why don't you come speak to my class. That cool?"

"That would be dope, man. Let's do it."

I followed Boogie down the hallway, and we approached the door of his classroom. I could hear a bunch of students inside laughing and talking. When I walked in, the room went dead silent, and all the students beamed at me.

"Wassup, guys. I got someone here that's special to me that I grew up with. He's here to talk to you. So please show him respect and give him your undivided attention." Boogie stuck out the palm of his hand toward the ground and motioned to me that the floor was mine.

When I spoke, I had a fundamental choice: I could either give them some rehearsed brochure speech about USNA or speak an undiluted truth from the heart. Although this was labeled a recruiting trip, I personally didn't view it that way. I knew that many of those kids didn't have the slightest idea about a Service Academy. But who was I to judge? If I spoke to these youths about Annapolis, I would spend most of my time attempting to explain what the Naval Academy was and how it's different.

That was time I didn't have.

I stepped forward and stood before the class, taking in their silence as energy. I looked out at their sea of faces, wondering who I was and what I was going to talk about. My emotions began to get the best of me when my eyes met theirs—because in them, I saw myself. There was this clear, untapped power and cry for help among them. After twenty seconds of just silence, the atmosphere of the room elevated to an awkward, sit-on-the-edge-of-your-seat anticipation of my first words. I said a quick prayer to God and asked that he guide the words that I was about to emit from my mouth.

Then I spoke.

"On the South Side, I learned at an early age that the greatest potential lies within the graveyard…Think about all the people buried beneath the hard, rich soil who never accomplished their dreams or lived life to the fullest…How many books that were never written…How many athletes that never made it to the league…How many regrets…."

As a speaker, your job is to go out there and serve the audience. I was honest with them about life at the Naval Academy, my struggles to adapt, and how I got there. That I, too, came from a working-class family with parents who did the best they could amid the struggles of life on the South Side. I expressed the importance of continuously striving to learn. I hoped that when they looked at me, they said to themselves, "If he can make it, I can, too."

I spoke of the memories and actions of my past life: pistol whipping the guy who wanted to jump my brother, standing up to a childhood bully when he had me at gunpoint, the drive-by shooting, the fights, and the importance and power of learning to read.

I was in the middle of talking when I noticed this kid in the back of the classroom who kept talking and cracking jokes with a young man next to him.

"Yo! My man, stand up!" I said aggressively. The boy's eyes grew so wide all you could see was the white circles. The young man rose to his feet.

"Do you want people to respect you?"

"Ah...yeah," he said hesitantly. His demeanor was hard, yet I could see his mind racing, trying to figure out what direction I was going to take my question.

"Then why would you be back there talking while I'm talking? If you were up here, I would give you my utmost attention. I demand the same. I don't get paid for this. I'm up here trying to give back to you so that you learn from my mistakes and become better than me. I know for a fact ain't nobody else coming up to this school to speak to you. Do you understand?"

The young man was silent.

"I said do you understand me?"

"Yeah."

I continued to speak. "My gang affiliation shaped my identity as a man growing up. How I perceived myself and others and how I acted was through the lens of what gang life had taught me. I..."

"Man, fuck that sappy ass story about wanting to belong," the same young man interrupted.

Boogie and I exchanged looks.

He nodded his head in approval.

I walked over and placed my hand on the young man's shoulder. I grabbed it hard and made his eyes lock with mine. His face tightened and his body squirmed a bit from the pain of my grip.

I could tell I now had his undivided attention.

"Why are you trying so much to prove that you are hard? For attention? Acceptance? Huh?"

"What you talkin' 'bout folks? Get outta here, yo."

I looked at Boogie. He gave me a head nod. I turned back to the young man.

"I see you, yo. I see you. This rebellious energy you have inside you. This tenacity. It's a good thing. Use this to accomplish your goals in life. Use this to defy the odds. Use this to take risks and start a successful business. I want to help you," I responded.

"Yo, G. We good. Let me go. I ain't mean to disrespect you. I was just giving you a hard time," the boy responded, tapping my arm.

"I see you like to learn from the school of...." I stopped mid-sentence and loosened my grip. Was that how I acted toward my parents as a young man? I sounded like Dwayne. Or was I actually becoming just like the man I despised the most?

"Alright, guys, I think that's enough. Let's thank Mr. Evans for his time today," Boogie said while bringing his hands together in a clap.

I stood by the door and shook each one of their hands or gave them a fist bump. Like the superhero Flash, I imagined myself transferring a lightning bolt of energy to each of them. I truly believed that by making some type of contact, taking a photo, or giving them USNA memorabilia, I could somehow give them a piece of "me."

I wanted to give every last one of those youths something. Hope. A dream. A new perspective. Proof that life was possible beyond the walls of the city of Chicago. Something. Even if they didn't listen or ignored what I said, at least I opened their eyes and altered what they used to know by letting them physically see me in the flesh. My only hope was that they would use it to rise out of their circumstance and uplift others in return.

Boogie and I walked outside the school together, and he stopped me on the sidewalk right next to my rental car.

"Good lookin' out today, Dre. Appreciate you for speaking to my class," he said while giving my chest a soft punch.

"Anytime, man. I'm glad you got out and started a different journey," I responded.

"These kids have to work twice as hard just to keep up with the rest of the world. Most of them don't even start the race until it's already over. This is the least I can do."

"Yeah, I feel you, bro. You know what's crazy?"

"What?"

"Damn," I said while shaking my head and pointing toward the sky. "Smoke would have been proud of us. If only he was here to witness this shit. Like, look at us, yo. Seriously, can you believe it? Who would have thought that we both would escape the streets and make something of ourselves?"

During my plebe year at Annapolis, Smoke was walking down the sidewalk when another Black man approached and shot him point blank in the face. He died instantly.

The cold truth is that could have been me had I stayed in.

I know it's not easy, but deep down I wished Smoke had found a way to escape life on the streets as well. Maybe he felt trapped? Maybe he felt he couldn't leave because he was the leader and had already been in the life for so many years? Or was it his pride and ego that got in the way? Or did he want to escape but was afraid to ask for help?

But none of that even mattered because he had now become a statistic, one of tens of thousands of Black men killed by senseless gun violence.

"Your destiny in life is a matter of choice. It's not dependent on where you come from. You showed me that, Dre. Smoke made his choice to stay in. And we made ours. At the end of the day, we were determined to want something better," Boogie commented.

That was the realest thing I ever heard Boogie say.

We are so quick to judge thugs and those who join street gangs, but people forget that they're just "people" too. Many kids don't even have a choice anymore and are forced into gangs depending on the block they live on or family ties. Everyone has their own way at figuring out how they belong and where they fit in this world given the circumstances handed to them. Boogie was a prime example of that.

In the end, I formed a partnership with the USNA admissions department. That same year, I joined a gang called the Writing Center that helped tutor mids in writing. Two of my mentors who were in charge of the center, Dr. Joan Shifflet and Dr. Robin Taub, helped further coach me on my speaking. I spent the majority of my weekends traveling around the country speaking to youth at schools in underprivileged neighborhoods, and it's easily been one of the most rewarding things I've ever done in my life. I cared about those communities because I had grown up in one too. But when I wasn't engaged in outreach, I spent the rest of my time with the gang that adopted me back in Annapolis.

* * * *

BECAUSE MY BROTHERS and I had a good experience with the Rosanders, at the start of Plebe Summer, we signed up for the sponsor program at the Naval Academy. We had a brief in Alumni Hall, where the detailers explained how the program was run in detail, and we even had a chance to meet our sponsor family.

And that's where things went wrong.

We were greeted by an older Caucasian gentleman and his young daughter. My brothers and I were in the process of saying hello and that we were from Chicago when the daughter said, "They don't look like us, Daddy. They look weird."

I looked at my brothers and gave them the look that says, "Here we go."

"Shhh. Be quiet. You can't say that out loud in front of these people."

My brothers and I politely excused ourselves and never saw them again. The rest of our plebe year, we went without any involvement in the sponsor program. But in the summer of my youngster year, something in my gut told me to try signing up for the program again. This time I would go to the office and indicate some criteria in what I was looking for.

Along the main p-way, the admin office was located on the far left, down a long, bright white corridor.[13] Like spiders, rectangular cork bulletin boards hugged the Bancroft walls, providing a rainbow display of information to the midshipmen and staff who walked past. Some designs were as simple as a

---

13 The Main P-way, or "Striper Alley" as it was also known, was the hallway where most of the senior Officers and ranked midshipmen had offices and/or lived.

quote while others involved detailed, hand-drawn pictures. Yet again, another responsibility of being a plebe was designing the boards themselves within a certain allotment of time. The punishment typically involved something physical if you didn't finish in time.

The brown door squeaked when I turned the gold knob.

"Hello, is it too late to ask for a sponsor? I would like to see if they could adopt my brother Alex as well," I asked.

"No. Sure, hun, you definitely can. Here, fill out this information card," the nice lady at the desk responded.

Two weeks later, my email pinged. It was around eight in the morning when Tara Bandes emailed my USNA Gmail account to inform me that she'd be my new sponsor. The subject line read GREETINGS, and Tara's face filled the Google account contact box. Within the body of the text, she mentioned a husband named Craig and two children: Brooke and Hayden. I first met the Bandes family one day in the middle of Tecumseh Court, or simply "T-court" as we mids called it.

The bright sun beat on the steaming white cobblestone and on Tecumseh himself, a bronze figurehead of a Native American mounted on gray Vermont marble that served as a warrior symbol for midshipmen. Also known as the "God of 2," Tecumseh was originally constructed out of wood to decorate the bow of the USS Delaware. Considered the "Guardian of USNA," the grim statue overlooked the courtyard of Bancroft Hall and all that passed by. Mids said prayers or gave sacrificial penny offerings for good luck with exams and athletic games. For decades, it has played a vital part in various traditions at Annapolis, including being decorated with paint for parades, Army and Air Force weeks, Parents Weekend, and Commissioning Week. T-court is also the location where noon meal formations are held.

"Hiehhhhhh! You must be Dre! Come hereeeee."

Her voice was high-pitched and full of excitement. She walked right up to me with her arms extended in a "Y" shape for a big hug.

A native of Southern California, Mrs. Tara was beautiful. She was White with flowing, curly blonde hair, and her sweet voice suited her bubbly personality. She definitely had serious Cali vibes for real. Mrs. Tara exhibited an infectious positive spirit and loved to engage in art projects and photography. She maintained an extensive fashion wardrobe. She was also great at listening. Sipping coffee in the kitchen while we engaged in deep conversations became a thing for us. Something about her made my entire demeanor relax. I felt at ease opening up to her about girls, Chicago, or life at the Naval Academy because no matter what I said, she never judged me. Mrs. Tara's commitment to Alex and me as a mother cannot be overemphasized. If we had a daunting academic test or project coming up, she remembered. Having a tough time at the Naval Academy or feeling homesick? She'd make frequent trips to the yard, drop off care packages, or text us encouraging words.

Next came Craig. After Tara finished embracing me, he leaned forward and extended his hand.

"Hey, wassup? How's it going, man? Nice to meet you."

Craig was short with an average build and was more laid back. Raised on the concrete of New York City, he was known for his slick, sarcastic jokes. Mr. Craig preserved a more serious demeanor and spent a great deal of his time in Baltimore or traveling around Asia, networking and sustaining his nano-technology business, Pixelligent. I've watched that man make many sacrifices for his family just so he could give them the world. From day one I respected his hustle.

At last, standing behind their parents' legs were Brooke and Hayden.

The little sister I always wanted, Brooke, or Minion as I called her, was an adorable, lovely girl who had a burning passion for art, dancing, and fashion. Minion and I bonded right away through our interest in art. I would visit the house and draw with her at the kitchen table. She would sketch me little pictures, and out of support for her, I would tape them to the inside back window of my car and post them around my room in Bancroft. In a funny way, people started to think I had a daughter or something.

Hayden was a boy wonder who took my breath away the moment I met him. Even at a young age, he had a sharp photographic memory and mature ethos. His short, coarse brown hair highlighted his subtle eyes and pale skin. Like his father, Hayden loved history and could recite major battles, figures, and dates with ease. Aside from history, Hayden loved LEGO, action figures, and filmmaking. Growing up around Annapolis and two midshipmen sponsor brothers, Hayden expressed a keen fascination about life at USNA. He never missed an opportunity to question Alex and me about our daily midshipman duties, drill practice, or classes. Hayden made us feel like real-life superheroes.

I realized how much the Bandeses cared when I visited their home at 601 Randell Road for the first time.

The neighborhood was full of greenery and peaceful. The moment I entered the home, I walked down the stairs into a huge basement and followed Mrs. Tara to another door in the corner.

When she opened it, there were two twin-sized beds within the center of the room with a small brown dresser separating them both. Against the wall to the right were two large white closets. To the far left of the room was a full-sized bathroom.

"This is yours," she said with a warm smile.

"No way. No, it's not."

"No, really it is. We want you all to feel like family. This is your room."

I looked at Mrs. Tara in disbelief. *Why was she being so nice to us? We had just met, and she already planned a full room for Alex and me and gave us a key to the house. What did she want from us?*

There had to be a catch. I was so used to the South Side of Chicago where people had ulterior motives and were usually only nice when they expected something in return. I was not used to sincere, plain kindness like this. My brothers and I saw it first with the Rosanders. But the Bandes family took it to another level. And this was my first lesson in the art of just being genuine and a good person. The power of how your actions can make a large imprint in people's lives. Mrs. Tara taught me that.

"I don't know what to say. Thank you so much for this. Really." I gave her a big hug.

"Anytime, sweetheart," she responded. Sweetheart was a common word she used every time she talked to us. "We had to really search to get the extra long sheets and beds because we know you all are tall. Craig and I hope that everything is comfortable. This is your home, too."

After giving me a tour of the house, she took me upstairs to the kitchen where I sat at this huge, white marble island in the center. There was a variety of black, copper, and stainless-steel pans hanging from the ceiling above my head. The kitchen felt heavenly with all its white cabinets and walls.

I opened up my chemistry textbook and notes. Before I started studying, I took out a separate sheet of paper and wrote out affirmations for that study session.

"I will get an A on this assignment and on my next chemistry quiz."

I was at the table studying for about an hour when Mr. Craig returned home from work.

He walked up to the left side of the island and gave me a serious speech.

"Hey, Andre, can I talk to you about something for a second?"

For a moment I thought I had done something wrong or was in trouble—and I had just gotten here.

"We had to take this very strict course at the Naval Academy about our responsibilities to you as your sponsor family. One of the main topics was about giving alcohol to midshipmen. We take underage drinking seriously, and we will not break the rules. Is that understood?"

He paused and looked deep into my eyes to make sure I understood everything he was saying. The room felt awkward and tense. Mrs. Tara watched in the background with her head down in nervousness.

I let Craig finish his whole speech.

And then in one short breath I responded, "I'm twenty-one."

Like a hot air balloon being burst, the room instantly turned warm again. "Oh, well in that case, do you want a beer?" Mr. Craig asked with a chuckle. He handed me a Jamaican beer called Red Stripe. Over the years, Red Stripe came to be one of my favorite beers and a signature drink that grew the bond between Mr. Craig and me.

Mr. Craig later recalled how he felt so uncomfortable having that conversation with me. He rehearsed what he would say multiple times and didnt want to make me feel uncomfortable, especially after first meeting me.

The second time the Bandes took my breath away was during the holidays.

It was December, and Christmas break was right around the corner. By now, Mrs. Tara and Mr. Craig had become Momma T and Papa C. Momma T asked if Alex and I could watch Brooke and Hayden for the night while they went on a date. We happily agreed. When we arrived at the house and walked into the living room, I noticed a large Christmas tree and all the holiday decorations Momma T had put up. In the center of the living room was a fireplace with a green wreath above it, and along the mantel hung seven stockings.

"Do you like them?" Momma T asked.

"Like the stockings? I mean, yeah, sure. It all looks nice."

Then she walked over to a large, fancy gold stocking on the right and turned it around to the front with a smirk.

Stitched in cursive brown letters it read: "Dre."

There were a bunch of little wrapped presents inside, which turned out to be art supplies. Momma T knew I was an artist and wanted to support me in that gift.

My jaw dropped. She did it again. Here she was doing something sweet and genuine that unexpectedly took me off my feet. It meant the world to me because growing up as a kid I always enjoyed decorating and all the festivities that came with the holidays, but that stopped when Dwayne came into our lives. What always amazed me about Momma T and Poppa C was that they listened, and they supported Alex and me in our passions and interests. I ultimately feel that all children and young adults need these types of qualities from mentors and parental guardians. It is critical in their development and growth, and it's something I aspire to provide for the kids I'll have in the future.

* * * *

MY MOST SIGNIFICANT milestone as a 3/C was starting courses within my major. At the end of plebe year, to help 4/C facilitate the selection of a major, all the academic departments hosted various open houses. The idea of settling on a major was a mix of excitement and nervousness. *Courses were already demanding as it was. Why make it worse by choosing a difficult major? After all, wasn't the purpose just to graduate?* No matter what my major was, it wouldn't determine my service selection. My writing affair at NAPS led me to strongly consider English. My exposure at West Point SLS led me to contemplate physics. Then I attended the engineering open house.

According to *U.S. News & World Report* and *Forbes,* the Naval Academy is ranked as the number five undergraduate engineering program in the country and the number one top public college in America. With a student to faculty ratio of eight to one and free education paid for by the Navy, why not get a degree in engineering? Plus, no one in my family was an engineer. What I did know was that I loved art. In my mind I thought, if engineering involves the design of things, it should be the perfect fit. There had to be some way I could use my artistic instincts and imagination within the engineering discipline. Maybe I sound weird saying that. At the same time, though, a little voice in the back of my head was telling me "no."

Ever since I first started school, I've always struggled with math, especially when it came to fractions and geometry. My mind would go into some sort of mental shock. We all hear and perceive the stereotype: you must be good at math to be an engineer. The voice in my head was speaking from a spirit of fear.

I was all over the place. The expensive, top-notch facilities caught my attention, in particular the 120-foot towing tank, coastal engineering basin, and circulating water channel in the Naval Architecture & Marine Engineering Department (NA&ME).[14] There was something worthwhile about the fact that the challenging courses students took ultimately led to the design of an operational structure. We were at the very end of the tour when the instructor told us to follow him up a flight of red steel stairs.

"This is the 380-foot towing tank. It is primarily used by 1/C students during their final design projects, faculty, and engineers from other schools such as MIT."

---

14 120-foot Tow Tank: Can test ship models and submarines up to six feet in length. Models are towed down the tank to study ship resistance and sea keeping.

Coastal Basin: Creates waves to study the effects of wave action on coastlines/various structures.

Circulating Water Channel: Flow visualization studies of how water moves around propellers, hydrofoils, rudders, and submerged bodies.

When he said the letters "MIT," my eyes widened, and something in my gut jumped. I considered that a sign. It was right then and there that I knew I would major in naval architecture and marine engineering.

One of the smallest majors on the yard with roughly twenty-five to thirty students each year, what made the NA&ME department stand out was how supportive and close the faculty seemed to be. The small size allowed labs and design projects to be hands-on and encouraged a close-knit atmosphere. You could ask questions without judgment, and my classmates and I helped one another often. As a whole, everyone wanted to see each other succeed.

I'd joined another gang.

I was excited about my first few engineering classes. Deep down, being a naval architecture major made me feel special, like I was stepping in my purpose to be an architect like I'd always wanted to do as a kid. It made me feel closer to my biological father Tony—even though he didn't want to be a part of my life.

I operated within my gift as a naval engineering major. Most of the assignments involved utilizing a computer program called MAXSURF to design ships and submarines, but I drew everything by hand. For me, it was easier to visualize. Art was one of the few things in life that always made sense to me. Not an avid fan of computers, I could draw everything in more detail and faster than the computer program could. My professors and classmates alike were blown away by my ability to turn in fully hand-drawn assignments. The work was still right, and I received good grades. In the end, as design projects grew more advanced and multiple calculations and design changes were necessary, I adapted and learned the computer-aided design software.

But those positive emotions were quickly replaced by feelings of intimidation and being out of place. Many of my classmates grew up on the water sailing or being on boats, so they knew a lot right away about basic ship hydrostatics and how they are built. This became very apparent in class. The professor would reference things or discuss topics related to naval architecture that just went over my head. A lot of my other classmates would naturally know what he was talking about. I know I could have asked questions, and the professor would have happily answered them. And I know my classmates wouldn't have judged me, but I still couldn't help but feel like the fact that I was from a city like Chicago was a disadvantage. I'd be lying if I didn't say that, in the first few weeks, I felt like I was still suffering from the lack of education I received growing up in the Chicago Public School system.

Once again, I had to work twice as hard.

* * * *

I WOULDN'T NECESSARILY say I had a love for school. On average, I got about three to four hours of sleep each night. Call me crazy, but after some time, I became numb to it. "I'll sleep when I die" and "short-term loss for the long-term gain" were the anthems I marched to. Since the first day I stepped on the yard, one thing was clear to me: I was the underdog. Nobody would hold my hand and push me through Annapolis.

I had to labor for it. In my head, there was too much work to do. I knew I wasn't the smartest person in the room—never have been—but I always wanted to be known as the hardest worker. Whatever classroom I walked into, I made sure that when the professor thought of the name Evans, the impression was clear: passionate effort. I would make up for my inner-city shortfalls and the feeling of affirmative action by allowing my effort and grades to speak for themselves.

The number of times I harassed my professors should be a crime. Without hesitation—almost every day—I was in their faces, reviewing my homework, labs, projects, and asking questions. I received extra instruction so frequently that there was no point in emailing them. My professors knew I would be there. I made sure they remembered me and knew how serious I was about my education. I honestly didn't care if they labeled me annoying. I had to do what I had to do to make it.

I learned early on at NAPS that asking for help doesn't make you slow. I knew the importance of help and where it could take me. I didn't play when it came to academics. Not only would I see my professors frequently for one-on-one help, I would also take advantage of the other forms of academic resources and instruction. There were paid civilian teachers that held tutoring workshops at night, and then there was the Midshipmen Group Study Program (MGSP), where midshipmen ran peer study sessions.

I set a rule that I would never study in the hall (there were too many distractions). I only allowed myself to work in the library or the engineering classrooms. By changing my environment, it allowed me to stay focused. It was always a war with the books, but it was a battle I had become experienced in. I wrote my academic goals down monthly, and I used every opportunity I could to study.

Waiting in between classes?

Study.

Waiting for a military brief to start?

Study.

Traveling on tour with the gospel choir or to a destination to complete urban outreach?

Study.

I even carried pieces of my notes in my pocket to get a quick glance at a subject if I was going to a place where I couldn't bring my backpack or a book. I had an unusual ability to consistently study bit by bit during all the small little pockets of my down time. I got the idea for this tactic of always studying during my spare time from when I was a plebe learning *Reef Points*. In the end, it paid huge dividends in my success at the Naval Academy. That was my secret to academic excellence. If only I could have applied that same level of control to swimming.

I made it to my youngster year and was still delinquent from failing the 200 meter multiple times. Regardless if you failed or not, midshipmen were required to move on and take the 3/C year swim course. An expansion from plebe year, the underwater swim assessment was longer, and the final test was 400 meters.

I was leaving McDonough Hall after swimming one night when I felt like I wanted to quit. I was having a down moment.

Like the sound of rotating helicopter blades, angry rain droplets smashed against the outside of the building. The sky was charcoal black, and the clouds were gathered in a gang when I walked outside. The roofs of the cars in the mid store parking lot made a *pink, pink, pink* sound from the spray of the impacting water. Mids sprinted for cover under the buildings. I didn't even try to run. You ever had that feeling where you felt like the weather matched your mood? I was tired from all the hours I'd spent practicing in the pool only to fail again and again. At this point, I swam twice a day: at 0500 in the morning and later during sports period. Each droplet that touched my body weighed me down. My breathing slowed, and the pace of my steps shortened. I stopped and let the cold rain trace paths around my skin and clothes. I didn't care that I was dripping wet. I soaked in my defeat.

I was so exhausted.

"Why do you look so defeated?" a calm voice rang out from the darkness.

I looked to my left. It was Ms. Nisey. She was standing in the corner, near the outside entrance of the mid store, with the same black bag hung over her shoulder. I could hear the *phut-phut-phut* of the rain running down the black umbrella that covered her.

"What are you doing out here, Ms. Nisey?"

"I'm waiting for my ride. What's wrong with you, sweetie? Talk to me."

I'd managed to lift my head just enough to look her in the face when the tears came rushing down.

"I'm tired, Ms. Nisey. I'm having a down moment. This swimming thing isn't working out. I have to pass to graduate…I don't want them to kick me out like they did Anthony."

"What happens if they do?" she responded.

"Huh? What do you mean?" Her question took me by surprise.

"You said if you don't pass swimming, you'll get kicked out. What happens to you if you go back home?"

"For the first time in my life, I would truly be on my own both physically and emotionally. I'd be gang-less."

I went on to explain that my brothers wouldn't be there. There would be no street gang to turn to for protection anymore. That means I would have to watch my back even more. Or, worse, I could be walking toward my very death. Who's to say I wouldn't be shot at again?

Not only that. My spirit as a man would be crushed. I would have let down Boogie and everyone in Chicago who supported me. And most importantly, I couldn't bear to imagine telling my mother I didn't make it. I'd never forget it.

I needed to make it through this place. USNA was supposed to give me a new sense of purpose.

"Then use that pain as motivation to fuel you," she said. "If you know the consequences of going back home would break you and potentially lead to death, then you know what you gotta do, Evans. You better not quit. Remember, the best things come from being at the bottom. Trust God. It'll all work out at the right time."

Minutes later, a white Nissan rolled up, and Ms. Nisey climbed in. The car drove off.

The day of the test, I thought about the talk Ms. Nisey and I had had in the rain.

I will make it through this. God wouldn't put me through something I couldn't handle. Keep going, Dre. Don't stop. Keep going. Just take it one day at a time.

* * * *

THE CLEAR GRAY goggles fit tight on my face when I adjusted them in the cold pool. My body was still adapting to the temperature. I stretched my arms out and let them hang against the edge to preserve my energy and stabilize myself. I was in the farthest left lane. I checked to make sure the string on my navy blue trunks was tied tight.

"EVERYBODY READY?" the coach in his USNA gold shirt and blue shorts called out.

I said a quick, quiet prayer to myself.

He had a shiny black whistle placed at the tip of his mouth to signal when to start.

FWEEEEET.

I was off.

With all my might, I lunged forward and allowed the momentum of my push-off to guide me through the water as far as possible. Then I kicked my long legs violently to propel myself through the water. I breaststroked the first four laps. My momentum was good. *Stroke. Stroke. Stroke. Stroke,* I said to myself each time I brought my hands back to part the water. Every few strokes I took a gulp of air. Then, like the flip of a light switch, I was on the fifth lap when my energy began to fade. I started to sink lower. The vapor of the chlorine water sprinkled my nasal hairs, and my lungs gasped for the slightest taste of air.

It was happening. I was failing again.

Like a fish pulled out of the water after being caught, I jiggled my body and forced my limbs up and down to survive. With every stroke, more adrenaline flooded my system. I slowly made progress down the lane. But it felt like someone was holding me down, pulling me to the bottom of the pool to my demise.

I fought the panic in my chest and tried something different. Instead of using the breaststroke technique for the entire test, I decided to rotate on my back.

I used my long legs like propellers to drive myself through the water. Then, *WHAM*, I hit my head on the edge of the pool. There was this ringing scream in my ears. By instinct, I grabbed the back of my head, which was in pain from the force of the blow.

I started to sink again.

Fear came back and danced around in my mind. My head was pounding. I had to kill that spirit of fear because if I didn't, it would continue to come back.

I swam back to the surface and persisted on my back.

When I touched the gray wall and turned around again, the faces of my mother and grandmother appeared to me. I could see them clearly, right within the middle of the big "N star" on the ceiling. My eyes welled with tears.

I don't want to be a failure. I wanna make something of my life. I wanna make you both proud.

And something inside me awakened.

I swam those final laps like I was possessed.

I probably looked like a mad man, splashing with fury through the water. An extra jolt of energy surged through my body. I thought about all the hours I'd sacrificed practicing. I thought about Anthony. I thought about fighting for my life to survive growing up in Chicago. I thought about the fights, the gun shots. It's funny how that works. When you work so hard at something, you refuse to consider failure as an option. I came to a point where I refused to go back home and tell my family I didn't graduate from the Academy because I couldn't pass a swim test.

Fuck that.

This gang would have to force me out, or I would die trying.

But as determined as I was, my muscles began to ache in pain again after a few minutes. My bones had no more strength.

My whole head went underwater.

I crawled so dramatically to get back to the surface. I could see the silhouette of the instructor hovering over me on the left edge of the pool.

I didn't know how far I had left. But in one final effort, I turned back around under the water and made the biggest wing flap I could to push my body forward.

My body kept sinking!

My heart was racing with passion. I refused to be defined by a swim test.

I squeezed my hands and feet tight together to glide as far as possible. I held my breath.

I thought I heard the buzzer ring off, but I wasn't 100 percent sure because of the *pop-pop-pop-pop* of the bubbles my mouth made underwater. Every cell in my body begged for oxygen.

I splashed up and touched the edge. I didn't have anything left to give. I turned around to look at the instructor. He looked back at me with a serious face. *What the hell?* He wasn't giving me an immediate answer.

I sporadically swiveled my head back and forth. I searched the crowd of midshipmen. I looked at the other coaches.

Could someone give me an answer please?

Everyone's face was blank. No response. I was the last one to finish.

I looked back at the instructor.

"Did I pass?" I yelled.

He glanced down at his watch.

BUZZZZ. The black clock on the wall went off.

I passed!

I climbed out of the water and collapsed to my knees. Water dripped profusely from my head as I leaned over with a shortness of breath. I silently thanked God for giving me the strength and courage to succeed.

I said to myself, *The best things come from being at the bottom.*

The next day, at 0600 in the morning, I took the 200-meter test and passed that as well. Talk about being backward.

CHAPTER 16

MASSACHUSETTS INSTITUTE OF TECHNOLOGY

I NEED TO BACKTRACK AND TALK ABOUT MY GOSPEL CHOIR TOUR IN ATLANTA, GEORGIA. My back was pressed against the purple-blue tornado patterned seats. We were en route to our next performance.

"What's wrong, Evans? You look down," Adriana asked from the seat across from me.

"I just got a lot on my mind, and I don't know what to do."

"You should talk to Dr. Scott about it. She's really good at listening and gives great advice."

"Yeah?"

"Yeah. Go. Go up and talk to her." She motioned me forward and gave me an endearing touch on my hand. The choir became a comfort zone for many of the Black midshipmen on the yard. At the center of that judgment-free environment was Dr. Scott. I took 1/C Adriana's advice and slowly walked to the front of the coach bus.

"Hey, Dr. Scott, you got a sec?" I asked.

"Sure. Join me, Mr. Evans."

For the next ten minutes, I did my best to explain many of the struggles I faced with my stepfather. Dr. Scott gave me a straight face as she listened.

"I just don't understand him. He's done so much damage to me and this family. But then there are these weird times when it seems like he really does care. It's confusing."

She let me finish speaking before she uttered one short phrase: "I think you should write him a letter."

That was not the response I expected or wanted to hear. "Wait... what? Why?"

"I know you feel like he's the adult and that you shouldn't have to be the bigger person, but it might help," she said.

That night I sat down and wrote out some of my frustrations in a letter to my stepdad:

Dwayne,

Crafting this letter was a struggle for me. But a mentor of mine advised that I write this to clear my head and get things off my chest. So here it goes. Ever since you came into my life I feel like you have never understood me. You've been quick to judge and label me. You always give me a harder time than Anthony and Alex. I'll never forget the words you said to me in the basement when you said I couldn't accomplish anything. It cut me deeply. I've tried to communicate with you, but you always seem set in your ways and never seem to listen. I just don't know of any other ways to get your attention. So maybe writing this letter will start a path of communication.

Sincerely,

Andre

The next day, I mailed it to the house.

Days went by.

Maybe he hadn't checked the mail yet?

Then weeks.

I never received a response back.

There was one more conversation Dr. Scott and I had on that long bus ride: about my work ethic. I came to a point during my second-class year (junior year) where I felt frustrated. I toiled away at whatever I put my mind to only to come up short again and again. I began to wonder if it was worth it. *Was I wasting my time? My energy?* I got caught up sweating the tangible results instead of continuing to trust the process.

"I feel like I'm working so hard, yet everyone around me is passing me by. I'm doing all the right things. I barely drink. I'm focused. I go to church every Sunday. I pay my tithes. But I'm still not getting the results I feel like I should."

"I want you to read Isaiah 49 and meditate on it daily," Dr. Scott said. From the New International Version Bible, Isaiah 49 reads:

> Listen to me, you islands; hear this, you distant nations. Before I was born the LORD called me; from my mother's womb he has spoken my name. He made my mouth like a sharpened sword, in the shadow of his hand he hid me; he made me into a polished arrow and concealed me in his quiver, He said to me, "You are my servant, Israel, in whom I will display my splendor." But I said, "I have labored in vain; I have spent my strength for nothing at all. Yet what is due me is in the LORD's hand, and my reward is with my God."

I learned a valuable lesson that day not to get overwhelmed with trying to accomplish so much at once and to trust God with the timing of things.

Isaiah 49 made me realize that God was shaping me into the man I needed to be. No matter how stressful things seemed, the work I was putting forth would reap fruit. It may take months or maybe even years, but eventually, *eventually*, my diligence would show. God allowed Dr. Scott's advice to come at the right time.

What happened next was a domino effect.

The email subject read, "USNA SUMMER ENGINEERING INTERNSHIPS." I clicked on it and opened up the attached Word document to scroll through the list. My eyes zoomed right to the word "MIT." At that point, I didn't care much for the other programs listed. Earning a degree from MIT had been a dream since I was a child interested in architecture.

As a youth, I spent most of my time playing around in the clouds. I daydreamed about the buildings I would design or what life looked like working for a prestigious firm. When my mother drove my brothers and me around town in her red Honda Odyssey van, I leaned my head back on the gray seats and imagined buildings in various shapes and sizes. I marveled at the sight of the city skyline, especially at night. An array of colorful lights illuminated the mass of skyscrapers that stood watch over the metropolitan area. In my head, I was Picasso, and the city of Chicago was my mental landscape.

Like the biggest dude on the block whom nobody messed with, everyone knew that MIT held the crown for anything related to the STEM fields. There was a problem though. I didn't believe I was smart enough to get in. You have to realize, it's not like guys on the South Side applied for internships or college at Ivy League schools on the regular. Naturally, when I opened up the link to review the application requirements, I was intimidated.

I barely met the standards. Most of the people who applied for those types of programs had a 4.0 GPA and were at the top of their class.

Sheesh. That definitely wasn't me.

Not only that, but I had been down this road of doubt and rejection before. When I was a junior in high school, I'd applied to MIT's six-week minority engineering and science summer program and was not accepted. It was supposed to target students like me who came from underserved or underrepresented communities.

Fear surged in and crowded my mind.

I'd been hesitant to apply to the program in high school, but I took a shot anyway and was still rejected. How would applying to an MIT internship in college be any different? In the back of my mind, I just didn't think I was smart enough or had access to the same type of resources and responsibilities as the other students who applied.

Why put myself through that same type of rejection yet again?

For some odd reason, I still went to the information session. A couple of days later, I walked into the auditorium of Mitcher Hall for the engineering internships brief.

"You're in the wrong place, aren't you?" I heard a voice say from a corner seat near the doorway. I glanced over to my right. A White male midshipman looked up at me from his chair.

"What's that supposed to mean?"

"I thought this was something you guys didn't do."

I looked him dead in the pupils of his eyes. I stared him down like I would an adversary in the hood. My fists were balled.

"Nah, I'm in the right place," I responded with aggression. "There are some of us who do engineering." The tone of my voice was dark.

This is not a hit against athletes (I have many friends who played varsity sports who are great leaders and also did very well academically), but at the Academy, my experience was the perception that if you were Black, the only possible way you could have received admittance was because you were a recruited athlete. Yes, the sports industry is dominated by people of color. But that doesn't mean that all Black people are athletes; we are talented and successful in other disciplines, too.

In my case, I was six foot five with a slim, athletic build. On countless occasions, midshipmen, locals, and staff members would make comments about my Blackness. This makes me flash back to my youngster year. It was a beautiful summer day, and I had just walked through the main gate into downtown Annapolis to grab some food. I was dressed in my clean, creased, all-white Navy uniform. An older Caucasian couple stopped me on the street and asked, "What sport do you play?"

"I don't play sports. Actually, I'm an engineer."

The look on their faces was shock. I saw that same look of wonder even after I graduated from Annapolis and was a Naval Officer in the fleet. Many of the White Officers couldn't seem to comprehend how a Black man from Chicago could gain admittance and graduate from the Naval Academy without being a recruited athlete. Their eyes threw sharp daggers of judgment. I've found that many of the Officers would not know what to say to me in a conversation, so, in order to break the ice, they almost always brought up playing sports to break the tension.

Again: there is nothing wrong with being an athlete. But there's a difference when people label you as one and assume doors have only opened for you because of that. That's like saying all White people are the same, and that's clearly not true.

I walked toward the middle of the auditorium and took a seat. I did my best to try to focus on the brief. However, as you can imagine, there was another side of me that was angry. Internally, I knew I wanted to say more and speak my mind. It was hard not to curse him out and beat his ass. Lord knows I wanted to.

I thought about the many conversations in which Ms. Janie Mines would tell me about what she went through as the first African American woman to graduate from the Naval Academy. The stories of racism and struggle she told me left me speechless. I first met Ms. Mines when she worked at the Pentagon. She had a motherly spirit, her hair firm with natural black curls, and she wore casual attire. Right away, there was something about her energy that felt welcoming and nurturing. Over the years, I've witnessed how Ms. Mines never hesitated to devote her time, money, and resources to help and mentor midshipmen and young Black adults. She played a major role in my success at the Academy. She later went to MIT for her MBA.

Meeting Ms. Mines was no coincidence.

So I thought, *If Ms. Mines could keep her cool and get through that, then I too can remain calm in this situation.*

I directed my energy and anger another way. Losing control would have allowed him to "win" over my mind, and I would have embarrassed myself and my family in the process. I couldn't give him the satisfaction or that type of power.

All I could do was prove him wrong.

He gave me the final push I needed.

The next day, I started the application for the MIT internship.

I applied to Los Alamos International Laboratory as a backup internship. The lab appealed to me because of its history as the design and test site for US nuclear weapons during World War II. I thought it was cool. Being able to say I interned at such a place drew me in. Plus, I'd never been to New Mexico before. A week after submitting the application, I was accepted.

I put my best foot forward on applying to the MIT internship, but there was a question in the application that kind of surprised me: "Have you applied and been selected for other internships?" I didn't think it was a big deal. Maybe the Academy was just curious if I had other offers, so I selected "yes."

I received an email from Professor Bean two days later. She was in charge of submitting midshipmen's applications and all the logistics that pertained to the MIT-LL internship.

> Midshipman Evans,
>
> You needed to be specific and list the name of the internship that selected you. If you don't, I will remove your application and not submit it to MIT.

At first, I thought, *Who the hell does this woman think she is? Two, who was she to remove the application I worked so hard on? She didn't have that right.*

I called my mother for some savage Mean Person advice.

"Hey, honey, how are you?"

"Wassup, Ma, can you talk?"

"Sure, what's going on?"

"I applied for an internship at MIT. But the lady who reviews and submits the applications on our behalf told me if I didn't tell her about the other internship, she would cancel my application. I'm concerned she might call and let Los Alamos know I applied somewhere else as well. And end up losing my backup intern spot in the process."

"Don't tell her the name," my mother said. "Trust God. Everything will work out fine." Then she prayed for me on the phone. "Lord, you know the desire of Andre's heart. You know the amount of effort he put into that application. I put this situation in your hands. Give him a clear sign on what to do. In Jesus's name I pray. Amen."

I knew she was speaking from experience. She'd experienced racism and sexism from her boss when she worked in sales at FedEx. She was one of the best at her job but was constantly given a difficult time by her boss. But she never stopped. She never gave up. And because she didn't, she ended up being the best and one of the most respected managers on her team.

The next day, I was sitting at my desk in my ship hydrostatics class when that sign came. It was morning, and Professor Greg White, a crusty sailor turned naval architect guru, was lecturing about the importance of weight distribution on ships when he went on one of his usual tangents.

"MIT also has a great master's program in naval architecture. A lot of my former mids have gone there to study."

My jaw dropped right there in my seat.

I couldn't believe it. That was my sign.

So what did I do? I didn't tell Professor Bean shit. In fact, I didn't respond back to her email at all. At least I faced my fears and took a shot at applying for one of the most prestigious internships in the country.

One week later I got an email in my inbox.

It was from MIT.

Dear MIDN Evans,

Congratulations! We are pleased to inform you that you have been selected to participate in our summer internship program at MIT Lincoln Labs.

It was like a punch in the chest.

I swear there's something special about that prayer stuff.

* * * *

MIT LINCOLN LABORATORY was a Department of Defense advanced research lab located in Lexington, Massachusetts. It was founded in 1951 when scientists from MIT worked there to develop our nation's first air defense system during the Cold War era. Today, it continues to be used extensively as the premier research depot for national defense.

At the front entrance, a tall flagpole with the American ensign flew gracefully in the wind. The building itself was marble white with a unique parallelogram shape and a multitude of glass windows that covered the main building. It even *looked* like a majestic and scientific place, like a bunch of smart people and ideas emerged from it. As I stood before the lab, I remember taking a minute to let the experience sink in.

You made it, Dre. Not too many people get a chance like this. Make this shit count.

When I walked inside, there was a large white reception desk located on the left in the main lobby. Everything inside was white, blue, or sea green and had a futuristic sci-fi look.

"Good morning, ma'am. I'm checking in for my internship with the Mechanical Engineering Division, Group 71. My sponsor is a guy named Mark Silver." I showed her the welcome packet I'd received via email. She gave me a friendly smile and began typing away at her computer. "Okay, great, just a sec. Let me look him up and set you up with a security badge."

"You must be Andre," I heard a soft-spoken voice say from behind me. "Hi, I'm Mark Silver." He extended his skinny pale hand, and I shook it with a firm grip.

"Yes, that's me, nice to meet you."

"Well, I figured it was you. Professor Bean sent me your midshipman photo. Plus, you're in uniform, so you stick out," he commented in his square-framed glasses. "Come on, let me show you around."

We walked forward and exited the lobby. The existing main building from the 1950s was attached to the modern front complex. I remember how low the ceilings were. The top of my head damn near touched the ceiling. In a square, grid-like pattern, research departments were grouped in their own sections within the main building, not including the top-notch facilities such as the flight test hangar, autonomous robotics lab, virtual reality center, and space surveillance complex. Reaching some of the other buildings required a car or transportation via the shuttle. The various research departments included Engineering, Cyber Security, Air Traffic Control, Space Systems, and Air Missile Defense, among others.

Mark and I made it to the Group 71 area and took a seat inside his small corner office.

"Again, welcome. I spend most of my time here in the office. You'll probably end up doing the same. The main project I want to assign you is to design a swivel fabrication device for a high-powered laser. The laser would be tested in the Autonomous Systems and Flight test facilities with an overall goal to be mounted on Navy ships, Air Force planes, and Army vehicles. How's that sound?"

"Sounds good to me, sir. That's actually pretty cool."

Engineers found it difficult to assemble the various laser components on one side of the center amplifier plate (where the energy beam is emitted), while the others remained on a hard surface because the fragile components would break. As a result, I was tasked with designing a fixture appliance that would allow engineers to simply rotate and lock in place whatever side they desired to build upon. I was also asked to design an aluminum plate that could be attached to the center of the amplifier to hold all the wires in one central location.

"Do you know how to use Solid Works?"

A common engineering design software, Solid Works was a database also used extensively by naval architects in designing

ships and performing stress and fatigue tests. I was very famil-
iar with it.

"Okay, great. Aside from that, I'll probably also assign you
other little tasks such as ordering parts or completing engineering drawings. I recommend you make time to visit the
other departments and facilities around here as well, like the
3D print shop or the OMAX water-jet machine."

* * * *

THAT AFTERNOON, ON my first day on the job, I met someone.

His name was Jamal Grant. He, by the way, also has an incred-
ible story. Jamal had a calm demeanor and a slim build and
was an African American man born and raised in Boston in
a hood called Dorchester. His participation in an after-school
STEM program led him to pursue an undergraduate degree in
mechanical engineering from the University of Massachusetts
Lowell. Dealing with a sick father and the pressure of failing to
maintain the best college grades made Jamal feel trapped. He
needed a way out to continue moving forward, so he sacrificed
his summer break and flung himself full force into a Draper
Lab internship. Jamal hoped that it would allow him to gain
valuable connections and open the door for an internship
opportunity at his dream job: MIT Lincoln Labs.

Eight months later, it did.

His final goal was to eventually earn a full-time spot working
in the mechanical engineering department after completing
his co-op as an intern. Unfortunately, Jamal felt depressed on

the first day. He thought he would be working on cool projects but instead found himself spending countless hours ordering parts. I met him in the cafeteria.

I was wearing my khakis that day.

"Hey, wassup, man?" Jamal asked when he walked up to me with food in his hands.

"What's goin' on?"

"Nothin' much. Are you here on a tour, or are you new working here?"

"Nah, bro. I just got here today for an internship. I go to school at the Naval Academy."

It never occurred to us that the two of us would be office mates. I saw him sitting at my computer going through some files when I walked in.

"Ah, hell nah. You're the new guy Mark said we had coming?" Jamal said, pointing at me with his right index finger.

"Hahahaha," I laughed. "Yeah, bro. Me." I extended my hands in the air.

"This ain't no coincidence."

Right away, Jamal and I hit it off and became close friends. I mean, this dude was solid. We'd sit in our small office space and talk for hours. We shared the same views, were both passionate about outreach in urban communities, and had a lot of hobbies and interests in common. According to Jamal, he labeled it as "Black Excellence." Years later, while catching up with him on the phone, he reminisced back to the first day we met.

"Man, Dre, I remember walking back into the office from lunch that day, and you had this cross prop with the words 'God is my rock' etched into it. And the rest of the table was full of all these motivational quotes. Right away, it caught my attention. I was like, who is this dude that is bold enough to display a scripture in such a scientific environment? Seeing someone else believe in the same faith moved me immensely."

Meeting Jamal was a blessing. He took me around Boston and showed me the city, from a great twenty-five-cent wing place to the main MIT campus, nice bars, and more. But what I learned most from Jamal was how to network with people effectively. Everywhere we went, he knew somebody.

"How do you do that? How do you know so many people?" I asked him one day over drinks.

"I just keep in contact with people."

Jamal pulled out his wallet and handed me a white business card. It was his. "If you don't have one, make one. Pass it out to everyone you meet." Then he taught me about the Rule of 48: calling or emailing anyone you meet within forty-eight hours. He explained the importance of the concept and what a great introductory email looks like. An example would be as follows:

Good morning/evening [insert title and name of person],

I hope that this email finds you well. It was important for me to take the time to send you a note to say, "Thank you." Thank you for taking the time to speak with me about your experiences. [Include any other relevant specific details about the person and/or your conversation you found impactful.] I truly appreciate it.

Thank you once again for your valuable time, I look forward to hearing back from you, and have a blessed day.

I've used that same email format for years, and it has never failed me. In hindsight, Jamal's wisdom on networking allowed me to foster a multitude of fruitful relationships throughout the rest of my time at the Naval Academy and in life. If it wasn't for him, I wouldn't have been able to build a network of mentors who would help assist me in planning multiple outreach events.

In the end, Jamal not only received a full-time job offer at MIT-LL, but also founded his own nonprofit called the NET Mentorship Group. Never in his wildest dreams did he think he would work with NASA and nuclear scientists or work on satellites at such a prestigious lab. Today, Jamal is currently a full-time scholarship student studying public policy at the Harvard Kennedy School.

There was also my man Monti. Jonathan Monti was a stocky White guy with an average height and an infectious warm spirit. He was also a devout Christian. He came into our office one day and introduced himself to all the interns. Come to find out, he was a Marine Corps Officer and Naval Academy grad. That's when we clicked. He opened my eyes and showed me what it meant to be a military professional: intelligent and a constant pursuer of education yet competent as a war fighter. He challenged the status quo by being a Marine and receiving a graduate degree in mechanical engineering from MIT. Countless nights I spent crashing at his apartment, smoking cigars on his rooftop that overlooked downtown while we drank beers, or just chillin' at bars. He even let me borrow his old black Pontiac to drive around the city when I wanted to and never asked for anything in return. It was my first true taste of the power of the brotherhood within the Naval Academy network as well as the power of having a giving spirit. Looking back, it still blows my mind how God brings people into your life at the right time.

In retrospect, I wasn't hung up on the fact that I was placed within the Mech E department or upset about any mundane tasks assigned to me. In my world, just being at MIT-LL was a blessing. It gave me a taste of what life could actually be like as a practicing engineer. My level of knowledge was elevated from all the workshops and seminars I attended, and most importantly, I left Boston with two lifelong friends and a pocketbook full of mentors and valuable contacts.

I'd joined another gang.

CHAPTER 17

SERVANT LEADERSHIP

THE FIRST TIME I FLEW TO SAN DIEGO, I HATED IT.

It was spring break, and I was participating in another STEM outreach event. My flight landed late that night, and the event was scheduled to start the next morning at 1000. But first, I needed to get some sleep. I was exhausted.

I woke up the next day in my hotel room and threw my headphones over my ears. Each morning, I listened to motivational speeches from speakers like Eric Thomas, Bishop T.D. Jakes, and Les Brown to set my mind in the right direction for the day. I enjoyed those speeches because I often felt like God used them to speak directly to me. There were hundreds of speeches, and each had a different message or theme. Depending on the adversity I faced at that moment in my life, a particular speaker fed my spirit, so I replayed the message on repeat over and over. Then I read one chapter of Proverbs and prayed for wisdom, knowledge, and understanding.

Ping.

It was a text message from the Mean Person: "Hey, honey. I hope you landed in San Diego safe. Papa passed away this morning."

Fuck, man.

I was just in Chicago three weeks earlier on another outreach trip. Papa had been in and out of the emergency room multiple times, battling with dementia and other health concerns. After speaking to a group of students on the South Side, I met up with my mother and grandmother. I remember the vibe of the small, dusty hospital room. It was cold—spooky even. There was an eerie quietness to the air. The only thing I could hear was the *BEEP* of the various medical devices they had hooked up to his bed and his hard, long, and slow breaths. I almost didn't recognize him. He looked so weak and frail.

The way Papa layed there struggling to breathe, it made me reflect on the time Smoke shot a man in the neck and he bled out in the street.

It was a warm day, and Smoke and I were chillin' in his black BMW, smoking weed. I took a long puff off the joint and passed it to him.

Cough. I put my fist up to my mouth. "Yo, man, I got a question. And I want you to be real wit' me."

"Wassup, Dre? Shoot."

"What was it like for you on your first time? You know, pulling the trigger. I'm just curious."

I had proved to the guys I was committed. I was fortunate I didn't have to live with the moral reality of killing someone.

"Damn, Dre...Hold on, let me get one more hit." *Swuuuuuu.*

Cough, cough. Smoke began his story.

"My shit was raw. I was at the mall leaving Foot Locker from buyin' some shoes when this tall dude bumped into me so hard I dropped my bag.

"'Yo, what the fuck?' I said. The guy kept walking.

"'Watch where you goin', n*gga,' he told me. Barely turning his back to look at me. I wanted to fight his ass, yo. But one of the other guys I was with nudged me and said we should follow his ass. We'd get him when he left.

"So we did. Me and my homie stayed at a distance and followed this dude out the mall to his car. Then we followed him home. The moment that n*gga got out the car, I pulled out my piece and pointed it at him.

"'Talk that shit now,' I said. He put his hands up in the air and his face turned white. He was mad scary.

"'My bad G. You got it. We good. I ain't meant to bump you, just let me go. I'm sorry,' the guy responded.

"'Nah yo, light that n*gga up. You gotta show people they can't disrespect you,' my homie said.

"I think the dude saw it in my eyes that I was gonna pull the trigger cause he instantly just took off running."

Pop, pop, pop. Smoke imitated a gun shooting motion with his hand by curling his right index finger inward to his palm.

"I let off like three shots, Dre. The next thing I knew, that dude was lying on the pavement bleeding out. When my homie and I walked up, like melted ice cream, bright red blood spurted out his neck and stained the concrete. The dude grabbed his neck and struggled to breathe. Each last breath was fierce and determined. Like he was choking, he gasped for air.

"'Damn, I smoked that motha fucka,' I turned and said to my homie. Ever since that day, everybody just called me by the name Smoke."

"Damn yo," I said.

"You cool people, Dre. You easy to talk to, man. Imma bring you under my wing and look after you, like on some big brother shit."

I've always known Smoke to be laid-back and collected. You could tell from his confidence in the way he walked and talked and the fierceness in his eyes that he was very comfortable with himself. He had accepted the fact that the streets would be his life for years to come, yet he was smart. He wasn't emotional with how he reacted to things and always tried to look at the bigger picture in situations.

I might not have killed anyone like Smoke did, but I'd seen death close at hand the same way he described it. I was out with one of the guys when shots rang out. I don't know who the bullets were intended for, but they did claim a victim that day. What I saw lying before me on the cold concrete, dead instantly, was a child.

They never found the shooter.

Sadly, this has happened many times on the South Side.

My mind faded and focused back on Papa. He had been in the hospital for about three days then, but he looked weak and frail, like a gray zombie. It was as if life was being sucked right out of him before our very eyes. I'll never forget the image of my Papa, with his sarcastic and quick-witted spirit, now helpless. It was depressing. At the time, I knew in my gut he didn't have long. I just didn't realize that would be my last time to see him.

Then I thought about when I was a child and my mother would take my brothers and me to visit our grandparents at least once or twice every week. I spent most of my time at the kitchen table drawing or talking to my grandmother. On occasion, Papa would run to the market and pick up a nice, fat, juicy watermelon. This would later become a tradition for us. My bones would shake with excitement whenever he came home with one. We would sit at the table and cut through the thick green skin of the melon and then cut it into square or triangular slices. Papa also had an old brown chair and a small, square television tucked away in the right corner of the living room.

When he wasn't working, he would retreat to his den and watch baseball. Always the Chicago White Sox. I would sit with him and watch. In the long run, spending solid quality time with my grandparents each week allowed us to be that much closer.

* * * *

DEATH HAS A weird way of revealing to you how short and precious life really can be. It is not to be wasted. In my usual habit, my brain moved from one reflection to the next. There were so many thoughts flying around my mental space. I concluded that when I died, I didn't want to just be remembered as a Military Officer with a Naval Academy degree. In my heart, I wanted more. I have businesses, books, speeches, mentorship programs, and so much more in me to offer the world. At Annapolis, I made frequent trips to the cemetery. The grim reaper and I have had quite a few encounters over the years. I would literally walk around the tombstones, touch them, and say to myself, "This will be me one day, and when that time comes, I don't want people to just make up stuff I did. I want them to say Dre really did use his life to give back to the world."

When I die, I want my children and their children to look back at my life and say to themselves that my daddy or grandfather was a beast.

* * * *

AN EMAIL TITLED "Truman Scholarship" jumped out at me from my inbox. At the time, I didn't realize what I had stumbled upon or the new journey I was about to take. Created by Congress in 1975, the Harry S. Truman scholarship serves as the official federal memorial for the thirty-third president. It offers graduate school money, leadership development training, and employment opportunities to young people who deeply value public service. It's one of five prestigious scholarships issued every year. The others include Gates, Marshall, Rhodes, and Cambridge Scholars.

What caught my attention in the message was the fellowship's mission to take a risk on and invest in youth who answered the call to servant leadership. The foundation encouraged its scholars to study policy, engage in nonprofit work and community activism, serve in the Armed Forces, and make a difference in politics. Its alumni consisted of people from all walks of life, including Stacey Abrams, Michelle Alexander, Eric Greitens, Madeleine Albright, Susan Rice, and John King (to name a few). It sounded like something I fit the mold for.

I was all in.

The Academy had its own application process for the scholarship. Professor Brendan Doherty, a political science professor who taught policy, was the lead representative for the fellowship at USNA. He was notorious for his big goofy smile, frizzy brown hair, and assortment of colored ties that he always paired with a casual gray or blue blazer. We were given a few weeks to complete the packet before Doherty and his team of professors reviewed our responses and selected the handful of mids who would advance to the next round: the interview phase.

It was the middle of sports period, and the hallways were empty when I walked down the thick black staircase toward the basement of Nimitz Library. One of the many things that made

Annapolis unique was its jigsaw of underground corridors and paths that connected the academic buildings. Midshipmen could travel between a brief in Michelson Hall, engineering classes in Rickover, and studying in Nimitz, all in one sweep without ever stepping foot outside. My interview took place in a small classroom located in the languages and cultures corridor, a hallway adjacent to Rickover and the library.

I opened the stiff, creaky door to find Professor Doherty and three other instructors present at the table. The rest of the teachers' names I can't recall. Right away, the panel proceeded to question some of the inputs I'd provided on the app, specifically a statement I made in an essay question: "I have many ideas on how to help prevent gang violence on the South Side of Chicago."

"Tell us more. We want to know what those ideas are."

"You fight street gangs with other gangs. Our sense of who we are, how we behave, how we speak, and to some extent how we think is determined by the various gangs we join and identify with. Even from a psychological perspective, Maslow's hierarchy of needs confirms this. The desire to belong, self-esteem, safety, and security are essential human needs for maintaining a fulfilled life. What I'm trying to get at is that youth will switch to different gangs, but they have to be motivated to do so. I speak from personal experience. I would use fraternities, STEM programs, hip-hop and dance clubs, or any type of gang that would appeal to youth in a cool way as mentorship platforms. I'm not saying I have all the answers and that this can be accomplished overnight, but I think these could be great additions for positive change."

The panel of adults stared at me with perplexed faces, like they couldn't believe what I'd just said. Then they picked up their pens and started writing a bunch of words on the notepads before them.

At the end of the interview, a woman on the panel asked the typical question, "Why do you want to be a Truman Scholar?"

"One of the greatest inventions of the human race is gangs. They provide us the means to accomplish more as a team and learn from others. I believe the Truman Foundation is a gang I identify with and can use to give back to Chicago and, most importantly, other hoods as well. Whether that be through politics, policy, education, or another avenue," I responded.

"Stop right there, Mr. Evans," the woman blurted out. She took off her glasses and placed them on the table. "You keep using the word 'gangs' a lot. I just want to be clear I understand you right. What are you saying? That the Truman Scholarship is a gang?"

"Yes, ma'am. That's what I'm saying. The same way the Naval Academy is. The same way fraternities and sororities are. The same way sports teams and political parties are. They all operate under some form of ethical or moral code of conduct with symbols, colors, and dress codes just like a street gang. They are all gangs, whether we want to acknowledge it or not."

"But what about the violence? All the organizations you named don't commit crimes."

"Yes, you're right. There are gangs that do commit violence, but not all of them do. The media gives street gangs a bad rep.

Movies and documentaries over-adrenalize our fear about them. There are good people, good positive role models in gangs. There are gangs that do good for their neighborhoods and have the right intentions. It's only bad when they resort to violence, and that's what's glorified by the media. At the end of the day, gang is another word for group, tribe, family, team, or organization. Gangs are a healthy part of society."

The interviewers looked at me like I was crazy.

"Alright, Midshipman Evans, I think we have all we need. Thank you for your time. We'll be in touch," Professor Doherty said and escorted me out of the room. I walked back to Bancroft feeling like I'd just bombed my interview.

Of all the midshipmen interviewed, four were selected to represent the Naval Academy and apply for the actual scholarship on the Truman Foundation website.

God gave me the opportunity to be one of them.

* * * *

I SPENT MY entire winter break stationary at the dining room table. For hours, I worked on the tedious Truman application. Every now and then, my brothers and parents would poke their heads in the room and ask if I needed or wanted to do anything. "Nah, I'm good. But thank you, though," I responded. I'd barely raise my head from the computer screen and the cluster of papers spread out before me. My family knew not to bother me too much; when I put my mind to something, I won't stop until I get it done. Working on the Truman application was no different.

After two or three weeks, I received an email from Tara Yglesias, the Truman Foundation's deputy executive secretary. I'd advanced to the next round with a scheduled interview at the Superior Court House in Washington, DC.

Four students were already present in a small, glass-walled conference room when I walked in.

"What school are you from?" one of the candidates asked.

"Umm, the Naval Academy."

"What is your major?"

"Engineering."

The group gave me a bunch of smug, judgmental faces.

"Is there a problem?" I asked. I've never been a person to avoid addressing the elephant in the room.

"No, there's no problem. It's just different. That's all. Truman Scholars usually come from a background in political science, policy, or English. Not engineering."

As each of the prospective scholars went around the table and shared the school they attended, their major, and what they wrote their policy proposals on in the application, they sized one another up. I sat there in the black chair and thought, *These motherfuckers have no idea what I had to go through and the amount of work I had to put in to get here.*

I didn't try to pretend I was more intelligent than everyone in the room. Instead, I ignored what I perceived as distractions before me. I didn't have time for this. I was here to get a job done. At that instant, Tara walked in.

"Andre Evans?"

"Yes," I said, standing up.

"Great. Please follow me."

They say that a normal heart beats fifty to eighty times per minute. I could feel the adrenaline surging in mine as it began to contract and beat faster inside my chest. Down the hall now, I followed Tara until I stood outside a much larger meeting room.

Heart rate: one hundred beats per minute.

I closed my eyes, prayed, and remembered the scripture Dr. Scott asked me to meditate on my entire 2/C year, Isaiah 49.

"Andre, we are ready for you. Come on in," Tara instructed.

Heart rate: 110 beats per minute.

I walked in the conference room. At the center was a lady named Laura Cordero, a born and raised Chicago native appointed as a judge to the District of Columbia Superior Court in 2005. She was African American and had full lips, bobby-flowy brown hair, and a slim frame. Judge Cordero served in the Domestic Violence Unit, where she presided over the issuance of civil protection orders. She also served in the Family Court, overseeing cases involving abuse and neglect, adoptions, juvenile delinquency, and juvenile drugs. To the left of her was Andrew Rich, the executive secretary of the Truman Foundation. Andrew was a Caucasian man with a very skinny frame, a soft voice, and hazy gray-blue eyes. To the right of him was Tara. Two other men sat at the opposite ends of the table, but I can't recall their names. The interviewers stared at me. They were studying my uniform and everything I said.

I was so nervous I could feel my heart beating through my chest. My mouth dried up. I couldn't taste any saliva or moisture around my lips.

Most of the questions asked of me were similar to what Professor Doherty and his team of professors addressed in Annapolis. But what stood out the most to me was Judge Cordero's question: "I am planning a non-violence conference panel, and whether or not you are selected for the scholarship, based on your background, I would love to have you come and speak. Would you be willing?"

"Of course, I would love that." Three weeks later, true to her request, I delivered a speech to over two hundred judges and court officials at the Newseum, located on Pennsylvania Avenue in Washington, DC, and was paid to do it. After I spoke, officials rushed toward me and shook my hand, gave me hugs, and handed me business cards (which led to even more paid speaking engagements).

I was in my barracks room at the Naval Academy working on an engineering homework assignment when I got the call.

"Hello. Is this Midshipman Evans?"

"Yes, who's speaking?"

"This is Admiral Michael Miller, the Superintendent. I wanted to personally give you a call and congratulate you on being selected for the Truman Scholarship."

I got a national scholarship! I screamed in my head. Someone later told me that I was only the second African American to be selected for the Truman Scholarship in over ten years at USNA. Receiving a call from the Superintendent was in itself an honor. At USNA, we were used to seeing senior Officers, but having contact with the Superintendent was rare.

The news blew my mind, largely because I didn't think I was smart enough based on the stories and resumes I heard from the other candidates. Some may say to me, "You need to stop saying that" or "You are smart enough." That may be so, but mentally, it was hard for me at times to believe that. I drifted in and out of this mental rut because I still struggled to see myself as academically capable due to my South Side education. This is why I understand, psychologically, how youth from the hood or people in general who come from environments where achieving academic recognition is uncommon, struggle to believe in themselves at times. It's hard to dream something you cannot see. For many young African Americans, their perception of success is limited to a tunnel view of the basketball court, football field, or music studio. I'm not taking any power away from those dreams. I do believe that there are people who are called to those disciplines. But as a people, we need to develop the courage to challenge our youth to expand their minds and step into the dreams they are destined for. I hope this is a testimony to those like me who feel that way.

The next day, I got the email from Dr. Rich that I was selected for the Truman Scholarship. The Truman Foundation took a risk investing in me, a risk I will forever be thankful for.

I'd joined another gang.

CHAPTER 18

NUCLEAR POWER

IT TOOK ME LESS THAN TWENTY MINUTES TO MAKE TEN THOUSAND DOLLARS.

Each year, a small group of second class midshipmen, who are seeking an initial service assignment within the nuclear Navy, may be offered the opportunity to compete for appointments as Admiral Frank Bowman Scholars. My desire to service select nuclear submarines had remained an interest in the back of my mind since West Point SLS. Dr. Gillich's support and belief in me laid the foundation. Despite the strong gravitational pull around me, I remained open minded about all the service communities (jobs) within the Navy. I'd watched firsthand the dreadful effects of not doing so my plebe year.

One of my first class midshipmen at the time (let's call him John), had a yearning desire to service select Special Warfare. I'm not exactly sure if this dream started in his childhood or upon his arrival at Annapolis. Either way, from the moment he introduced himself, it was apparent he wanted to be a SEAL. He walked around wearing SEAL team shirts, and most of the leadership references that emitted from his mouth came from books written by Navy SEALs or from "sea stories."[15] Midshipmen and alumni from Annapolis know how daunting the selection process for SEALs can be. Mids are required to finish an in-house Naval Special Warfare screener with SEAL Officers and senior enlisted, as well as complete summer training under the evaluation of a SEAL team unit. The punchline is this: by the time service selection rolled around, seniors who passed these demanding prerequisites had a pretty good hunch if they would be selected or not.

I remember being gathered in a cluster around my classmates, waiting down the hallway corridors in excitement for our first class to emerge from the Wardroom with their service selection results. Next to me were a couple of chairs and barber clippers set up to shave the heads (completely bald, of course) of the seniors who service selected Marines, another USNA tradition. See, at Annapolis, service selection day is a yearly ritual in which all the seniors learn what their job will be.

Essentially, midshipmen submit a "dream sheet" of their preferred assignments, and based on the current needs of the Navy and Marine Corps and their class rank (a combination of academic standing, military performance evaluations, physical fitness, and conduct), each mid's fate is determined. They say that nine out of ten mids receive their first or second

---

15   In the US Navy, "sea stories" refers to the tales told by sailors recollecting their memories serving within the armed forces. This includes combat-mission oriented adventures or silly encounters.

choice. For every Academy graduate, it's one of those days you will never forget, a day full of anxious tension etched in the back of your brain. For some, it's a culmination of earning their dream job.

"I'm gonna be a pilot!"

"Yut!! Marine Corps!"

"SWO Mama!"

Various upperclassmen screamed their job titles as they emerged from the Wardroom holding their service selection certificates in their hands with big Kool-Aid smiles smeared across their faces. There was only one standout: John.

John was not selected to be a Navy SEAL. I watched as he burst from the room in tears. Here was a man who'd successfully completed all the required waypoints to become a Special Forces operator, who had everyone convinced the job was his, and still came up short. He bitterly passed the remainder of his time at USNA.

Another plebe responsibility was grabbing the upperclassmen's laundry every week. Each company had these large blue metal crates with wheels on them located at the end of their hallway. On a certain assigned day, laundry personnel would pick up the crates to clean and then deliver them back a few days later. It was then the responsibility of the plebes to sort the laundry and deliver it to the door of each upperclassman with the company.

That night, I was running around with three blue garment bags looped around my arm when I ran into Ms. Nisey in the p-way.

"Hey, Ms. Nisey, how are you today?"

"I'm blessed today, Evans. How are you?"

"I'm good. Just delivering some laundry. I'm sure you saw all the 1/C got their service selections today. Most got what they wanted. But one of ours didn't. It was surprising. He completed all the requirements to become a SEAL, but he didn't get it. He was distraught. I kinda felt bad for him. It was fucked up. Seemed like he wasted like three years of his life pursuing something he didn't even get."

"It's never a waste of time. Everything that young man went through is preparing him and leading him to the thing he was supposed to do originally. God never puts us through a situation we can't handle. Stay open to every opportunity that comes at you while you are here at Annapolis, Mr. Evans. That's what separates those who are great and rise above circumstances from those who don't."

"I understand. Thanks, Ms. Nisey. I gotta go finish this up before I get in trouble."

"Go ahead. I'll see you around. Have a good day. I love you."

After hearing Ms. Nisey's words, I promised myself I'd never let that be me. Although the goal to be a submariner was my first choice, I did my best to listen and let God guide me where he best saw fit.

Applying for the Bowman Scholarship was no different. Prior to being officially selected as a scholar, candidates are interviewed for the Navy's nuclear training pipeline. If selected for nuclear power and subsequently as a Bowman Scholar, the student would participate in a tailored research internship during one of the summer training blocks and partake in an independent research project their last year as a midshipman. To top it off, upon graduation from the Academy, scholars are offered graduate education at the Naval Postgraduate School, resulting in a master's degree in a technical discipline.

I didn't get the Bowman Scholarship, but I did become a finalist. As a result, I was able to complete a nuclear internship at the Air Force Institute of Technology (AFIT), a graduate and research facility located on Wright-Patterson Air Force base in Ohio. It also opened the door for me to join another gang.

* * * *

I WAS ASKED to interview early for the Navy nuclear power program. Unlike with the other service selections at the Academy, midshipmen with a desire to qualify for the nuclear pipeline onboard submarine and aircraft carriers could do so early their junior year. My Battalion Officer, a submariner at the time, pulled me into his office for a talk on the matter.

"Would you like to interview early for nuclear power? I saw you became a finalist for the Bowman scholarship."

"I'll think about it, sir."

He proceeded to speak to me about his career. But he didn't try to sway me. He more so talked about what it was like for him. The conversation itself was actually refreshing because he didn't sound like a salesman. It was personal. After my initial conversation with the CAPT, I was asked three more times by other submarine Officers on the yard if I wanted to interview. The answer was always "no." It's not that I didn't want to go subs, I just didn't want to rush the process. I wanted to be sure that the decision I made was the right one. If I did not early select now, I still had senior year to interview as well.

I called Ms. Janie Mines for advice.

Everyone needs a mentor who will keep them accountable and whom they look to for advice who understands what they are going through and can provide solid wisdom. For me, that person was Ms. Mines.

Between the two of us, we had formed our own little inspirational gang.

"They keep asking me to interview. I don't know what to do," I said. I called her every week.

"Just do it, baby. Give it a shot. You never know where God will take you," she said in a sweet Southern accent. She had a momma bear personality.

I never had the chance to study much for the interview due to my busy engineering workload, so the night before, I didn't do any schoolwork. I stayed up late and studied.

I racked out of bed at 0400 the next day and boarded the large blue USNA coach bus that took us mids to Naval Reactors (NR) in Washington, DC. As expected, we were excused from our classes and the Academy's strenuous daily routine. I tore off my service dress blue jacket and placed it on the seat next to me. Around the rest of the bus, a few mids chowed down on their cold box breakfasts while the rest of us slept the whole commute.

In a nutshell, NR is a government agency responsible for the safe operation of the Navy's nuclear power program. The building itself was located on the Washington Naval Yard, a former ordnance/shipyard now turned administrative base. Walking into the building, I vividly remember being escorted to the "waiting room," a small conference room full of chairs and dead silence. Back then, the first part of the two-stage interview process focused on technical questions in physics, chemistry, and math administered by two different NR staff members. They were usually active duty or reserve nukes dressed in civilian attire. With our school transcripts in hand, the guardians of NR had a slight perspective on the level of knowledge we mids should possess and what courses we struggled with the most. They used this to their advantage to attack us poor mids with challenging questions tailored toward our majors as well. For those smart midshipmen forced to go nuke who pretended to act stupid because they didn't want to be selected, NR staff took notes on their performance and forwarded it to the Admiral.

We sat there within the dimly lit waiting room in silence, scared that if we spoke the staff would listen in on us.

The wait was unreal.

No one dared leave the room for a bathroom break or any variant of refreshment in fear they'd miss their place in line if their name was called. Every now and then, a staff member would enter through the door, call a name from a sheet of paper, and direct us to follow the footsteps on the floor plan. I twiddled my thumbs between my hands for what felt like hours until someone finally called my name. I followed a Lieutenant outside the room, and he escorted me to a roughly eight-by-eight-foot one-person office space where I would meet my fate. I wouldn't see my classmates again until the end of the day.

At the other end of the desk, a man wearing a blue dress shirt and black tie stared back at me. My stomach turned with nervousness. A speckle of light beamed from his glasses when he asked me to sit down.

"Let's start simple," he said.

He took a sheet of paper from the cabinet and drew out a physics problem for me to solve. The multipurpose copy paper scraped against the gray desk as he slid it before me. I glanced down to observe what looked to be a classic mechanics momentum versus friction problem. I picked up the yellow pencil. Its barrel was greasy to the touch from my moist, frantic fingers. I solved the problem after a few minutes.

"Okay, good. Try this."

The gentleman pulled out another sheet and created a question that involved concepts of water buoyancy and the Archimedes principle. *Damn, it was a topic from my naval architecture major.*

I tried to write out the "givens" for the problem but ended up short in concluding a final answer. "What about this?" "What about that?" The NR member threw me a few bones for hints, but not enough to give the solution away. After struggling through for a few more minutes, I somehow managed to obtain the correct answer.

"Okay, that's it. You're done. Walk out and follow the floor plan to your next interview." I shot to my feet and scurried out.

I don't remember much about my second interview. My most vivid memories at NR revolve around my first evaluation and final talk with the Admiral. Nonetheless, what I do know is I didn't fail either of the first two interviews. If I had, I would require a third one. It took another three hours of waiting around, playing on my cell phone or watching the movement of the second hand on the wall clock before I realized my name wouldn't be called again.

Holy crap, it looked like I passed.

The middle of the day commenced with my classmates and me being escorted to a cafeteria area where we could buy lunch. It was hard for us to eat because we knew the process wasn't over. We still had to be accepted into the program by the Admiral. Sitting around the table, we shared stories of our interview experiences, many of them similar in nature. That was by far one of the most nerve wracking adventures I had ever been on. Like an artery about to burst under pressure, most of our feelings were heightened by the fact that we'd waited around in anticipation for so long.

My final interview was with the director of Naval Reactors at the time, CAPT John M. Richardson. My classmates and I gathered into an enclosed briefing room and waited for our names to be called. For those of you who haven't heard the rumors that come with interviewing with the nuclear director, the process has changed dramatically since Hyman Rickover's time. Admiral Rickover would make candidates stand in a broom closet for up to three hours if they gave him a response to a question he deemed was a stupid answer. Or he might have them sit down in a chair with purposely shortened front legs. The list of creative antics he employed was endless. When I interviewed, nobody was asked to do anything out of character or ridiculous except write reports on books the CAPT thought were interesting.

"Evans," a Lieutenant Commander (LCDR) called and directed me to the director's door. I stood outside waiting, still unsure of whether or not I wanted to select submarines or nuclear surface warfare (SWO). It's a job similar to being a submariner except that my leadership and advanced schooling would be applied to the maintenance and operation of nuclear power on board US Navy aircraft carriers instead of submarines. I knew my life would be drastically different depending on the job I picked, so I pulled two Officers aside—one a submariner, the other a nuke SWO—and asked about their experiences.

"Excuse me, can you two go through the advantages and disadvantages of subs versus nuke SWO?"

Like a great debate, they went at it. The two seasoned Officers argued back and forth right in front of me about why their respective community was better. Five minutes passed before

I saw one of my classmates emerge from the door. I was next. After hearing the debate, plus what I already knew, I followed the feeling in my gut and decided subs. I slowly walked into CAPT Richardson's office and sat down. A Naval Academy graduate, he was a skinny man with a long oval head, pointed ears, and a large forehead. Not to be stereotypical or anything, but the man just looked smart.

"Why do you want to go subs?"

"I like how tight knit the community is. Everyone genuinely wants to be there and feels like they belong. Plus, nuclear power has always fascinated me. Many of my mentors are submariners," I responded.

I told him the story of my nuclear physics exposure at West Point SLS. He didn't say a word or seem to acknowledge my answer. He just kept staring down at an open file on his desk. It was my academic record. He looked up. Then he began attacking me on certain grades I had achieved at USNA, in particular, my scores in cyber class.

"What happened in cyber security? You did really well in all your other technical courses. Why is that?"

"I'm not sure, sir. I did the best I could."

He also questioned my class ranking and why it was so low. The entire time, his tone was not abrasive or condescending but stern.

"You can leave."

I walked out of the office not knowing what my fate would be. The LCDR walked back into the CAPT's office and asked me to wait outside. Two minutes later, he emerged from behind the door and shook my hand.

"Congratulations. Welcome to the naval nuclear power program."

That was my five minutes of fame with the director of nuclear power.

I'd just joined one of the most secretive, esteemed gangs in the world.

A few days later, I woke up from a nap to my phone chiming. I picked up the device and glanced at the notification message from USAA. "A deposit of $10,000 has posted to your checking account ending in XXXX."

It was my nuclear bonus.

* * * *

THAT WEEKEND I went by the Bandes home to visit. Craig manned the grill and made his famous barbeque wings. Momma T and the kids went around the dinner table and shared stories of their week. At about 2200, the house was still. Tara and the kids were sound asleep. Craig and I stayed up to have a serious talk. Because he was a man of few words when it came to advice, Poppa C and I seldom had deep conversations, but when we did, they stuck.

"Dre, I want to talk to you about work-life balance. I remember when you first came by the house. You sat right there at the kitchen counter and didn't move for hours. We went to the store with the kids, cooked dinner, and watched a family movie, and you studied the entire time. I know you work your ass off, and I respect that, but you have to make time for yourself. Trust me, I was the same way at your age. But Tara taught me the importance of balance," he said while taking a sip of his Red Stripe Jamaican beer.

Over the years, beer had become a common ground for Poppa C and me. The majority of my visits to the Bandes home usually began with one being thrust into my hands with the phrase, "You want a beer?" or "Have you tried this flavor yet?" Their tall gray refrigerator was a stockpile of an assortment of flavors.

"It's hard, yo. There are so many things I have to accomplish in what feels like so little time. I just want to be able to lay my head on my pillow at night, look up at the ceiling, and know that I made the most of the gifts God put in me and the opportunities presented to me. I want to look back on my life and say I died on 'E,' that I truly emptied out my potential tank," I responded.

"It's great to be driven, but balance is important, too. Try to complete as much as you can, but use your weekends to relax and recharge. I know you've seen and been through a lot. But that's the past. You're young. It's time to start really enjoying life now. If you don't, you'll look back on it in regret. And I don't want to see that happen to you. Okay?" Poppa C got up from his stool and gave me a tight hug.

Poppa C was right. My greatest strength turned out to also be my greatest weakness. I worked so hard that I would stress myself out. Craig's advice came at the right time for me in my life. When I stopped to think about it, I was burned out by school, by all the military training, by the long hours of studying, and by pressure. His words of wisdom resonated with me and allowed me to enjoy the rest of my junior and senior years at the Academy.

CHAPTER 19

THE PASSION OF COMMAND

DEFY ALL ODDS.

Believe in yourself.

Step outside of what you think is possible.

That's what God pushed me to do in that season of my life.

At the end of my 2/C year, the usual crowding of my USNA Gmail began. I received various messages about internships and military training billets open for the summer. Because I'd graduated from NAPS, I entertained the idea of going back to Newport to become a detailer. It seemed like a sweet gig based on what I'd observed during my time there as a student. My tenth Company Officer at the time was CAPT Drexel King, a tall African American Marine Corps Officer and former USNA grad. Throbbing veins navigated his arms and neck, and his athletic build only confirmed his former days as a football player. Generally speaking, your Company Officer oversaw the well-being of the midshipmen within his or her respective company.

On the other end of the leadership spectrum was our senior enlisted leader (SEL) Chief Lori Files. She was a passionate, Christian woman with a high-pitched voice that complemented her short stature. There was never a day where she failed to wear a hard smile on her face. She was always positive and exhibited a kid-like sphere of energy. As an SEL, she was the most senior enlisted service member and acted as an advisor to the Company Officer. In order to qualify as a detailer for NAPS or Plebe Summer, 2/C were obligated to complete an interview with a panel of midshipmen, Officers, and enlisted chiefs. I remember standing outside the small Second Battalion conference room for mine.

"Midshipman Evans," a voice said from within.

I guess that meant they were ready for me.

Following standard Navy procedures, I knocked three times on the door and blurted with confidence, "Sir, Midshipman 2/C Evans, respectfully request permission to come aboard."

"Come aboard," the voice commanded.

I briskly walked in, feeling the smooth surface of the blue carpet under my polished black shoes. I sat at the end of a narrow rectangular table in the center of the room.

At the beginning of the evaluation, I mentioned to the board my desire to become a detailer at NAPS. "Why do you want to be a detailer?" and "What could you bring to the table?" were questions I recollect. I knew I didn't fit the mold of a typical or model midshipman, but the ammunition I carried with me was my authenticity. I was barbarically honest about my thoughts on leadership and what the Naval Academy meant to me. I didn't attempt to speak from my lips what sounded good or what I thought the panel wanted to hear.

Take a step back and think about it. If you enter an interview as the underdog or if everyone around you is just as qualified, what makes you as an individual stand out? What are you going to do or say that will make them remember you?

Tell a story.

My opportunities with public speaking taught me that people respond best to and remember stories. If asked a question, stop, think about it first, then share a compelling narrative that relates to the question at hand and answer it.

In the end, the interview felt like it went by fast.

The next day, CAPT King approached me in the p-way after morning meal formation. His notoriously stern Marine gaze met mine. Aligned with the way my parents raised me to listen or communicate with others, I looked CAPT King back directly in the eyes. "Evans, you made it to the next round. You have another interview with the Battalion Officers and the Brigade Commander tomorrow."

I didn't give much thought or response to his order. *Sure, I guess that's good*, I thought. I was under the impression that I did well and that this next board would be to consider me for a more senior billet at NAPS, such as Battalion or Company Commander.

At Annapolis, the Brigade Commander is the most senior ranked midshipman who sports six striped shoulder boards, and leads roughly 4,500 midshipmen daily.[16] A rewarding position only given to a select few, he or she has frequent contact and mentorship from the Commandant, Superintendent, and the four Battalion Officers.

Today was interview day. I glanced over at my dress blue navy uniform hanging on a black curtain in my barracks room. The beam of sunlight cast a glow over the four colorful ribbons placed above the blouse breast pocket. I preferred wearing dress blues over whites because the uniform was easier to clean and looked like an actual suit. To get ready, I wrapped the white dress shirt around my chest and fastened the clear buttons. I fit the ironed black tie snuggly around my neck. My pressed black trousers were held in place with a belt and fit flush with my polished shoes. I looked at myself one last time in the mirror to check for discrepancies.

It was time.

The interview took place in the Commandant's office located near the main entrance of Bancroft Hall. Coliseum-like cherry

---

16 See Addendum for the full breakdown of midshipmen striper leadership positions.

doors greeted me when I walked up to enter his office quarters. At the top of the doors, large gold letters read "COMMANDANT OF MIDSHIPMEN."

I knocked on the door.

A silver-barred Lieutenant Officer appeared before the entranceway and asked me to step in. I believe it was the DANT's (short for Commandant) aid. *SLAM.* The doors closed loudly and echoed in the hallway. My eyes glanced around. To the left and right of the passageway were trophy cases of awards of all shapes and sizes from Naval Academy varsity athletics. Looking up, I saw portraits of all the noble men and women who'd served as the Commandant since the school's founding decorating the walls. Toward the back left of the entryway, there was a brown door where midshipmen could find the DANT's personal office and his assistants. Directly in front of me was the conference room.

Again, following my plebe training for entering a superior's office, I knocked three times and respectfully asked for permission to enter. "Enter," I heard a deep male voice say. I walked through the door. The conference room table was so long I had to square my feet around it to get to the center of the room. When I made it to the middle of the table, I stood there at attention, my fists rolled tightly in quarters and pressed against the sides of my trousers. From this vantage point, the long table faced me horizontally, and a board of Officers and midshipmen sat on my left and right sides. Just like my last interview, I started off by attempting to explain my interest in wanting to serve at NAPS as a detailer, but I was quickly cut off. This interview was different.

"Mr. Evans, it does not matter what you desire. Every midshipman we interview will first be considered for Regimental Commander (REG CMDR). Other positions will be assigned based on how we see fit," Colonel Kohmuench, the senior board member asserted.

Similar to the Brigade Commander during the academic year, the REG CMDR was the highest ranked midshipman in charge of Plebe Summer. The face of the Naval Academy, he or she led parades, completed news interviews, issued the oath of office, and was featured in countless USNA brochures, articles, and photos.

"One of the hardest challenges with being the Regimental Commander is leading your own peers. What would you do to engage them when motivation is low?" the Brigade Commander asked.

I thought about Hadiya Pendleton, the fifteen-year-old girl shot to death in broad daylight on the South Side of Chicago. An honor student at King, Hadiya was enjoying a warm January day with a group of classmates when a gunman opened fire into Harsh Park. How could a girl, with light brown skin, a sweet smile, and innocent face be mistaken for a rival gang member? Her death still cuts deep at the bone for me. Hadiya was shot just a mile from where President Barack Obama lived in the Hyde Park community, and blocks away from my alma mater high school. Just like my brothers and me, who'd performed at Obama's first presidential inauguration with the marching band at King, Hadiya was a majorette who performed for his second. Hadiya's murder became a symbol of Chicago's struggle to adequately address gun violence, which claimed more than a thousand lives that year. First Lady Michelle Obama attended Hadiya's nationally televised funeral, where she met some of the girl's closest friends, including my cousin whom I grew up with, Quiana Flynn. I was in my room at the Naval Academy when I saw the news. Seeing Quiana hurt and crying on TV angered me. Then they showed the gunman and his getaway driver's photographs. They were my classmates at King, Michael Ward and Kenneth Williams.

I sat in class right next to Hadiya's killers.

"Mr. Evans, what would you do?" someone said.

I snapped back to the present. At this point the room had grown silent for several moments.

But I remember my response like it was yesterday.

"My 'why' that wakes me up every morning are my family and the experiences I went through growing up in Chicago. I translate that into my role as a leader. I'd stay connected to my classmates by continuously engaging with them on the deck plates.[17] I'd leverage their unique talents and skills and empower them to lead. I'd listen to their concerns and build key relationships with other leaders in the Regiment who would help carry and spread my vision. This would in turn convert others who did not yet fully believe or were hesitant. They'd see my passion through the way I speak to others and how I conduct myself before the Regiment during physical training, military evolutions, and

---

17   A Navy way of saying "floor." The "deck plates" are referred to as the common areas where the people you lead see you most.

parades. I'd remind my classmates to never fail to be selfless in our leadership and impact on others. As detailers, let's not look back in regret that we didn't give our all to train and lay the foundation for future Navy and Marine Corps Officers."

To conclude my session, a few other questions about my class ranking were posed before I was asked to leave.

The interview lasted twenty minutes.

"Midshipman Evans, can you please come see me?" It was CAPT King. His tall, built structure blocked the entryway of my door. I was sitting at the desk in my room, busy completing school work, but I got up immediately and followed him into Chief Files's office. They shut the door. CAPT King's eyes and serious face beamed at me for what felt like minutes before he finally spoke.

"You've been selected as the Plebe Summer Regimental Commander," he said. I tilted my head to the side and squinted my eyes at him. My entire demeanor turned serious. *He's gotta be playing a joke on me, right?*

"Excuse me?" I replied.

"The Naval Academy has selected you to be the Plebe Summer Regimental Commander."

"I'm sorry, sir. I thought that's what you said. I just don't believe you. I asked to be a detailer at NAPS. There's gotta be a mistake."

"No, Evans. They picked you for a reason. It's yours."

I was told by multiple staff, alumni, mentors, and peers that I became one of the first Black Plebe Summer Regimental Commanders in Naval Academy history.

I would be the face of the United States Naval Academy.

Giving news interviews, speaking with parents, leading drill parades, leading PT each morning, and briefing and meeting senior officers. The number one person in charge: me.

I was truly humbled and thankful.

I didn't measure up to any of the stereotypes associated with what a "model" midshipman selected for a high-ranking leadership position was supposed to look and act like. Instead, I was a Black boy from the hood of Chicago, wasn't ranked at the top among his peers, wasn't White, and did not have perfect flowing blond hair.

"Ironic, isn't it?" CAPT King said.

"How is that?"

"Your youngster year—remember how we used to meet weekly for mentorship? You sat right there in my chair and vented about the midshipmen in leadership and the lack of diversity. You said you would do things differently if given the chance."

I slouched back in the brown chair and shook my head in disbelief. Then I looked up to stare at the stale white ceiling as if hoping for God to appear and speak before me. *What are you doing, Lord? What the hell is going on?* I had a hard time trying to wrap my head around the fact that Annapolis would let me be a prominent symbol for the school. I couldn't see it at the time, but I was struggling to recognize the power of greatness God put inside me.

The battle was in my mind.

Being Black at Annapolis had its challenges. Right out of the gate, the odds were stacked against us. Although admission rates have risen, I looked around and still didn't see many midshipmen who looked like me. Statistically, at that time, White students composed roughly 64 percent of the midshipman population while Black students composed only 7 percent. White students came from wealthier families and had a higher rate of graduating.

On the other end of the spectrum, many of the midshipmen of color unknowingly held themselves back. Society did a number on me *and them*. Imagine saying all your life that you would prove the naysayers wrong and yet end up doing the exact opposite by cowering away. I noticed that the adversity fed the insecurities Black mids felt and strengthened the chip on their shoulders. It's social conditioning, a version of Stockholm Syndrome, that lets you believe that you can't do better because the "White man" is going to hold you back. Many fell into this "us versus them" mentality.

I became president of my own gang at Annapolis: the Midshipmen Black Studies Club (MBSC).

It was a senior billet, but I was chosen as a junior. I spoke to many Black mids who felt hopeless. They used racism as the reason why they failed to succeed academically. I did my best to plead with them not to drop out, including sharing my personal story about Anthony.

"My brother was kicked out of the Academy when I was a plebe. I don't want you to make a short-term decision based on how you feel now and regret it later," I said. "I literally know kids in Chicago who would kill you for your spot here at USNA. Don't waste that."

Black culture is vastly different from that of White; social interactions vary. But learning how to engage with people from different backgrounds is a necessary part of life. Although I do acknowledge that the road may be harder for us, that is not an excuse to quit or not perform to the best of our abilities.

You control how you allow people to affect you and the amount of effort you give toward work.

I'd always thought that the mission of the MBSC organization was important, and I believed it was vital for minorities to provide guidance and support for one another, especially behind the walls of a military environment where some of our disadvantages were hidden and not even known. Poor public perception and cynical attitudes toward the organization were my main obstacles. Every day was difficult. Reestablishing relationships with Officers and midshipmen to support MBSC was tough and required patience. I was trying to change the narrative of not only the Brigade, but also of how Black midshipmen viewed themselves. I wanted them to be filled with hope and promise and to see themselves as more at Annapolis.

It was hard.

So how did we do it?

The first step was engaging the community. My staff and I sent out over twenty emails to the Brigade, posted flyers, and even recruited through word of mouth. Within three months, we welcomed over 138 new and returning members—and not all Black. Persistent, I pressed on. I'll never forget how, when we first started, MBSC only had $129.48 in its operating account. My team and I established a fundraising committee, and within four months, MBSC raised over $17,707. We used these funds for outreach in the Maryland and DC area and USNA. Our programs spread far and wide—activities that included feeding the homeless, tutoring youth, financial workshops, engineering workshops, and leadership/mentorship socials. We even established partnerships with other groups on the yard and hosted joint events. This motivated me to dream further. That summer, I wrote a letter to Michelle Obama, requesting she speak at USNA in honor of MBSC for Black History Month.

I sent Mrs. Obama over thirty letters.

On August 30, 2014, I received a personal letter from her.

She could not attend because of prior commitments. But she thanked me for my diligent outreach efforts. She thanked me for sharing my story and for my service, and she thanked me for being from Chicago.

It still took me another two weeks to process the fact that I was selected as the Plebe Summer Regimental Commander. Once

I overcame the initial shock, I had to prepare for the role and convince myself that I deserved it. I had a mix of emotions all in one: nervousness, fear, and excitement. What occupied my mind the most was what I would say to my detailers and plebes for the first time. I could picture their bulging eyes and faces standing before me, hanging onto whatever words I spoke out of the crevices of my lips. We all know just how important first impressions are, especially in a leadership-driven laboratory like USNA.

I'd been given the opportunity of a lifetime. Would I rise up and defy statistics, or fold?

I made myself ready through hours of mental visualization. I pictured myself in the role until it felt normal. At around 0300 in the morning, the streets of Annapolis, Maryland, were deserted. Like a zombie apocalypse, it was as if human life was no more. No cars could be found rumbling on the roads. Everyone was inside the comfort of their homes sound asleep. Yet my spirit had a different agenda. My fear was the alarm clock that woke me in the middle of the night one weekend at the Bandes house. I slid on my neon-green New Balance shoes, threw on some basketball shorts, and headed outside.

"You're not good at art; you're not good at playing trombone; you're not smart. You ain't shit."

Dwayne's words rang in the back of my head. I took off jogging with a slow stride. I didn't bring any water, and my stomach was empty. I could feel the insides of my intestines moaning and scratching for food, making the first few moments of the jog painful. Truthfully, my body wanted to stop. *Keep going,* my mind said. I needed to reinvent myself. I had to prove him wrong.

I pressed on.

After a while, like an hourglass being filled with sand, I could feel my levels of confidence rise. The blood in my veins grew hot. Sweat dripped from my shirtless body while I ran in the middle of the street. I was focused. Running at night, alone with myself, allowing the weight of my thoughts and my fears about the adversities I would face run off my shoulders...it was liberating.

I dug deep and envisioned myself in the future. I imagined myself leading the Plebe Summer Regiment on a jog. The more I reflected on that image, the more confident I grew, and the more I continued to believe in myself and trust the process God was putting me through. The humid Annapolis sun beat down on our perspiring bodies. I could see a gang of plebes dressed in white shirts and a company of detailers sporting bright yellow tees. And I was their leader. Me. Out there late at night, with my feet slapping the pavement with each stride, I redefined and sharpened my ideology on leadership.

"WE STARTED...TOGETHER...WE GONNA FINISH... TOGETHER...WE STARTED...TOGETHER...WE GONNA FINISH...TOGETHER," I screamed. In my mind, the Regiment repeated my chant after me.

I made it to the Naval Academy bridge and continued the chant under my breath. I always hated the run up because it was more difficult. I extended my stride and tried to run up the bridge to get to the top faster. My hope continued to grow.

Slam.

I tripped on my feet and landed on my face. It came out of nowhere. I let out a long, frustrated puff of air and shook my head. I allowed myself to lie there in the middle of the road. For several minutes, I didn't move. I let the darkness of the night and road swallow me whole. I thought about Ms. Nisey's words the other day when she stopped me in King Hall.

"I heard about what happened. All us Black servers here in King Hall. We talk. And we know what goes on within these walls of Bancroft."

"I don't know what you're talking about, Ms. Nisey," I responded with a scrunched-up face. "Why you talkin' crazy?"

"Boy, don't play me. Stop that right now. You know what I'm talking about. Being the Regimental Commander." She slapped me on the hand.

I put my head down. "I have mixed feelings about it."

"Raise your head up right now. Look at me."

I kept my head bowed down toward the floor.

"I said look at me." She gripped my two cheeks together with her right hand and raised my head up. I looked into her dark brown eyes. An army of freckles surrounded her face.

"Dontchu ever put your head down as a Black man. You hear me? You can do this. You have to do this. This is bigger than you. Not every day we get a Black Regimental Commander. You are making history. You have to do this for us," she pointed to her skin and rubbed it. "We are counting on you. We are so proud of you Andre."

A tear rolled down her cheek.

Then Dwayne appeared before me.

And he said those words.

"You ain't shit. You won't be anything."

I'll prove you wrong.

My gut screamed with fire.

I have to show Chicago...my family...everyone at the Naval Academy...that I am made of something.

I rose from my feet slowly and looked into the sky.

It's time. At some point there is no excuse. Either you'll do everything it takes to make it happen, or you don't.

I got up and finished my jog back to the Bandes house. The sun began to peek over the horizon.

When I walked through the front door, I was reborn as a new man. Realizing my potential is what my journey has been all about. After that night with myself and the dark, I learned to accept my new destiny and face it head on.

I learned a critical lesson: don't belittle your worth. You are capable of achieving unimaginable success if you embrace the energy God put inside you and allow it to direct you forward.

Envision your success and where you want to be in life.

* * * *

LIEUTENANT COLONEL WILLIAM Kohmuench (or LCK for short) was the Officer in Charge (OIC) of Plebe Summer. He was responsible for the overall leadership and direction of all the Officers, senior enlisted, midshipmen, and plebes. Rumor has it that in the warzone of Afghanistan, he was known among Marines for his infectious ability to inspire and lead—his guidance of combat logistics patrols and rescue of a downed aircraft in the heat of battle made this evident. A die-hard Marine, he wore a serious poker face and had a shiny, egg-shaped bald head. Around the yard, he was known for his awkward sense of humor.

Because I was the Regimental Commander, I had the privilege of working alongside him. At the time, I had never interacted with a senior Officer one-on-one for a significant amount of time. Each day, I visited his big square office located across the p-way from my room. I could literally poke my head out the door and see LCK with his black square-framed glasses that dangled on the tip of his nose, usually an indication that he was reading something. Like any good mentor should, Colonel Kohmuench made an effort to groom my proficiency as a leader—starting with my appearance.

"Try on all your uniforms and come see me for inspection," he said one morning. Top to bottom, bit by bit, he tore me apart. With my feet firmly placed together, I stood tall at attention in my bright white uniform in the middle of the p-way outside his office.

"When you inspect a sailor, you start at the top, and in a snake-like pattern, make your way down their entire uniform." He demonstrated with his own hand. His fingers were pressed completely together to make a flat palmed gesture we like to call the "knife hand."[18] In similar fashion, he started at the top of my head by examining my combination cover. Midshipmen and Officers know just how hard it is to keep the top cloth-like layer of the hat clean. You must rewash the material and hope all the stains are removed or buy a new one. Any mark of dirt or blemishes on the cover was considered a "hit."[19] Gold colored buttons that screwed in on both sides held a black strap in place that ran alongside the bottom seam of the cap. The trick was to use superglue to keep the gold eagle infused buttons upright.

"Remove your cover." I did as I was told and placed it upright, facing forward, in my hand. LCK leaned forward to examine my Navy regulation haircut: neat, clean, and well-groomed with no hair to extend greater than three quarters of an inch, and no hair on the back of the neck touching the collar.

---

18 The "knife hand" is one of the most effective weapons at the disposal of a military leader. It's used by drill instructors to instill fear and respect in new recruits, discipline troops, emphasize a point while talking, and point out things that are deemed important.

19 A "hit" is a common term used in the military to refer to errors or discrepancies.

Pass.

Moving on, he inspected my nose hairs and critiqued the quality of my clean-shaven face. No loose follicles. No missed hair spots.

Check.

He whipped out a small blue ruler and placed it under my ribbon rack. It was correctly centered and placed a quarter of an inch above the pocket. Every small string of fabric that protruded from the uniform was cut off.

Double check.

The next critique was my shoulder boards. LCK removed them, took out a lighter, and used it to burn the edges to give them a crisp finish. He brushed the top surface of the mesh-like material.

"Make sure you do this any time you purchase new shoulder boards. People will notice how clean they look."

Roger that.

He made his way to my waistline and examined my belt buckle. It was supposed to be polished and wiped clean of any fingerprints. Loose strings from the belt loop were to be removed.

Check.

One last thing: my shoes.

"Just a sec, I'll be back," LCK said. He ran back into the office and emerged from it holding a black ball point pen. "Turn around." I did as I was told and pivoted my body.

Tap. Tap. Tap.

To test if my heels were worn out, he would attempt to slide a pencil or pen under the back heel of my shoe. If he could, it was concluded I needed new heels.

I failed.

For the next hour or so, LCK examined every uniform I had in my closet and made me fix the discrepancies until each one was perfect.

At the end of my senior year, LCK retired from over twenty years of service as an Officer in the United States Marine Corps. I still keep his retirement pamphlet tucked into the center of my Officer cover.

Looking back, I appreciate LCK for taking the time to show me the importance of maintaining a proper uniform.

"Perception is reality" was a common phrase spoken from the lips of staff and midshipmen alike at Annapolis. I didn't realize it then, but when you speak and engage with others, your naval uniform is the first thing people notice. If your black shoes look like polished glass, your attire is wrinkle-free, and your uniform is sharp looking, you have already proven, without speaking, that you have honor in your appearance as a man and military professional. I learned that more than half the battle in being a great leader is about the image you portray and how you carry yourself.

That day, I distinctly remember the eyes of the workers. The way they watered and glistened with pride when LCK informed them I was selected as the Regimental Commander. The community of service professionals went above and beyond to make sure I not only looked good in my uniforms, but they also reminded me on a daily basis of who I was—a hardworking, middle class kid from Chicago. "Make it count, Evans," they would say. "Make it count."

And make it count, I did.

Wednesday, July 1, 2015

Annapolis, Maryland

1800 EST

"You guys ready?"

I bellowed in a deep voice to alert the attention of my staff members. Everyone lined up and took his or her place within the "wedge," a five-person military formation that depicted the shape of a half-cut diamond. At the very front was the Commander. Shoulder left behind me was my Regimental Adjutant. Behind me to the right, my Regimental XO. To the left and right at the very ends of the wedge, my Regimental OPS or another senior "striper." I glanced down and touched the gold handle of my long silver sword that hung at my side. I made sure the black belt that held it in place fit snugly around my waist. I then looked down at my feet to check my shoes. Great, they were tied. Everything seemed to be in place the way it should be.

"Forward, march!"

A shot of nervousness surged through me when my staff and I began our processional march out the large dungeon-like corridor doors of Bancroft Hall. As I approached the first descending temple of gray steps, my conscience said, *Dre, you can do this.* The magnitude of the large group gathered within T-court came clearly into view. It was mesmerizing. I could see reporters with microphones and white light TV cameras posted near the flagpoles. Families and friends congregated behind the low white cobblestone walls that prevented crowds from entering the center of T-court. And then there were the 250 detailers and 1,192 plebes, all dressed in their blinding, bright all-white uniforms. I'd never stood before a crowd this vast in size. There had to be at least 3,000 outside. My staff and I stood there at attention for roughly ten minutes while the immense crowd just stared at us. The sun was still in full bloom as it beamed down on us before the start of the Oath of Office Ceremony. It was my moment. *Now, Dre, now.*

"REGIMENT!!! AHHH-TEN-HUT!!!"

I yelled at the top of my lungs to command my detailers and plebes to snap to attention. Superintendent Vice Admiral (VADM) Ted Carter walked out of the corridor and approached the church-like podium placed at the top of the stairs. The roar of the crowd grew silent. Thousands of eager eyes stared at

VADM Carter in his very own dress white uniform as he leaned his thin lips toward the black mic to speak.

"Here, more than ever before, you will be challenged morally, mentally, and physically. It's not supposed to be easy. Plebe Summer is pressure with a purpose."

At that moment, it felt as if everything in the atmosphere stopped moving. The birds stopped flying and took position within the trees that lined Stribling Walk. The squirrels perked up. VADM Carter's words echoed across the yard.

Commandant Colonel Stephen Liszewski was the next to speak at the podium. He had a slim athletic build, with veins that protruded from his arms and neck, and he limped slightly whenever he walked. When he spoke, his baritone voice was composed and confident.

The last step in the ceremony was to issue the Oath of Office to the Class of 2019 plebes. Colonel Liszewski slowly raised the palm of his right hand to the side of his crisply pressed uniform. Then he commanded the plebes to do the same.

"Class of 2019, raise your right hand."

The next set of words that came out of his mouth would change their lives forever and mark the official beginning of Plebe Summer.

"Having been appointed a midshipman in the United States Navy, do you solemnly swear (or affirm) that you will support and defend

the Constitution of the United States against all enemies, foreign and domestic; that you will bear true faith and allegiance to the same; that you take this obligation freely, without any mental reservation or purpose of evasion; and that you will well and faithfully discharge the duties of the office on which you are about to enter, so help me god."

"I DO!!!!!!"

The entire Plebe Regiment screamed back in response at the top of their lungs. Plebe Summer had commenced, and I didn't mess up on my first day as the Regimental Commander. Immediately, my detailers began yelling at the plebes to hurry inside. Family and friends watched as their loved ones disappeared behind the walls of Mother B. You could see the fear on the plebes' faces, many of them thinking, "What the hell did I just get myself into?" At the top of the stairs, two Gunnery Sergeant Marines stood at parade rest. They came to attention and then proceeded to close the enormous front doors of Bancroft Hall.

SLAM.

The doors shut with a thunderous roar that echoed across T-court.

That summer, and for the rest of the year, God gave me the privilege to finally turn the negative narrative of my plebe year. I received positive comments from my peers and was ranked at the top of my class. I felt thankful.

CHAPTER 20

GRADUATION

Monday, May 23, 2016

Annapolis, Maryland

1210 EST

IT WAS COMMISSIONING WEEK at Annapolis, and I was dressed in my whites. In two days, I would march across the stage and graduate. I walked down the long spiral staircase in fifth wing and into one of the side doors entering King Hall. The moment I walked through the double white doors, I saw Ms. Nisey leaning against the wall. I approached her.

"Hey, Ms. Nisey, how are you today?"

"I'm good, baby. Look at you all dressed up. You look so hand-some," she remarked with a bright smile. Over the years, we'd developed a close relationship with all our talks during meals about life at Annapolis, God, and family. But her next set of words I'll never forget.

"I'm so proud of you. You completed your journey," she said with a serious face. I could see a line of water begin to form in her eyes.

"Why? I didn't do anything."

"Yes, you did. Everyone has twenty-four hours...twenty-four hours... You had the same amount of time as the rest of these midshipmen running around here, but you chose to do something different with it. You did a lot for us and this community. Never forget that."

She touched my arm.

Everyone needs a reminder of what is important in life or a kick in the ass to get them on the right path. I've been blessed to have many mentors like Ms. Mines, CAPT King, and LCK, but I've come to realize that Ms. Nisey was the guardian angel that looked out for me at Annapolis.

Wednesday, May 25, 2016

Navy & Marine Corps Stadium

0500 EST

I finally made it to graduation day at the United States Naval Academy.

I couldn't have done it without God and the support of numerous teachers, mentors, friends, and family. It took years of hard work and stress: over 465 hours of studying, 1,460 days of little to no sleep, and over 500 hours of extra instruction from my professors. Now was my time to bask in that appreciation.

It was like any other beautiful May day in Annapolis. The sun's rays were bright and beamed down on all 1,076 of us. I was in my choker white Navy uniform. In the service, they called it choker whites because the collar fastened high around the neckline. Gold circular buttons with an eagle imprint in the middle ran down the center of the choker blouse. My other lucky classmates who were selected to commission as Second Lieutenants in the United States Marine Corps wore a similar uniform, except that their suit-like blouse was black and paired with straight white pants.

The day was perfect: clear skies and a slight breeze off the Severn River. The surreal moment and mix of emotions of it all was too big to put into words.

We were grouped, by company, in two long lines at the top of the Navy-Marine Corps Stadium. One end would walk in from the left, the other from the right. Rows of seats arranged in a square, divided alphabetically by company, awaited us in the center of the field. A large black stage was constructed, and at the edge stood a brown podium that had the Naval Academy crest embedded in its center. The same large screen used at the mandatory football games we had to attend damn near every weekend towered over the black stage. The words "Lockheed Martin" were printed at the top. The screen's image was big enough for everyone to see the graduation, no matter where they sat.

The music began, and we marched out slowly and took our seats. The gray foldable chairs felt firm against my butt while we waited for the stadium to be filled. The guest speaker for the graduation was the Secretary of Defense, the honorable Ash Carter. What's unique about the Service Academies graduations are the speakers. The President, Vice President, and Secretary of Defense rotate between West Point, Annapolis, and the Air Force Academy. Ash Carter's speech dragged on, and the hot sun baked us in our seats. It felt even longer waiting in eager anticipation for the moment I would walk up to receive my diploma from the Superintendent and Commandant. I'd gone through so much to get here. I didn't know how I would respond on stage.

Finally, after what felt like several hours, my time had come. "ANDRE EVANS," I heard my name called as I waited at the bottom of the steps. I walked up slowly, taking in the moment. I was excited but weirdly nervous at the same time. I thought about all the people who'd poured into me and supported me during this journey. Then coolness poured over me. I walked up and shook the SUPE's hand, while receiving my diploma in the other. Colonel Liszewski looked at me keenly and extended his hand. I shoved my hand into his, the impact making a hard slapping sound, and we both gave each other a firm grip. He pulled me in close for a moment.

"I'm going to miss you, Dre. Do great things." We pulled away from one another, and I looked him back in his eyes.

"Thank you, sir. I appreciate that. It means a lot," I responded.

After everyone's name was called and people had taken their seats, our elected class president, Eric Kellogg, walked up to the stage to deliver the closing remarks. What I remember most were his final words.

"Three cheers for those we are about to leave behind."

"Hip-hip!"

"HOORAY!!!" the entire class of 2016 shouted in response.

"Hip-hip!"

"HOORAY!!!"

"HIP-HIP!!!"

"HoooRAAAAAYYYYY!!!!"

And into the air my hat went. It was another iconic image of thousands of covers flying through the air and Naval Academy graduates jumping off their feet, shouting with joy. Except this time, I was a part of it. Since 1912, the famous tossing of the covers symbolizes the end of the graduates' old lives and marks the beginning of new ones as Commissioned Officers. I launched my cover toward the sky as if offering it to God as a token of gratitude. It was all over: the exhausting responsibility of leading other midshipmen, being tossed and turned through a structured yet evolving military schedule on a daily basis, and all the rigors of studying. I now really knew what the Naval Academy Blue & Gold experience was all about.

At the conclusion of the ceremony, families gathered on the leafy green turf to take photos and present their graduates with their new Officer covers and shoulder boards. With my mom on one side and my dad on the other, they removed my first class midshipman rank and replaced it with my much larger Ensign shoulder boards. Next came the first salute: a sacred military tradition in which an enlisted service member, Officer, mentor, or family member who served has the honor of presenting you with your first salute as a commissioned Naval Officer. It's a sign of respect and gratitude. Although deviating from traditional naval customs, I decided to let my minion (Brooke) do the honors.

"You ready, Brooke?"

"Yeah, I'm ready," she said in her soft little voice with a big smile.

She raised her small hand and saluted me. I saluted back. I don't use the word cute in my vocabulary, but there's no other word to use to describe it.

The shit was adorable.

Looking back, there is no place more special than the Naval Academy. It's one of the toughest places in the world, but the best place in the universe to be from. Often seen around the yard are T-shirts that read "N*ot College." In fact, Annapolis wasn't your average college. It was a place that never accepted short cuts. Attending was like getting punched in the face every day. The drip of blood from your face, plus the very fact of being punched in the first place, brought a mix of emotions.

Over time, you become resilient. You adapt. You learn that pain is weakness leaving the body. Plain and simple, USNA is hard.

And while in the moment it sucks, it's one of the reasons that, over time, make it such a unique place. All graduates would agree. It's the reason why every year, you see crusty old alumni fill the yard, trying to relive their midshipmen days. They long for it. They miss it. Unlike in a normal college where you can go back and take additional courses or attend graduate school, your time at Annapolis is limited. After four years, you're done. There is no going back to experience what you felt as a mid.

I left as a distinguished graduate, Black Engineer of the Year (BEYA) award recipient, MIT Fellow, Air Force Institute of Technology Fellow, Truman Scholar, Plebe Summer Regimental Commander, MBSC president, Mandell Rosenblatt award recipient, urban outreach youth activist, and motivational speaker. I had a job at the Pentagon for the summer, and I was awarded the Community Volunteer Service Medal. The big homie, my man God, blessed me immensely.

* * * *

One final thought before I close this chapter. For me, attending the Naval Academy and serving in the military was a tool. It was my way to get my foot in the door and ultimately a gateway to other opportunities that wouldn't have been remotely possible without it. Once I made it to Annapolis, I worked my ass off with a vengeance. Although I did have a lot of internal self-doubts initially, I did not act on them or allow them to control my destiny. I looked my fears—which are really just fake emotions holding us back—in the eyes. I surrounded myself with mentors, and I acquired skills that furthered my development. My mind evolved, and I went from having a victim mentality to being powered by adversity.

Just like the military, I urge youths, especially my young Black men, to treat sports in the same regard. Athletics is just a tool to get you where you need to be: out of the hood, safety for you and your family, or initial financial security. Like a drag strip, don't confine yourself to just one lane. Consider basketball superstar Lebron James, who, in addition to basketball, has his money invested in multiple businesses and meets with his mentor Warren Buffet regularly. King James is just one of many examples. It's not about one career. There is a bigger picture at play in the immediate background. Use all your gifts and talents to help and inspire others. You're so much more than one thing. You need to see that the military, education, sports, etc., are powerful forces that, if used the right way, have the potential to separate you from the pack.

So ask yourself, what's going to separate you?

Brigade of Midshipmen Rank Insignia Sleeve Striping

Midshipmen Officers

Midshipman
Captain
(CAPT)

Midshipman
Commander
(CMDR)

Midshipman
Lieutenant
Commander
(LCDR)

Midshipman
Lieutenant
(LT)

Midshipman
Lieutenant
Junior Grade
(LTJG)

Midshipman
Ensign
(ENS)

Midshipmen Other Than Officers

Midshipman
First Class

Midshipman
Second Class

Midshipman
Third Class

Midshipman
Fourth Class

Shoulder Boards

Midshipmen Officers

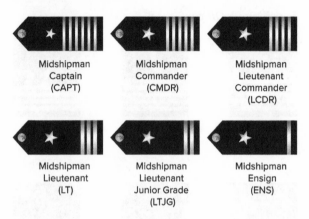

| Midshipman Captain (CAPT) | Midshipman Commander (CMDR) | Midshipman Lieutenant Commander (LCDR) |

| Midshipman Lieutenant (LT) | Midshipman Lieutenant Junior Grade (LTJG) | Midshipman Ensign (ENS) |

Midshipmen Other Than Officers

Midshipman
First Class

Midshipman
Second Class

Midshipman
Third Class

Midshipman
Fourth Class

Collar Devices

Midshipmen Officers

Midshipman
Captain
(CAPT)

Midshipman
Commander
(CMDR)

Midshipman
Lieutenant
Commander
(LCDR)

Midshipman
Lieutenant
(LT)

Midshipman
Lieutenant
Junior Grade
(LTJG)

Midshipman
Ensign
(ENS)

Midshipmen Other Than Officers

Right	Left	Right	Left	Right

Midshipman
First Class

Midshipman
Second Class

Midshipman
Third Class

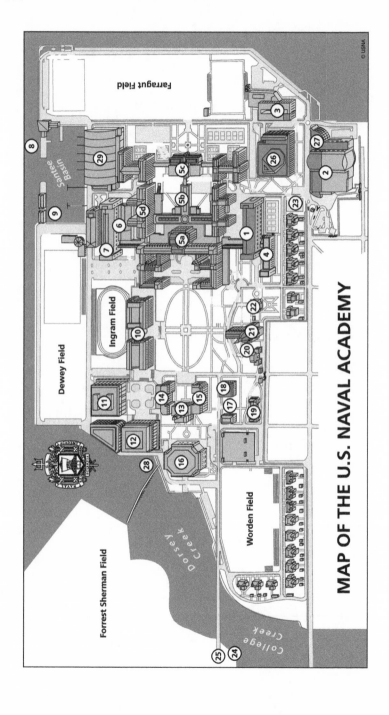

MAP OF THE U.S. NAVAL ACADEMY

Walking Paths

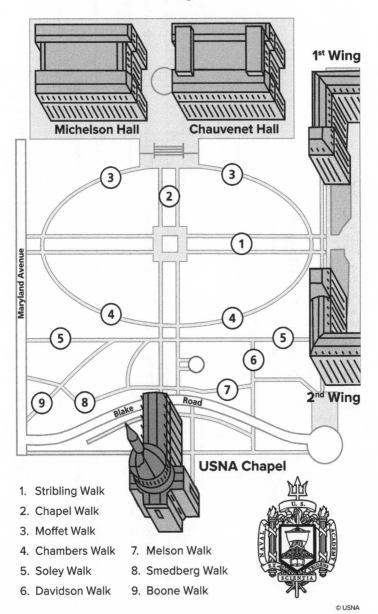

1. Stribling Walk
2. Chapel Walk
3. Moffet Walk
4. Chambers Walk
5. Soley Walk
6. Davidson Walk
7. Melson Walk
8. Smedberg Walk
9. Boone Walk

© USNA

Prove Them Wrong

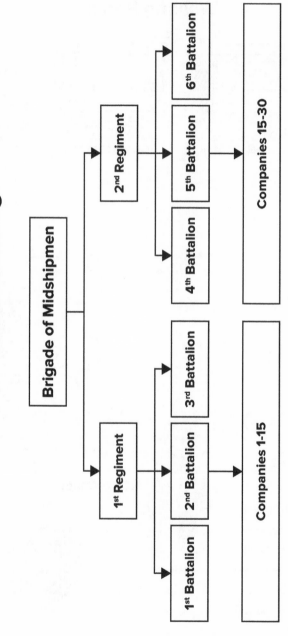

Structure of the Brigade of Midshipmen

ACT III: DYING EMPTY BY LIVING LIFE TO THE FULLEST

A friend of mine said something powerful at his grandfather's funeral. He said that the greatest lesson from his grandfather's life was that he died empty, because he accomplished everything he wanted, with no regrets. I think that, along with leaving a legacy, would be the greatest sign of success.

—MARVIN SAPP

CHAPTER 21

THE PENTAGON

DWAYNE WAS CRYING.

During one warm spring afternoon my final year at the Academy, a group of 1/C midshipmen boarded a bus to head to Arlington, Virginia for a Naval Submarine League (NSL) luncheon.[20] The guest speaker was Admiral Charles Richard. His elongated head encompassed his naturally grim face and pointed ears. He had thick, intense eyebrows, was clean shaven, and the wrinkles in his face suggested that he didn't smile much. Admiral Richard was the director of Undersea Warfare (OPNAV N97) at the Pentagon.

His fifteen-minute PowerPoint slideshow focused on how the US Navy utilizes underwater drones in the submarine force. At the end of the demonstration, he paraded slowly around the square meeting room and interacted with Officers and students. I was standing next to a group of other midshipmen when he walked up and began to question a few of us.

---

20 NSL is a nonprofit organization that promotes the importance of the US Navy submarine force to national security through luncheons, mentorship sessions, briefs, and other activities.

"What's your major, MIDN Evans?"

"Naval architecture, sir."

His face lit up.

"You know, the Navy is trying to develop a submarine that can launch and recover unmanned underwater vehicles (UUVs) and unmanned aerial vehicles (UAVs).[21] You're a naval architect. What do you think about that?"

Like a spark going off in my head, Admiral Richard's words struck an idea for me—design a sub that could launch and recover drones for my senior capstone project.

For my major, it was the final engineering assignment that involved designing a ship from the ground up. A culmination of applying all the knowledge from the rigorous courses we took for three years, the project required detailed boat design schematics, lots of mathematical calculations, and a large, handcrafted model. Each group consisted of four to five members. At the end, teams would present their final assignments to the engineering faculty, alumni, NAVSEA representatives, midshipmen, and other members of the naval architecture community.[22]

---

21   A UUV is an underwater drone. It's a robotic vehicle that operates underwater without a human passenger. Thus, it allows the submarine force to complete many strategic and dangerous missions in secret and without placing human lives at risk. A UAV is a scientific name for a regular aerial drone. It is an aircraft piloted by remote control.

22   NAVSEA: Naval Sea Systems Command. Headquartered in Washington DC, NAVSEA is in charge of the Navy's warfare centers and all of its major shipyards.

Roughly eight months later, we presented our submarine design and received the Mandell Rosenblatt Award.[23] It was given to the group with the best aesthetic design. Because it was hard to build an actual model that would show the working mechanisms of the drone device, we created a virtual 3D rendering of the submarine that showed everything in operation. At the end, Admiral Richards took a second to pull me aside.

"Mr. Evans, great presentation. What are you doing for the next three to four months after graduation before you report to nuke school?"

"Nothing planned yet, sir."

"How about you come work for me at the Pentagon and present your project there as well if you're interested?"

Say what? Did this man just say what I think he just said? Hell yeah.

"Sir, I would like that. It would be an honor."

Two days after graduating from Annapolis, I got in my car and drove to Washington, DC.

I called Dwayne during the commute.

---

23 The history behind the award is significant. "M. Rosenblatt and Son Naval Architects and Marine Engineers" was a reputable firm that played an integral role in the design of half the ships in the United States Naval fleet for over fifty years.

You have to understand: calling my stepfather to let him know I would be working at the Pentagon was complicated. A part of me felt obligated to tell him because, ever since my brothers and I attended West Point SLS, he'd frequently say to us at the dinner table, "One of you is going to work at the Pentagon or for the Secret Service." *Whatever*, we'd say to ourselves. *This dude is crazy. Ain't nobody working for the Secret Service or the Pentagon.* In our minds, we felt those types of jobs were for the elite and out of reach for us. If only we knew that Dwayne was breathing life into the three of us. He spoke our future into existence. Deep down, he wanted to live vicariously through us.

In hindsight, it's remarkable that I worked at the Pentagon and that Anthony became a Secret Service agent. Words are powerful. There is truth in one's ability to prophetically speak greatness over others.

Another side of me made the phone call just to prove to him once again that I was going places and had made something of my life despite all the negative comments he'd said to me over the years.

And then there was the sincere part of me that finally just wanted his approval as a son.

"Hello?" he answered.

"Hey, Dwayne, how are you?"

"I'm good. What's goin' on, Andre?"

"I just wanted to let you know that I'll be stationed at the Pentagon this summer."

The other end of the phone went dead silent.

"Hello, are you there?" I asked.

I still couldn't hear anything. I thought the reception must be bad, when all of a sudden: *Sniff. Sniff.*

Dwayne was crying. I could hear the sobs coming from his mouth and nose from the other end of the line. "Congratulations, Andre. I'm so proud of you," he said.

I'd never heard Dwayne say he was proud of me before.

I was so used to fighting with him that I didn't know how to respond. This time our interaction was different. Genuine even, like a father and son should have. I was observing him, I realized, in a moment of sincerity. He cared. Maybe his response had something to do with the letter I wrote? He never responded back, but maybe he wanted to but just didn't know how?

His reaction made me think back to when I was in elementary school. The first time Dwayne showed concern for me was when I cut my arm open.

Most of the fences that encompassed backyards or surrounded homes on the South Side were made of metal. The fence post tops varied in style. Some had a rounded out point at the top while others featured sharp, twisted wire in an X pattern. In those days, for me, hurdling over a fence to avoid a cop, chase after someone, or to avoid a group of guys, was essential. In some instances, depending on how fast I was running and the height of the fence, I could use my momentum to hop over without touching it at all.

On a humid Chicago summer day, my Grandma Martha was in town from Detroit for the weekend. A bunch of my family had gathered at my Grandma Mildred's house in celebration. My exact memories of what in the world I was engaged in before my accident are pretty scattered. I just recall running to hop one of the twisted wire fences, but when I attempted to lunge myself over, the next thing I knew I had slipped, and my arm was caught hanging on the fence. The sharp metal from the top of the gate pierced through and latched into the flesh of my arm. My arm peeled back. It was stretched out and bloody. Like a cow hanging from the ceiling after being slaughtered by a butcher, I stayed there pressed against the gate, motionless, until my brothers came to help free me.

I was afraid to show my mother in fear of how she would react, so Alex ran inside to tell her first. "Andre hurt his arm on the fence."

When I finally walked through the back screen door of my grandmother's house to show them what happened, my T-shirt was covered in blood. I looked down at the gushing red liquid. Skin was hanging off, and my arm was cut open so deep I could see down to the bone. I vividly remember the white pieces of meat sprinkled and mashed up all around.

I had never seen anything like it.

Before my mother even asked me what happened, she rushed me to the emergency room. I didn't cry during the incident or the two hours it took the doctor to numb and stitch my arm closed. But Dwayne cried and complained the entire time. I remember looking at the TV to focus on the Lakers playing in the playoffs just to block him out. *Shit.* By the way he was looking at me, I was starting to get worried. My mother sat right next to me, calm as a cucumber. I was like, *What is wrong with this dude? I'm not even crying, so why are you?* Deep behind my stepdad's tough boy shell, he had a soft spot.

What caught my attention the most were the doctor's words: "If your arm had moved one more inch, it would have cut your vein, and you would have died." I knew God was looking out for me that day. He had more in store for me in life that I couldn't yet imagine.

* * * *

JUMPING OFF THE TRAIN to take a long escalator up to the front door of the Pentagon, our nation's symbol for military doctrine and power, was, well, just awkward. I had imagined there would be a greater divide between a major public transportation outlet and the headquarters of the Department of Defense. But that didn't take away from the fierce security that awaited me the instant I walked forward. For the sake of national security, I will refrain from discussing details about the security measures present. Instead, I'll focus on what I can. I recall the buzz of the Pentagon that made my first day feel like a blur. Civilian and military sophisticates scurried down the enormous bright hallways. Every door I passed was closed and looked high tech with a bunch of fancy security devices surrounding it. Armed guards patrolled everywhere. Numerous gray or black cubby bins were mounted against the walls for individuals to place their phones before walking into a space. Like a maze, even when you thought you began to understand the layout of the building, it still confused you. It took me the entire three months onboard to learn how to walk around without getting lost. The fitness center was top notch, and the food selection in the cafeteria area was superb. There were clothing and gift stores, a barbershop, laundry facilities, and even tailoring. The whole operation was like a small, self-sustaining city.

When it came time to work, I was placed in the OPNAV N97 division for Undersea Warfare, the department responsible for the planning, acquisition, and operational readiness of US Navy submarine forces. Right away, I was thrown into the mix to research unmanned underwater and aerial vehicles, a spin-off from my project at Annapolis.

At times I found myself twiddling my thumbs at my desk in boredom when the tasks assigned to me were complete and the schedule had slowed down. I knew it was uncommon to find a junior Officer working at the Pentagon—most of the military personnel were senior in rank—but I did my best to make the most of the opportunity. Growing up, my stepdad used to say to my brothers and me all the time, "Be the best. Even if you shovel shit for a living or serve fries at McDonald's, be the best shit shoveler and fry server there is." Not to say that people who work at McDonald's or handle waste are lesser people. No. But to make the point that even when you work at a less desirable job, position, school, or place, work as hard as you fucking can. It will build a work ethic in you that will translate to the things that you do enjoy. So when you finally receive an opportunity you want, you'll value it even more. And then there's just the appreciation of having a job in the first place, food to eat, and a school to be able to attend. I'm not saying it's easy. I have plenty of moments where I'm like *forget this*. But you have to make the most of it.

* * * *

I THREW UP in the middle of the street my first weekend working at the Pentagon. It was a warm DC summer day, and I was attending a party at one of the dorm rooms located on the campus of George Washington University. During the working day, I was a polished military professional. I wore my cleanly pressed khaki uniform, and I walked in sync among the hustle and bustle of crowds of people toward the Foggy Bottom train station to catch the blue line. But at night, once or twice a week, I was a public service fellow. In conjunction with my time working at the Pentagon, I participated in the Truman Summer Institute, an eight-week program for building stronger relations with my classmates, attending seminars focused on policy making, and participating in workshops. My peers interned at various nonprofits and corporate and government sector jobs around the city.

I vividly remember walking into an apartment room that night and seeing a stockpile of alcohol bottles resting along the kitchen countertop. Large black speakers boomed the sound of hip-hop and club music. "Take a shot with us, bro," someone said. The next thing I know I had a shot glass in my hand. The inside of my throat slightly burned from the 1800 Silver tequila I downed with one gulp. I ended up taking three more shots before I heard a loud knock at the door. THUMP, THUMP, THUMP. Still the closest person to the door, I opened it right away. I thought it was more people.

Nope.

It was the police.

Two mean-mugged officers stared back at me from the other side of the doorway.

"We have received multiple complaints about loud music and yelling from this room."

"Uhhh," I said with my mouth held wide open.

"Keep it down or next time our return won't be so nice."

"Yes, sir. Thank you."

I quickly closed the door and turned around to see everyone staring at me. The small apartment was so quiet you could hear a pin drop.

"YAY!!!!!"

Everyone erupted into ecstatic cheers and screams. You would have thought we were watching the Super Bowl or something.

"Let's play slap the bag."

"What's that?" I asked.

Slap the bag was when you took a bag full of wine, turned the knob on it, and chugged down as much red or white wine as you possibly could. Other participants timed everyone to see who could last the longest. I grabbed the plastic black knob on the bag and flipped it open. Like a waterfall, a surge of bitter tasting red wine flowed into my mouth as I gulped it down with ease. I finished 80 percent of the bag before multiple people stopped me. I could have kept going.

"Let's go out clubbing," someone said. It wasn't long before I found myself standing in front of a brawny, mammoth-like security guard. I extended my hand to show him my military ID only to find it swallowed in size by the guard's enormous hands.

"I can't let him in. He's had too much to drink."

What?

"I'm fine, bro. I'm good to come in."

"No, you're not. Step back."

I might have zigzagged a little when I walked, but overall, I felt fine. It's not like he saw me walk up, anyway. If anything, I was just a little "lit."

"Come on, sir, he's with us. We'll watch him," one of the guys said.

"No, he can't come in."

In disbelief, I turned around and proceeded to walk down the street. I just started to walk off alone. Maybe it was an attempt to head back to the dorm room to sleep. Who knows?

Only one thing was certain: the group of people I came with didn't follow or come looking for me. My head began to buzz from the alcohol settling within the membranes of my body. Like weights holding me down, my feet felt heavier with each step. My lonely journey down the DC concrete appeared to last forever. But I eventually did make it to the corner of the street. And I saw—at least it was what my eyes zoomed in on—McDonald's.

I walked in, climbed into one of the small cream-colored booths, and put my head down to take a quick nap. I was exhausted. It wasn't even two minutes before I felt a soft tap on my shoulder. I looked up slowly, my eyes red and my head heavy. It was the security guard working in the restaurant. "You can't sleep in here. Either buy some food and eat or leave," he said softly in his all-black uniform. I grudgingly nodded my head up and down in acknowledgment and walked out of the door. Then I leaned against the side of the McDonald's. The golden arch logo on the glass of the restaurant touched my back. My insides began to hurt and turn.

"Augghhhhhh."

Immediately, I bent over and proceeded to throw up on the corner of the sidewalk. I was like an animal in a zoo; people walked past and watched and pointed. I looked back at them in dismay. At that moment, I felt helpless. I closed my eyes and spaced out and thought about my time as the Regimental Commander.

"Every challenge is an opportunity," Nate (my Regimental OPS) said into the microphone at the center of the large podium.

"RISE TO IT!" the entire plebe class shouted back.

During my stint as the REG CMDR, I always looked for unique ways to motivate and engage the plebes. One of those ways was through my mantra: "Every challenge is an opportunity; rise to it." It started out with me saying those words in the morning at PT, on the drill field, or during conversations, but the expression quickly evolved into a mantra the entire Regiment adopted as its own. Before every meal, and at the end of every brief, my Regiment shouted those words with pride.

That day at Annapolis it was noon, and the plebes and detailers had all gathered in King Hall for lunch. Just like during the academic year, everyone sat and ate within their assigned Company. The senior stripers, however, in this case my staff and me, had our own table centered at the front of the main entrance to King Hall. We were enjoying our meal when my detailers walked up to speak to me.

"Dre, you got a sec, bro?"

"Wassup, man?"

"I've been having issues with one of my plebes. He has been disrespectful and isn't showing any type of motivation. Could he sit with you at the REG table? Maybe you can speak to him."

"Yeah, I got you. Bring him by."

Two minutes later the upper class detailer walked up with his plebe. He was a skinny, innocent looking kid with smooth skin.

The Black plebe stood directly behind his chair, stuck out a paw, and asked for permission to join the table.

"Sir, Midshipman 4/C Jackson. Respectfully request permission to join the table."

"Midshipman Jackson. Nice to meet you. You may sit down," I responded. He quickly sat down and fixed his gaze forward, eyes on the boat[24].

"You can look at me when I speak to you."

4/C Jackson turned his head.

"Where are you from?"

"Virginia, sir."

"Okay. Virginia. Nice. I hear you've been having some issues lately. What's going on?"

"You disgust me, plebe! Who do you think you are?!" one of my Regimental staff members shouted out of the blue.

For the next several minutes, as 4/C Jackson attempted to explain himself, she berated him rudely. It didn't take long before I became frustrated. She had the type of attitude I sought to demolish during my reign as a Commander: the belief that detailers were above the plebes and could treat them any way

---

24 "Eyes on the boat" was a phrase that meant you looked straight ahead and didn't move your eyes or head at all.

they saw fit. I remember how I felt the way Oxford and Fields treated me. I believed I could learn just as much from a 4/C as they could learn from me. The only difference is that I was more seasoned in my leadership and experience as a midshipman at the Naval Academy.

I cut her off.

"That's enough. I got it from here."

4/C Jackson explained how he struggled to remember his rates and was having a difficult time adapting to the rigors of his training. After questioning him further, I discovered that his father was a Colonel in the Army and that his mother was battling cancer.

"What's your WHY, Jackson? Like, what motivates you to get out of bed every morning? What drives you?"

"My parents, sir."

"Do you think they would be proud of you right now? Your mom is back home in Virginia battling cancer, and you're here at Annapolis with the opportunity of a lifetime. Don't waste that. You're not fully applying yourself."

"No, sir. They would be disappointed." Jackson started to tear up.

"Don't do it for yourself then. Do it for them. Be better."

At the end of the meal, plebe Jackson thanked me for my time, apologized, and gave me his word he would do better. Before finally walking away from the table with his detailer, he turned back around and said to me, "Sir, you inspire me."

I felt so honored.

I was humbled by the plebe's words because for me, impacting lives, even just one, was all that mattered. At the same time, I was extremely disappointed in the way my Regimental staff member carried herself at the table that day. We live in a world where some are placed in a position of leadership and others as followers, but mutual respect must always be present. One thing I learned as the REG CMDR was that a leader is nothing without his or her people. They need you just as much as you need them to accomplish a mission.

* * * *

I KNEW I needed help, so I fumbled my hands in my pocket, took out my phone, and called my brother Anthony. At the time, he was a cop working for the George Washington University police.

"Hello?"

"Hey, bro, it's me. I need you. I'm drunk. Can you come get me?" Five minutes later, he pulled up in his compact unit car, helped throw me in the back seat, and drove away. The next morning, waking up on my brother's brown leather coach in his small apartment, I felt ashamed. I could only imagine how embarrassing that was for him, and for that I'm sorry. I had just graduated from the Naval Academy and was commissioned as an Officer in the United States Navy. And there I was, throwing up on the corner of a busy street in the heart of Washington, DC. What if someone from the Pentagon identified me? What if one of my Officer mentors saw me? What about the midshipmen in Annapolis who looked up to me and could have been in DC that weekend? I was quick to judge my Plebe Summer Regimental staff member for her actions, but look at how I was behaving out in public as a Naval Officer. What if now-3/C Jackson saw me out in town? Where was that inspiration now?

But I knew the reason why. I'd allowed myself to get drunk because I was honestly afraid and frustrated with life. My stepfather and I were still on uncertain terms and argued often. In addition, I had all these feelings bottled up inside me. It felt weird that my demanding four years at the Naval Academy had finally come to an end. Truth is, I wasn't ready to let it all go. Nothing would be the same anymore. Neither my brother Alex nor my closest friends would be within walking distance. From what I had observed, most of the mids that graduate from Annapolis don't seem to outwardly speak about the transition from midshipmen to Officer. But it's difficult. You're no longer able to play the "I'm a midshipman card" and get out of things. Not only is more demanded of you, but society expects you to set the standard for what good character and leadership look like on a day-to-day basis. Even though we had been training for that moment at Annapolis for years, it was still nerve-racking. It's nothing like wearing the actual bars on your shoulders.

And then there's the added pressure of paying bills and figuring out what it means to live on your own. It doesn't take long before life gives you a solid uppercut to the lip and leaves you bleeding out on the pavement. Adulting hit me hard in the face the moment I graduated, and I found myself overwhelmed by the pace of life.

I failed to go back home and recalibrate myself. Even if I didn't have the means to travel back to Chicago, I should have taken some personal time for myself to reevaluate the battlefield.

Sometimes living life to the fullest is about being honest with yourself and hitting the pause button to self-reflect.

CHAPTER 22

LIKE FATHER, LIKE SON

IT WAS 0445 WHEN I PULLED MY WHITE FORD FOCUS INTO THE DARK PARKING LOT. The only light that danced on the concrete came from the tall, murky orange light poles that, like soldiers, guarded the outer perimeter of the lot. There were only two other cars present. I made a conscious effort to arrive before the school house opened at 0500 each morning. That way, I could get an extra two hours of studying in before classes started at 0700.

I didn't know it was possible to study so much your head would hurt. I made sure to leave my phone in the car and briskly walked toward the front door of the two-story brown brick building. Students were prohibited from bringing cell phones, smart watches, or any form of media device into the building.

The Naval Nuclear Power Training Command is a six-month school located in Goose Creek, South Carolina, that teaches sailors how to operate nuclear power plants aboard US Navy aircraft carriers and submarines. From the outside, it looked like every other dual military building on base. But the intense atmosphere that existed inside was a different story. The pace of the training was mind-blowing.

Even as an engineering major at the Naval Academy, it took one semester to complete an entire course. At Power School, we went through a course a week.

I nodded my head in respect to the watch stander on the quarterdeck while he observed me scan my ID badge at the front entrance.[25]

"Hold on, sir. I need to check your bag, and I need you to empty out all of your pockets." At Power School, it was normal to have random routine bag and personnel security checks to ensure students did not remove or transfer any of the classified material from the building.

"Sure, go ahead," I motioned while opening up my bag to let him look through it. The White man in uniform dug his fingers through my bag and rummaged around all my food. I had enough to last me the entire day. I wouldn't leave for lunch or go home after class until I felt confident I had studied enough to grasp the material, which usually meant staying at the schoolhouse until 2000 or 2100.

"Go ahead, sir. You're good."

---

25 The quarterdeck is the main ceremonial or reception area. Typically, it's the main entrance to any military building or ship. Traditionally, it was where the Captain of a sailing vessel commanded the ship and where the colors, or flags, were kept.

It was Monday morning, and I was already studying to prepare for my Nuclear Chemistry I exam on Friday morning. The first floor of the building was for the enlisted sailors. All the Officers took classes on the second level, which was really just a long hallway with thick white tiles and classrooms on the left and right.

"Hey, Dre!" I heard a voice behind me say while I walked to my assigned classroom. It was the fifth door on the left. My class number was 1701 and consisted of roughly thirty students. I turned around to find it was one of my friends, Bria.

"Yo, wassup?"

"You too, huh? Came in early to study, I see," Bria said.

"Yeah, I'm trying to make it, sis. It's hard to remember all that material in such a short period of time. I'm barely making it," I told her.

"Yeah, I feel you. I saw you did pretty well on your exam last week, so you are probably good," Bria said.

"Ah. Maybe you're right. I hate that, though. I hate that they post our exam scores next to our names at the back of the class for everyone to see. It's not like they remove it after we all looked to see what we got. It stays there all week until they put up a more updated sheet. It's embarrassing, yo, especially if you fail. I feel like that shit just adds more pressure."

"You know how it is, Dre. That's that Navy tradition stuff. The nuclear Navy is not about to change anything Admiral Rickover created," Bria said.

We entered the classroom. Along the left and right sides of the white room were columns of caramel brown wall lockers. Four rows of gray desks were positioned in the center of the room, with five desks placed next to one another to make one row. We unlocked our circular dial lockers and grabbed our packet of notes. Before sitting down, I made sure to date, initial, and indicate the time I opened up my storage locker on the security check sheet posted on the front. Each night, instructors and a security watch made sure all the lockers were annotated as opened and closed appropriately. If not, we got in trouble.

I laid out my snacks and my mini dry erase board and got to work.

"A nuclear fission chain reaction is a nuclear process when a neutron strikes the nucleus of a radioactive element, usually Uranium 235, and splits into two or more smaller nuclei fission products, neutrons, and releases a large amount of energy."

I couldn't just know what nuclear fission was. I had to remember the entire sentence verbatim. See, that's what made nuke school so difficult. The expectation was that we had to remember everything. I mean *everything,* including hundreds of equations and diagrams of systems. Even if I did remember all the formulas, it was difficult for me to mentally cipher through and know which equation to use for a particular problem. Oftentimes, being able to see all the equations in front of me on one sheet allowed me to pick the correct formula during my engineering classes at the Academy.

I tried repeating the text to myself in my head, and then reading it out loud or discussing it with Bria, but I couldn't recall the material exactly when I attempted to write it out. By and large, I did whatever I could to make the information stick as fast as possible. The only thing I could remember quickly was drawing out the diagrams of valves, nuclear reactor components, and chemical reactions.

"Hey, can you help me with this problem?" Bria asked, separating me for a brief moment from my frustrations with studying.

"Yeah, sure, I got you," I responded. Bria handed me one of the problems from our homework. The words CONFIDENTIAL were stamped at the very top and bottom of the page in bright red. All of our homework assignments had to be stamped with this label and completed on white or green graph paper in order for it to count as complete.

The shit was crazy. We had homework every night on top of being expected to take an exam, sometimes two, in one week.

I finished helping Bria just in time. One of our instructors, a short Caucasian man with a round egg head and box-like body, walked to the front of the room. It was 0655, and class was about to start. There was a small gray desk with a projector and computer that was located at the very front of the room. He opened up the PowerPoint slideshow and began to teach. The packet of notes they gave us was like a workbook with fill-in-the-blanks and pictures.

I sat there in the stiff chair and paid attention as the instructor went through the concepts. I adjusted my blue back pillow, which was wrapped around the seat. Most of us had cushions on the backs or bottoms of our chairs because of the long hours we spent in class or studying. When the instructor came to a slide that had a fill-in-the-blank in my notes—which was pretty much every slide—I copied it down. Example problems were usually at the end of each chapter, and the instructor would perform them on the chalk board up front.

And no, you couldn't get a copy of the slides from the instructor if you missed something. I went back to my old habits from Annapolis and harassed the instructors, studying over thirty hours a week. I also studied all weekend and night, to the point where I felt like I was forgetting information.

How could you study so much and still feel stupid?

Then the unthinkable happened.

My grandmother Martha passed away.

As Martha grew in age, she had unfortunately come to a stage in her health where she couldn't live alone. In his usual fashion, instead of stepping up as a man to aid his mother, Tony manipulated her and lived off of her money. He had simply failed to take care of her. Tony had people Martha didn't know visiting the house at all times of the night. It was probably drug-related, and she was scared. His actions added further stress and complications to the health equation. In need of help and aware of the situation at hand, a friend of my grandmother's called our cousin Caulet in Maryland. A short, beautiful African American woman with light skin, she was Martha's first niece. "Hey, Collette, I think you should come check on Martha. She's not doing too well." Very soon, Collette and her husband

Billy touched down in Detroit. After a few days, they made all the proper arrangements to move my grandmother to Bowie, Maryland. Martha lived with Collette and Billy for a few years before she was later relocated to Ohio to live with Tony again.

I remember the phone call from my mother clearly.

"Hey, Andre, you have a sec?"

"Yea, wassup, Mom?"

"Your grandmother Martha passed away."

"What? She passed away?" I said in a confused manner. "I don't understand. How?"

"At this time, I don't have a lot of details. But Tony had her cremated and didn't tell anyone. She passed away a couple of weeks ago. I only found out because Collette just gave me a call. It took a couple weeks before even she knew."

My heart sank. I didn't know what to say. I didn't act out in anger because I was still struggling to process the information. I was more shocked that Tony hadn't had a funeral and failed to include the family. That whole week, I tried to block out my emotions and focus on the demands of completing nuke school, but the real pain caught up to me a week later, the night before my Nuclear Chemistry II exam.

I couldn't sleep.

I felt numb.

Lying there on my air mattress, I struggled to close my eyes. When I forced them shut, my mind kept racing. My eyes began to burn and swell with tears. As much as I hated to admit it, and as hard as I fought to suppress my internal feelings, that conversation with my mother on the phone ripped me apart. All I could think about was my grandmother. I was more hurt that I couldn't give her a proper goodbye. When I finally let go and allowed myself to feel, I was angry that my biological father didn't have the decency to call us and let us know Martha had passed away. Deep down inside, there was still a small mustard seed that secretly hoped he had some measure of love for us. That moment solidified that he didn't.

I walked into the school house the next day to take my exam.

The instructor handed me the twenty- to thirty-page blank pink test packet, and for one hour I just stared at it.

I knew that stuff. I know I could have passed that exam. But my mind was elsewhere. I couldn't put the knowledge down on paper. At the end of the exam, I walked up to my instructor and told him my situation.

"I'm telling you right now, sir, that my exam is blank. I'm going to fail," I muttered.

"I don't understand. What's going on?"

"The exam is blank. There's nothin' there. My grandmother passed away. I couldn't focus or think straight."

"Okay. I'll look it over and discuss it with the department. I'll get back to you. I'm sorry for your loss." The next day after class, my chemistry instructor pulled me aside.

"I know you had a death in the family, but according to school policy, because this is the second exam you've failed, you're required to have an academic review board."

"When was that policy put out? I thought you only had a review board if you struggled to pass multiple exams? This was only my second, and I had a valid reason. Can't I just retake it?"

"I'm sorry, Mr. Evans. You have a review board with the Executive Officer (XO) tomorrow morning."

What lasted an hour felt like twenty minutes. As I attempted to answer questions related to electrical engineering, chemistry, and physics, my mind was elsewhere. I was thinking about my biological father, my grandmother Martha, and my family. I was exhausted, hurt, and fed up. I wanted it all to end. I know I could have finished Power School, but I didn't feel it was worth fighting to regain admission back into the program just to start over.

"We have to let you go," the Commander ultimately said.

My time as a submarine Officer was over.

The walk back to my car was one of the longest walks ever. My mind flashed back to senior year at the National Black Engineer of the Year Award (BEYA) Conference. It was February 18, and the forum took place at the Philadelphia Marriott Downtown. Admiral Michelle Howard, the first African American woman to command a US Naval warship and the first female US Navy four-star Admiral, presented me with the BEYA Engineering Student Leadership Award.

CAPT Roger Isom, the Diversity Officer at the Naval Academy during my plebe and youngster year, was there to support. He was a man rigid in structure. His handshake was firm. He had serious eyes paired with a round, bald head, and he spoke with great ethos and authority. Naturally, I would say I'm a pretty motivated person. My friends and family often comment on the amount of pressure I place on myself to accomplish certain goals. And then there was CAPT Isom, who pushed and challenged me even further. I didn't get to meet with him often, but when I did, his few words would carry me for weeks until our next encounter.

He walked right up to me and extended his large hands that day. I felt a circular object press against the center of my palm. I withdrew my hand and unraveled my fingers. A black, oval pin with the Navy's submarine dolphins warfare device pressed in the center, and the words CENTENNIAL 7 etched in gold at the bottom, stared back at me.[26]

The Oxford dictionary defines a salute as "a gesture of respect, paying homage, or giving polite recognition or

---

26 The "Centennial 7" is a term used to denote the first seven African American officers to command US submarines in naval history. Their names in order are as follows: CAPT C.A. "Pete" Tzomes, Rear Adm. Tony Watson, CAPT Will Bundy, Vice Adm. Mel Williams, CAPT Bill Peterson, Rear Adm. Cecil Haney, and Rear Adm. Bruce Grooms.

acknowledgment, especially one made to or by a person when arriving or departing." If I had to do the math, I'd say I have given over five hundred salutes in my lifetime.

For all the salutes that went out to superiors and peers, the most meaningful were those to Black senior Officers and colleagues. We *saw* one another, but not in the sense of seeing with your eyes. It was more like, "I see you overcame, and I see you thriving. You rose above the racist jokes and inherent biases. You made a conscious effort to go out of your way to introduce yourself because you know seeing a Black Officer is a rare feat." When I became a Naval Officer, each salute meant way more to me when I knew it could change a sailor's outlook or instill a sense of pride. It was my way of saying, "I see you, too. Keep doing your thing. Keep fighting forward."

I slowly raised my hand and gave Isom a salute.

"I'm proud of you. Look at you. A Regimental Commander and a submarine select. I want you to have this pin. Wear it once you start nuke school. You're one of us now."

He saluted me back.

"Thanks, sir," I mumbled.

I was proud and glowing inside at his words of acknowledgment, almost as if his confirmation was a check in the box of my rite of passage to graduate. I was now a part of the network of Black submarine naval Officers.

I'd joined another gang. Except this one kicked me out.

* * * *

I MADE IT TO my car and called my parents. As the phone rang, my mind was flooded with a mix of questions. What was I going to say to them? Would Isom be disappointed in me? Would Ms. Mines be upset? Did I let everyone at Annapolis down?

Dwayne picked up the phone.

"What's going on, Andre?"

"Hey, is Mom around, too? I gotta tell you guys somethin'."

"Yea, she's right here. Wassup?"

"I got kicked out of nuke school."

Based on past experiences, I thought my stepdad would blow up on me like he always did. However, this time he listened.

"Andre, it's okay. The only thing your mother and I ever asked for you to do was graduate from the Naval Academy. And you did that. Anything else is just icing on the cake."

In another rare instant, Dwayne surprised me.

Damn. He really has changed over the years. My mother's constant prayers and making him attend Bible study at church are working.

It's hard to admit this, as much as I love my mom, but growing up, I absolutely hated that she never stood up for us during all those punishments. I was angry and hurt. I said to myself, *How could she choose this man over her own flesh and blood? Her own children she gave birth to?* As a minor, I was never in the position to be able to ask "why." Years later, when I was older, I took the time to ask her about it.

My mother explained to me how painful it was to watch us be disciplined by my stepfather even when she didn't agree. But she said something on the phone that day that I didn't expect: "Never show kids you are divided as parents. Children will use that to their advantage. I saw that firsthand in my last marriage with Tony." Although my brothers and I didn't see or hear it, there were plenty of times when my mother would deal with Dwayne sternly behind closed doors. As a child, it was a concept I didn't fully comprehend. In the moment, all you care about is how you feel. I now understand as a man why she did what she did. The job of parenting isn't an easy one, and no matter how much you love and try to raise your children on the correct path, you will make mistakes. And that's the thing; my mother did the best she knew how.

"Lord, help him get his anger under control," my mother would pray. Yet at the same time, she said she used to wonder if there would come a day when he got so angry that he'd hurt her or her children. Should she sneak out of the house and just leave? She said that, despite the way she felt, she prayed for him constantly. *Tell him you love him*, the Lord would reveal to her, even in the heat of an argument. That was a hard turning point for my mother.

All our issues seemed to come to a head that day and were resolved. In the end, nuke school wasn't a waste of time. I learned how I study best, I mastered the importance of balance, and I started what would be the foundation of a great relationship with Dwayne. He and I talked more during that transition out of Power School than we ever had before.

It was then, and for the remainder of this book, that I first started to call him Dad.

* * * *

I TOOK TIME to fly back home to Chicago while I waited for my next set of military orders to pop. As always, being back on the South Side recentered me; it brought everything back into focus. It was a beautiful, breezy summer day, and I had spent most of it running the streets with my dad, assisting him with the vending business. My mother had just started working a new job with Southwest Airlines. Due to work, my quality time with her that week was minimal.

The hum of the engine from the F-150 was smooth as we drove down King Drive. "It's so nice out today. Let's grab a few beers and chill in the backyard," I said. My father and I pulled up to one of the many corner stores in the hood and grabbed a case of beer. The clerk glared at us from behind the bulletproof glass that enclosed the store counter while my dad paid for the green case of Heineken beers. There was a security guard wearing a gray shirt and black pants posted up near the entrance and a small security camera located in the back of the store. We were just about to walk out when a young Black boy walked in.

Dad froze and didn't take another step.

The boy couldn't have been more than twelve years old.

"Hey there, young blood. What do you want to be when you grow up?" my dad asked while extending his hand.

The young boy paused and just stared at his hand for a moment before proceeding to shake it. My dad gave it a firm squeeze and pulled the young boy closer to him so that he had his undivided attention.

"Look at me. You look a man in the eye when he's talking to you." He was old school and disciplined in his approach. "What do you want to be when you grow up?" he asked again.

"I wanna be a rapper," the boy replied.

"But everyone wants to be a rapper or an athlete. Have you ever thought about working at the White House or being an astronaut?"

You could tell that a light bulb went off in the child's head and that gears started to spin inside. He had never considered something like that before. Like Denzel Washington mentoring the young man who battled with life as a thug in *Equalizer II*, Dad pushed youths to think differently than what they saw in Chicago and beyond the sports and entertainment industry. He never missed an opportunity to engage in outreach.

Another trait we have in common.

Dad and I left the store and made our way home. We went straight to the backyard, pulled up two white lawn chairs, and sat in the shade drinking our beers. I'll never forget this moment because it was special: this was the first time I ever drank a beer with my father, let alone had quality one-on-one father and son time with him. I used this occasion to my advantage to become more open and personal with him.

"Dad, can I tell you something?"

"Yeah, wassup?" he responded.

"I have never told anyone this, but much of my success at the Naval Academy was because of you. My anger to prove you wrong fueled me."

Under the shadow of the table umbrella, I explained to my father that the harsh words he'd said to me the night he threw away my artwork never left my spirit. No matter what I accomplished at the Naval Academy, it never seemed like enough for him.

I'd been carrying that weight on my back and in my heart for years. It felt good to finally throw it down.

The slight drop of the beer from his lips was subtle after he gulped down a refreshing sip. He turned his head to look at me. In shock, he uttered, "Wow, Andre. I didn't know that. Look, for years I was always harder on you because I saw a lot of me in you. I didn't want you to travel along the same path of mistakes I did."

I don't want to paint a picture that everything about Dwayne was horrible. I don't want people to read this and view him as a monster—because he isn't. He's human. As I grew older and saw how God has completely changed his life around, I can now personally quantify and see what the power of prayer will do in someone's life. Consistently. Diligently.

Looking back, maybe it was a blessing. Maybe if he hadn't challenged me, I wouldn't have used that resentment to push myself to work as hard as I did in my studies and leadership positions. Through Dwayne, I found out that I had a relentless ability to *hustle*. And no one could take that away from me.

Despite proving him wrong every single time, I never boasted about it. I never called to let him know he'd been wrong about me for years, or that he, in fact, had not figured me out like he thought he had.

Dad was also sterner in his attempt to reach me because he had a fractured relationship with the two children from his prior marriage, Corey and Ketta. Dad supported and cared for his kids to the best of his ability. Unfortunately, his previous wife made it difficult for him to maintain any form of stable relationship. Even after they'd been divorced for years, she refused to meet Dwayne and continued to spread false rumors about him to the kids. As Corey and Ketta grew older and were able to make their own decisions as adults, a relationship did start to formulate, but was still crippled by the actions and words of their mother from behind the scenes. She gave the children ultimatums to choose between the two parents. I know this still hurts him to this day. When I look into his eyes, it's one of those pains in life I see he has to carry and deal with.

All things considered, one of the qualities I respect most about Dwayne is his acceptance of us. He took in triplet boys, and although the seas of our relationship were rough, he did the best he could to raise and view us as his own. "Those are my triplet boys," he would say to people in the street, even though we looked nothing alike.

Dad and I had been at odds with one another for twelve years.

But his journey is a perfect example of the power of grace, prayer, and not giving up on someone.

If I've never said it before, I hope these words illustrate my appreciation for you, Dwayne. You are the man I consider my father.

Life's crazy, isn't it? For years, you can go around thinking you have all the right answers. I went through my childhood and college thinking I knew what motivated me most and what it meant to be a man. The answer was not who influenced me the most, but what.

The real truth is that my greatest influence was my biological father's absence. I am motivated best by opposition. By unfortunate events. By proving people wrong. Most of the success I have received is in response to some form of resistance.

That statement is not meant to make my mother feel left out. She will always be the center of my world. Today, I realize that most of the frustrations and issues I have had stemmed from how I coped with my journey as a man. If Tony hadn't left, I wouldn't be the man I am today.

My father and I spent the rest of that sunny afternoon discussing life and our passion for muscle cars.

EPILOGUE

Friday, January 18, 2019

San Diego, California

0500 PST

It was the start of another routine morning. Or so I thought. I hopped right out of bed and walked into the bathroom to brush my teeth, wash my face, and throw on my blueberry-colored Naval Officer fatigues uniform. As I walked out of the house, the air was thick and the ground wet from the nightly rain. I remote started my Dodge Challenger Hellcat and slowly crept out the garage. I gripped the steering wheel and couldn't help but smile.

When Dodge released the Challenger Hellcat, they shook the world. With a 6.2L supercharged V8 engine producing an ungodly 707 horsepower, and more capability under the hood than most Lamborghinis and Ferraris, few cars in the world can match the raw, barbaric power of such a car. It throws you in the back of your seat. At full throttle, the obnoxious, intoxicating scream of the supercharger makes the car sound pissed off and strikes terror in the hearts of animals and people alike. The way the exhaust tips gargled and popped made my mouth water. At every second behind the wheel, it tested my self-control. More times than I can count, I would climb in my car and just drive. It was my high.

My drive was the same as always that day: light traffic moving on the 805 freeway exiting Chula Vista. The bass from the Harman Kardon subwoofers in the trunk of my car thumped to the sound of hip-hop music while I sipped my daily Starbucks coffee. I felt good. It was the Friday before the long Martin Luther King Jr. Day weekend, and I had plans to hang out with my guys. Although it was morning, the sky was still dark from the night. It was around 0600 when I exited the freeway and drove down Harbor Drive, a drive that would turn out to be one of the longest in my life.

I could see the first gate entrance to Naval Base San Diego when I clicked my turn signal on to switch into the left lane. Out of nowhere, a speeding car came from behind and almost rear ended me. It was common for military members to speed down Harbor Drive, eager to beat base traffic and arrive at work on time. I jerked the firm SRT steering wheel right to avoid the hit, but the 672 pound-foot of torque from the Hellcat had a different agenda. It kicked in and overpowered me. The massive Continental DWS tires failed to grip and slipped from the wet pavement. Like a rocket, my car slid right. The vicious scream of the supercharger engine made one final roar before being silenced by the impact. The next thing I knew, I slammed directly into a metal railing at full force.

It was hard to see or breathe, but I vividly remember the smell of smoke engulfing the car cabin. My eyes were red and stung uncontrollably. The only relief I received was the slight breeze of the outside air because the entire front windshield of the car was shattered. Deadly shards of glass showered the inside and were sprinkled all over my body. The front end of the car was completely crushed from the impact, and the metal moaned like a dying lion. My head rested against the deployed airbag in shock. It pounded in pain. The crash happened so fast.

The very first thought in my mind was: *Oh my god, I can't believe I crashed my Hellcat.*

Here's why: when the Challenger Hellcat was first released, my dad and I would watch hours of YouTube videos listening to others rave about the experience of driving such a car. I used to daydream about how I would feel and how much of a blessing it would be to own one. And that's the thing. It's one feeling to watch videos to try to gain an understanding of its barbaric power, but it's a completely different feeling to control that type of power between your fingertips on a daily basis.

More than just a hunk of metal, it helped solidify our relationship further and gave us something to bond over when I left nuke school. After I bought my Challenger, my dad bought one three months later. When we spoke during the week, most of our time went toward discussing our Challengers, what new mods we wanted to do next, or anything related to Dodge. For his birthday, Father's Day, and Christmas, I would send him parts and accessories for his Chally. He would do the same for me.

"I don't know any father who can say that he and his son both drive the same car," my dad said one day on the phone. He was right. I considered it a blessing and an extreme honor. For us, the Dodge Challenger was more than just a car. It was a symbol of our growing bond.

Then fear crept in.

Everything around me seemed to go silent.

The beat of my heart pulsated so hard I felt like it was about to burst through my chest. In a matter of seconds, my life seemed to flash before my eyes. The faces of my parents and brothers flickered before me. All I could think of next was if the car would blow up with me in it. There was so much smoke. I felt squashed. Everything was tight from the bent metal. I looked around. The large gray metal railing went straight through the front of my car, and the impact crushed my driver side door. I couldn't get out.

I was trapped.

I fought with the airbag and managed to push it to one side. I tried to squirm over to the passenger side to open the door, but something was holding me back. It was my seat belt; it was still fastened. Frantically, I searched for the latch. After a few seconds, it came undone. I made another attempt to scramble for the other side of the car, but my legs were still held securely in place by the crushed dashboard. I slowly raised my right hand over to feel for the door lever, but it was smashed as well. In a dire effort to escape, I pushed as hard as I could to pry open the door, but it wouldn't budge.

This was it. I would die in my dream car. Tears started to form. I sat there for a moment and began to accept the paralyzing reality that today might be the very day I met my maker.

Just when I started to give up attempting to free myself from the smoking cabin, the passenger door opened, and a pair of hands grabbed my upper body to pull me out.

"Are you okay? Are you hurt?" a voice said.

"I think so. I feel fine," I responded.

"Sit down on the curb."

The man directed me over to the side of the street. I looked over at my Hellcat. The car was totaled. I later found out that the man who rescued me was a Navy sailor on base. He called the police and paramedics.

I knew it was a blessing to be alive, and I knew God was looking out for me from above. The impact alone, in addition to the steel railing that went straight through my front windshield, should have killed or severely injured me. Yet here I was, unscratched. I survived what should have been a fatal accident with no internal bleeding or broken limbs. Every time I get behind the wheel to drive, I make it a habit to say a quick prayer and ask for safe travels. This particular morning, for whatever reason, I forgot to do so. I'd survived another bullet.

Neee-naw, neee-naw, neee-naw, the siren of the ambulance wailed as it pulled up along the damaged curb. Lying on the ground, I could see two police officers walk over to the paramedic at the back of the ambulance and inform him of the situation regarding the crash. They pointed at me.

"Sir, I'm going to ask you to come over to the back of the ambulance. I need to check you out," the paramedic, in his crisply pressed black uniform, instructed.

"Anything really in pain? Does this hurt?" he asked while poking around my joints, chest, and neck. I could feel his blue latex gloves dig into my flesh.

"No. Nothing really in pain. I'm just sore."

"Okay. That's expected given the crash you just had. I've seen crashes not as bad as this where people are killed or severely injured. You should be dead. You're a lucky motherfucker."

While the paramedic continued to examine me in the back of the ambulance, he stopped taking my blood pressure, looked up at me, and asked, "What made you want to join the Navy?" I reflected back on my life thus far and all I had accomplished. His words made me think about the question Smoke asked me that gory October evening in the basement, the question that started this whole journey.

"Why do you want to join a gang?"

"Shit. Umm. I wanna feel like I'm a part of somethin'. I want excitement. I wanna feel like I belong. Like a real family. I wanna prove people wrong. Ya know?"

I realized that gangs are good for society and a necessary part of it. Truth is, we learn and grow from each other. We find comfort in some form of identity. We all desire a life of excitement and social belonging, and gangs fill that void and help shape who we are, good or bad. The armed forces, fraternities and sororities, sport teams, and even the Naval Academy—are all gangs. Throughout life, I believe human beings join a multitude of different gangs.

Along that path of joining different gangs, everyone must also find their own definition of greatness and sacrifice. Ever since I took a leap of faith and started to share my story at the Naval Academy prep school, my professors, peers, and youths have advocated that I turn my attention to the pen and tell my story in writing. My mother's own writing has proved to me the power contained within the written word—its ability to touch souls. After she wrote her marriage novel, I witnessed people reflect on how her book has saved them and the impact it had on their relationships. As Malcolm X once said, "People don't realize how a man's whole life can be changed by one book."

The morning after my near fatal car crash, I started writing this book.

Life's too short. It's time for me to stop hiding.

It's time for you to stop hiding, too.

Prove yourself wrong. You have more to give.

Everyone has struggles of identity, happiness, death, pain, negative habits, rejection, family complications, peer pressure from social media and society, violence, being resilient, or combating laziness, to name a few. But the struggles we live through are what make us stronger mentally and emotionally. Our toughest things in life tend to be our best things in life as well.

No matter what your situation is, the key to "proving people wrong" and "proving your circumstances wrong" is hard work, discipline, faith, and wise guidance. These traits will see you through to a good place on the other side.

I look forward to seeing you there.

Did this book inspire or add value to you in some way? If so, I'd love to read your review and hear about it. Honest reviews impact the lives of other readers by helping them find the right book for their needs.

Thank you for your time and support.

THE PROVE THEM WRONG CHECKLIST

- Wake up at four a.m. or five a.m. Wake-up trick: (1) Place your phone away from you so that when your alarm goes off, you have to get out of bed. (2) On the bed stand, have a cup of coffee or energy drink you can drink to give you a boost of energy the moment you are out of bed.

- Write out your goals for the day and for the month every morning. Then, say them out loud to yourself as affirmations.

- Write out your goals for the month again on a sticky note or notecard. Tape this on the dashboard of your car so that you can always see it when you are driving. Every time you get in your car, read your goals out loud to yourself.

- Work out for at least forty-five minutes at least three or four days out of the week. Physical fitness is a must. You will look great, feel great, reduce stress, and be more productive.

- Have a healthy, balanced diet. Proper nutrition is a must in order to perform at a high level. Throw in cheat meals as appropriate.

- Work as hard as possible during the week and use your weekends to recharge.

- Whether you work a W2 job or not, commit to work on a goal/dream of yours for at least thirty minutes a day. You'll be surprised at how much you accomplish within a month.

- When you are in the car, commit to only listen to podcasts that educate you. You'll be surprised how much you learn and grow every week.

- Read for at least fifteen to thirty minutes a day.

- Do 10 percent more than everyone else, and you will succeed 90 percent more than other people.

- Minimize distractions: (1) Complete tasks in a quiet, productive location. (2) Limit social media.

- Surround yourself with positive, goal-driven individuals.

- Have a handwritten to-do list/planner. Writing things out forces your brain to accomplish them.

- Stay up to date on news and trends. Most media stations have a top five list that you can subscribe to that will be emailed to you daily.

- Nobody knows everything. Ask a lot of questions and be humble.

- Make business cards and network your ass off.

- Always look for solutions to problems: find a way.

- Never complain.

- View everyone as someone you can learn from in some way.

- Take risks.

- Time hack everything you do. Set time limits on completing tasks throughout the day. You will limit distractions and be more productive.

- Some days will be really hard or tiring. That's okay. Take it one day at a time. Each day is a fresh start to get better and grow.

- Give back to others and expect nothing in return.

CLASSROOM DISCUSSION STUDY GUIDE QUESTIONS

1. When you first meet Dre, what kind of person does he seem to be? What seem to be his strengths and weaknesses? What personality traits does he have that make him able to be a success? What strengths do you find in his family and home life? What negatives do you observe?

2. What factors or what major turning point led Dre to finally leave the streets and pursue applying to West Point?

3. In this story of a young man from inner-city Chicago, we see the negative and positive influences and consequences of gangs. Cite some examples from the story. After reading this book, has your outlook on how we use the word "gangs" changed? Explain your answer.

4. Make a list of the gangs you have joined in life. Why did you join each of them? What connections did you make? Mentors? What lessons did you learn from each?

5. Family and friends play a large part in the development of our lives. They can help shape our personalities and goals in life. How did the following people influence Dre? Use examples from the story.

   a. Adrienne (Dre's mother)

   b. Dwayne (Dre's stepfather)

   c. Ms. Nisey (King Hall food worker at the Naval Academy)

   d. Boogie (Dre's best friend in the street gang)

   e. Smoke (the street gang leader)

6. Dre grew up in the hood on the South Side of Chicago.

   a. How does this environment affect his actions and development as a young man?

   b. Discuss with students what constitutes an underserved community or "inner city." What challenges do youth who grow up in these environments face?

    c. Draw parallels between the neighborhood and background in which Dre grew up and that of students in your group. Explain how adversity and obstacles can appear in all kinds of neighborhoods.

7. What people influenced Dre most within the story? Think of the person who influences you most. It can be a sibling, a teacher, mentor, parent, or someone from the neighborhood. Share your response with the rest of the class.

8. What personal habits, traits, and/or characteristics are important for achieving success in life and overcoming failure and adversity as depicted in the story? How can you apply these same tactics to your personal life as well as in the classroom?

9. Masculinity and the role of father figures is a major theme present throughout the memoir. What does Dre do to prove his masculinity? List examples. How important are father figures and male role models? How important are mother figures and female role models? What happens if they are not present? Present examples from your own life.

10. How much of our lives is really a choice? Dre and his brothers took completely different paths. Does our upbringing and background truly determine our fate? Despite the statistics and the odds stacked against him, what things does Dre do to survive and overcome?

11. Discuss some of the mistakes and failures Dre made throughout the story. How did these experiences change him for the better? What can you learn from his mistakes? How can this be applied to students in the classroom when they struggle with learning concepts or fail to perform as well on an assignment or test?

12. During the Academy application process, as well as while being a midshipman at Annapolis, Dre often felt a feeling of hopelessness. What kind of impact could the feeling of hopelessness have on you as you aspire to achieve your goals? What are some measures you could take to combat this feeling?

13. Dre often did extreme things not considered "normal" and made sacrifices in order to not only complete his academics, but to do well at the Naval Academy.

14. What does this teach us about goals and determination? What does this teach students about studying and working hard in the classroom?

15. What specific tactics did Andre employ to do well in his studies? How can students apply and learn from this?

16. The gang and scenes of violence are important parts in the development of the story. Why do you think they are included? What steps can teachers, parents, mentors, and friends take to reach those influenced by life on the streets?

17. Why does Dre feel that joining as many gangs as possible in life is important? Do you agree or disagree that joining groups is crucial for developing our identity and discovering who we really are? What was your opinion of gangs before you read the book? Explain your answer. When you join groups and/or other gangs, what characteristics do you look for? What positive traits would you bring to the table?

18. Imagine that PROVE THEM WRONG is set to be released as a movie. Your graphic design company is selected to promote the movie. Design a poster, website, and/or social media page to advertise PROVE THEM WRONG. Have each group of students present their campaign project to the class, the rationale for why they chose the medium they chose, and its relation to the book.

19. Children today are faced with many challenges. Make a list and identify what challenges you feel they face in society today. How do these compare with the challenges Dre faces in the story? What difficulties are similar? Different? Discuss your responses with a group or with the class.

20. What are the main themes in this story?

21. Why was the author haunted by the words and actions of his stepfather? What was the reason Dre insisted on proving him wrong?

22. We often live up to the expectations projected onto us. How much do expectations from family, friends, teachers, mentors, and coaches play in shaping your life? Dre's life? At what point does personal accountability come into play?

23. Discuss the relationship between dreams and believing in yourself versus your environment. Can we dream what we cannot see? Oftentimes Dre struggled to dream and believe in himself as a result of his upbringing in Chicago. Most youth from his neighborhood only dream of being athletes and rappers. What effect does this have on youth that grow up this way? How does this relate to the classroom?

24. What motivates Dre most? As students, what motivates you to care about something?

25. Is the journey to finding answers about yourself worth the potential hazards and heartbreak you may face while doing so?

26. How can you make being "knocked down" work in your favor?

27. In the story, Dre's stepfather's harsh words have a great impact on him. He uses those negative words to fuel and motivate him. What are other examples of negative words and being able to find good from them?

28. Describe the program at the Naval Academy. What

is it about that program that helps shape Dre from his street background into a military Officer? What is it about the school that allows Dre to be successful? What difficulties did he have to overcome?

29. Describe the feelings Dre has as he graduates from the Naval Academy. Can you understand those feelings? Explain.

30. Explain the title of the book. What possible interpretations does it have? Give specific examples from the book.

31. Why don't more young men succeed like Dre and his brothers? What social and cultural problems prevent their success? What can be done to increase the possibility of success in other young men?

32. What did you learn about survival, success, adversity, pain, and determination from reading this book? How can it be applied to the classroom and in life?

33. Write a letter to Dre explaining your feelings about the book. What advice would you give him? What questions would you ask?

34. In the story, we see the power of speaking things into existence and writing our goals down on paper. What things does Dre speak into existence? What goals does he write down? Write down your goals and a list of affirmations you can say to yourself daily.

35. The trauma of gun violence is like the PTSD some veterans experience. In what ways do Dre's experiences growing up affect his mental health? If Dre had received the help he needed early on, how do you think that would have affected his journey? List some forms of trauma you may have experienced in life. This could include sexual assault, the death of a family member, a car crash, etc. How does dealing with trauma impact the learning process in the classroom? What are some methods and strategies teachers can employ to help combat this?

36. You are a reporter for a newspaper. Write a story for the following scenes:

    a. Dre and his brothers are accepted to the Naval Academy

    b. Dre has a beer with Dwayne in Chicago

    c. Dre as a student and studying

    d. Dre's first day at West Point

    e. Dre applies for and receives the Truman Scholarship

37. What do you think was the most inspiring part of Dre's PROVE THEM WRONG? The most surprising?

38. How does this book differ from other coming-of-age memoirs?

39. How did PROVE THEM WRONG make you feel at the end?

40. Growing up, Dre had a certain view about White people and race. What was his viewpoint and how did his upbringing form that belief? What is his viewpoint now and how has it changed?

41. Dre became an avid reader of books for inspiration. He is also a big fan of motivational speakers. What books stand out to you the most? What speakers inspire you?

42. What traits does it take to succeed at the Naval Academy? How can some of the lessons Dre learned at the Academy be applied to better your life?

MY GANG
MEMBERSHIPS

Triplet

South Side Street Gang

King College Prep Marching Band

US Naval Academy

The United States Navy

Naval Architects

Senior ranked midshipman striper

MIT Lincoln Lab

Truman Scholar

Writing Center

STEM Club

Midshipmen Black Studies Club

USNA Gospel Choir

Naval base Newport Chapel Choir

Apostolic Faith Church

Submarine Officer

Centennial 7 Black Submarine Officer Network

NAPSTER

What gangs have you joined in life? Make a post to social media with the hashtag #PROVETHEMWRONG and list all the groups you have joined that influenced you.

ACKNOWLEDGMENTS

WELL THERE YOU HAVE IT, FOLKS. *PROVE THEM WRONG.*
I'm not even sure where to start with this thanking people thing. It's one of the hardest parts of the book to write because, with so many people who have mentored and poured into me, I'm bound to forget someone. I hope I was able to achieve a level of honest candor in this book that compels others. Or maybe a text passed down from a mentor to a youth he or she believes would benefit from its contents. In the end, I hope that its profits later lead to the creation of a nonprofit or a scholarship of some sort.

So without further ado, I would like to take the time to formally thank everyone involved who supported me in my journey as an author and the creation of this piece of literature, no matter how major or minor. I would like to start out first by thanking God for the many blessings he has done and continues to do in my life even when I don't deserve it. Second, big thanks to my beautiful mother, Adrienne, for being the best mother a son could ask for. Thank you to my dad, Dwayne, for teaching me what it means to be a true man. Third: my two big-headed brothers, Anthony and Alexander. I love you guys and the tight bond we share.

And of course, one time for my Auntie Georgia, Auntie Sonaie, Auntie Nina and Uncle Caleb, Cousin Collette and Cousin Billy, and all my other family members and their prayers.

Thank you to Congressman Bobby Rush and his entire office for taking a chance and believing in my brothers and me.

I am grateful for my Truman family.

Big shout out to my boy Jamal at MIT.

One time for all the professors that held it down for me at the Naval Academy, who remained patient with me among all the hours of extra tutoring I received. To all my mentors and Naval Academy family, thank you.

Ms. Janie Mines, I don't even have the words to write how much I appreciate you as a woman of God and your guidance.

Shout out to Admiral Cecil Haney, for always pushing me to never stop learning.

One time for my close friends whom I hold dear to my heart. You know who you are.

And lastly, for my readers, thank you for your valuable time, and have a blessed day. Peace.

ABOUT THE AUTHOR

DRE EVANS is a top graduate from the United States Naval Academy with a bachelor of science in naval architecture and marine engineering. Hailing from the South Side of Chicago, Dre and his two brothers shocked the city and the Service Academies admissions process by becoming the first set of African American triplets to receive acceptance into the Air Force, Naval, and Merchant Marine Academies.

He is a recipient of one of the ten most prestigious scholarships in America: the Harry S. Truman Scholarship. Dre is also the host of the "Multifamily By the Slice" real estate podcast and is the CEO and founder of That's My Property, a commercial real estate investment firm. He has served in various military environments, including the Naval Nuclear Power School, the Pentagon, and onboard multiple naval warships.

Today, drawing from his personal experiences of violence, the military, and other obstacles, Dre is a sought-after public speaker and motivator who allows his life to be an inspiration to people across various cultural backgrounds.

All social media:

drmultifamily.com

multifamilybytheslice.com

@drmultifamily

ADDENDUM

MY ADVICE:
APPLYING TO A SERVICE ACADEMY

With an acceptance rate of only 8 percent and a complex, multi-tiered application process, admission into Annapolis is more difficult than most Ivy League schools.

So how exactly do you get into the Naval Academy?

It's true that there are several aspects to the application process, but below are four tips I believe will help future candidates have a strong shot at acceptance. Remember: even if all else fails and your child does not receive an acceptance offer, understand that their very preparation for applying will yield great dividends with other college applications, ROTC programs, enlisted service, or even a job in the civilian sector. Ultimately, I want to offer some practical advice from an actual graduate, different from the various articles and videos plastered all over the internet that all, to me, speak the exact same language with no real tangible advice. So without further ado, my four tenets:

1. Tell a Story

2. Visit the Campus

3. Apply for the Nomination

4. Attend Prep School

Tell a Story

There's a reason why I started with sharing your story first. In my opinion, for what it's worth, an honest testimony of a candidate's motivations and journey is the single most important pillar of the application. Just to give you an idea, when I interviewed for Plebe Summer and NAPS detail in front of several senior Officers and ranked midshipmen, what made me stand out was my story. With every question pitched at me, I caught it and found some way to relate it to my foundational core—my upbringing and experiences on the South Side of Chicago. I'd tell a quick story and relate it to the question at hand. I didn't beat around the bush or tell a vague story either. I was vulnerable and sincere in the stories I told, stories that I knew would catch their attention.

Years later, when I went on to mentor multiple mids at the Academy, I told them that exact same advice when they went up for interview boards. They all did exceptionally well. I'm not boasting here. Too many applicants get tripped up on trying to be the perfect candidate and just list all their accomplishments. Yes, it's important to let the board know everything you have done, but if the majority of the competition also have a long list of impressive bullet point accomplishments, then you need to have an honest talk with yourself in the mirror and ask, "How the hell am I going to captivate my interviewers? What am I going to say that makes it impossible for them to shake me out of their minds?" Take a glance at the Mission Statement and have it in front of you as you write. If you need a reminder, it says:

> To develop Midshipmen morally, mentally, and physically and imbue them with the highest ideals of duty, honor, and loyalty in order to graduate leaders who are dedicated to a career of Naval service and have **potential** for future development in mind and character to assume the highest responsibilities of command, citizenship, and government.

"Potential" is in bold print. Why? Because your story needs to paint a picture for your audience that, based on your upbringing and/or background and interests, you have the "potential" to be a Military Officer. The mission statement should be your guide.

And when you talk about leadership, don't just think that your leadership is limited to the four corners of a classroom or clubs at school. It includes church, outreach, volunteering, sports, and even employment. Not to beat a dead horse here, but remember, show them you have the "potential" to lead. In summary, telling a story during the essay section of the application is what allows the admissions board to gain a perspective of who *you* are as a person and your capability.

Visit the Campus

Complete an official registered visit (so that it goes on your record that you were there), attend Summer STEM (for ninth through eleventh graders), or participate in the weeklong Summer Leadership Seminar (for students entering twelfth grade). Of the three, attending SLS will provide prospective candidates with the most realistic exposure to what life is like as a mid at Annapolis. You'll sleep in the sacred halls of Bancroft, attend rigorous academic classes, engage in PT and competitive sports, speak to admission counselors, and, the best part, interact with actual mids. It's a huge addition to your application not only because it looks good, but because the application used to apply for SLS is carried over and also used as the preliminary application for applying to Annapolis. Overall, attending SLS, the STEM summer program, or an official visit lets the Naval Academy know you are serious about attending and allows you to leave an early mark on who you are as an individual. Make a lasting impression that leaves mids and faculty asking, "Who was that?"

Apply for the Nomination

Look, for many of you, I get it: you don't just have a congressman or senator on speed dial in your back pocket. While completing the application, this was one of the most intimidating parts of the process to me. Many of you are probably asking yourself, "How do I even start to reach out to my representative?" I recommend you Google the congressman in your area and senators from your state. Next, pay them a visit personally at their office. More than likely, someone will be present and direct you on how to apply for a nomination. I strongly encourage candidates to volunteer or intern. Get your foot in the door by any means possible. Do whatever you have to do to get noticed.

Think about it. Who's going to turn down an individual who is willing to volunteer at their office for free? Not many. Be engaged and ask questions. Learn all you can while you volunteer or intern. Establish connections with everyone and leave a lasting impression. Chances are that, because the entire staff knows you, you'll be more likely to receive one of the congressman's or senator's spots. Every little bit helps. Another tip: if you can, see if it's possible to claim residency in multiple districts as this will increase your chances of securing a nomination because you can ask multiple officials.

Attend Prep School

As a former NAPSTER, I'm biased toward the prep school. There are several benefits in attending. If anything, during the application process, be sure to indicate that you are highly interested in receiving an offer to the prep school as well. Chances are they will offer you a spot. In most cases, prep school is offered to candidates whom Annapolis believes would be a great fit but need extra help academically before entry to the Naval Academy. It's further proof that the Academies are looking for well-rounded individuals. Just because you don't have a 4.0 or stellar ACT/SAT scores doesn't mean you don't have a solid shot at admittance. It's an option I believe many people overlook. If anything, I believe it's more beneficial because it gives individuals a true taste of military life. If a candidate decides they don't want to continue forward, a direct acceptance spot isn't wasted, and they also gain valuable experience in the end. For those who do decide that Annapolis is for them, well, you now have a leg up on all your incoming classmates plebe year.

FINAL ADVICE TO CANDIDATES AND MIDSHIPMEN

One, Plebe Summer: don't take it personally or too seriously. The detailers are there to practice and hone their own leadership capabilities before graduating to serve in the fleet. They are human and will make mistakes. Some will turn out to be great and influence you, others will not. In the end, don't expect them to be perfect.

Two, the physical training during Plebe Summer can only go for so long and will eventually end. Think of it this way: although the days are long, you can't add more hours to it. Nor can you add more days to the week. You will find that the way to stay calm throughout Plebe Summer and the rest of your time at the Naval Academy is to take it day by day, meal by meal. Too many things are piled onto your plate as a midshipman. The schedule and hustle and bustle of the yard become too much to try to mentally process everything at once. You will stress yourself out by doing so.

Three, don't try to anticipate and understand every aspect of Plebe Summer and the lessons you learn during your time at Annapolis. Some lessons will be learned as you progress through the years, others not until you are in the fleet. Let your experiences be handled in your own way at the right time.

Finally, no matter how you feel in the moment, don't quit. NO alumni, after graduating from the Naval Academy, has EVER turned to his or her buddy after throwing their cover in the air and said, "I regret attending the Naval Academy. It was a big mistake." Like anything in life, you will feel uncomfortable at first, but it will pass. One day, one random day, all the things you considered horrible about USNA will be replaced with a feeling of pride. Every midshipman who has come before you will agree that the four-year journey at Annapolis honestly sucks but is so richly rewarding in the end. You'll think, *This is my school. I'm a midshipman.* And you won't be able to fathom how you could have attended any other learning institution. You'll be honored to be a part of the Brigade of Midshipmen.

CPSIA information can be obtained
at www.ICGtesting.com
Printed in the USA
BVHW051208251122
652755BV00001B/8